Mark Twain on the Lecture Circuit

From the *Seattle Post-Intelligencer*, August 14, 1895.

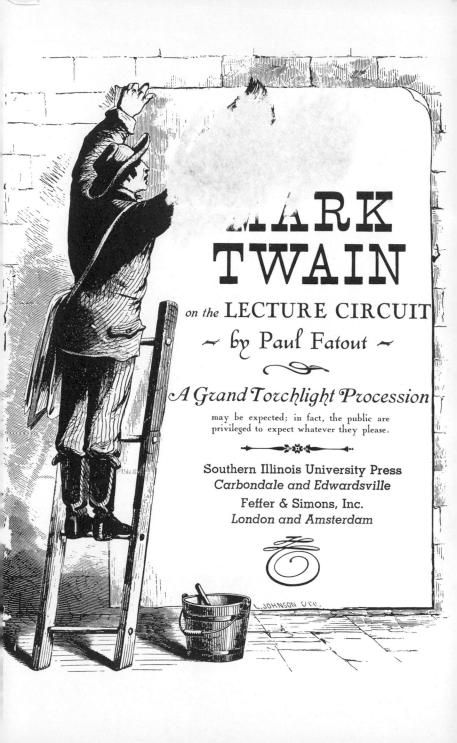

MARK
TWAIN
on the LECTURE CIRCUIT
~ by Paul Fatout ~

A Grand Torchlight Procession

may be expected; in fact, the public are
privileged to expect whatever they please.

Southern Illinois University Press
Carbondale and Edwardsville

Feffer & Simons, Inc.
London and Amsterdam

FOR EMERSON SUTCLIFFE

Preface

MARK TWAIN was so gifted a talker that, to those who knew him, his fame as an articulate person equalled, if it did not surpass, that of the writer. Capable of seriousness and occasionally of eloquence, he is probably best remembered for his ingenuity at provoking laughter. Timely evidence of this skill appears in the present success of Hal Holbrook, who, in "Mark Twain Tonight," impersonates the great humorist in makeup, voice, and manner. Today's audiences respond to the impersonation with the same delighted laughter that greeted Mark Twain, the same delayed reaction to a joke sprung offhandedly as an anti-climax. As of old, a minority of critics complain of what seems to them unfunny funny business, precisely as some complained of the original joker almost a century ago. These phenomena make him a living personality fifty years after his death, and testify to his ability to interest people, as one reporter put it, "in spite of themselves." Talking was an important manifestation of his character. A lecturer on the lyceum circuit, an informal monologist at home and elsewhere, an after-dinner speaker of such repute that in his heyday no consequential banquet was complete without him, he was also a sterling conversationalist undaunted by any company, and able to keep going indefinitely. This book attempts to view chiefly his platform performances and to glance, though less intensely, at his dinner speaking. Since no attentive Boswell took notes of casual talk, conversations can only be imagined from awed comments of listeners who marveled at Twainian versatility when he was not merely a jester, but an earnest advocate of theories philosophical, historical, political, and humane. His biographer and friend, Albert Bigelow Paine, was overwhelmed by the ranging mind and brilliant expression. Howells once remarked, after a visit from Mark Twain, that late hours, smoke, and Scotch almost killed him, but that he would not have missed the glorious experience. Others made similar observations about the magnetic Twain character and the fascinating speech that is now irrecoverable. Omitted perforce is another kind of oral expression also unfortunately unrecorded: Mark Twain's searing explosions of temper that were apparently Elizabethan in their rich prodigality of language and vividly metaphoric profanity.

I am glad to acknowledge my indebtedness to publishers for permission to quote: to Harper & Brothers for excerpts from the *Autobiography, Following the Equator, Huckleberry Finn, Joan of Arc, Life on the Mississippi, Roughing It,* and *A Tramp Abroad,* all by Mark Twain; from *My Father, Mark Twain,* by Clara Clemens Gabrilowitsch; from *Mark Twain: a Biography,* by Albert Bigelow Paine; from *Mark Twain's Letters, Mark Twain's Notebook,* and *Mark Twain's Speeches,* all edited by Paine; from *Mark Twain in Eruption,* edited by Bernard DeVoto; and from *The Love Letters of Mark Twain,* edited by Dixon Wecter. To Samuel C. Webster, editor of *Mark Twain, Business Man;* to Charles Scribner's Sons, *George W. Cable: His Life and Letters,* by Lucy Leffingwell Cable Bikle; to the University of California Press, *Mark Twain and the Enterprise,* edited by Henry Nash Smith and Frederick Anderson; to the Henry E. Huntington Library and Art Gallery, *Mark Twain to Mrs. Fairbanks,* edited by Dixon Wecter; to the Duke University Press, *George W.*

Cable, by Arlin Turner; to the Michigan State University Press, *Twins of Genius,* by Guy A. Cardwell; to Chester L. Davis of the Mark Twain Foundation, *The Twainian.*

For invaluable assistance in bringing this book into being I am grateful to my colleague, Emerson Sutcliffe, a perceptive critic with an encyclopedic mind; to Henry Nash Smith, Editor of The Mark Twain Papers, Berkeley, California, and to his assistant, Frederick Anderson, for their generous help during my several visits to Berkeley; to the staff of the Bancroft Library, University of California; to Dr. John B. Gordan, Curator of the Henry W. and Albert A. Berg Collection, New York Public Library; to C. Waller Barrett, New York; to the custodians of the Lilly Collection, Indiana University; to the Purdue Research Foundation for a grant in aid; to a host of librarians who have cheerfully run down notices of Mark Twain's lectures in some fifteen states; and to my wife, Roberta, for proof-reading and indexing, and for enduring the storm and stress of book-making: long journeys, long hours, cluttered study, clattering typewriter, pipes scattering ashes and burning holes in rugs, shirts, and trousers.

P. F.

Contents

Illustrations

1

Young Sam Clemens

ON EXAMINATION EVENING at Mr. Dobbins' school, admiring citizens crowded the flower-bedecked room, and rows of pupils squirmed: scrubbed, starched, beribboned, and uncomfortable. On a temporary platform sat the chosen performers, gawky boys intolerably burnished, self-conscious girls in a white froth of lawn and muslin. While proud parents beamed and simpered, small children haltingly piped nursery rhymes, and young ladies read original compositions: melancholy essays heavily didactic, poetry choked with sentiment and tears. When Tom Sawyer's turn came, he stepped forward boldly to declaim "Give me liberty or give me death!" with stern eloquence and dramatic gestures. But in the middle of it he succumbed to stage fright that tied his tongue. He floundered, gasped and sputtered, then retired in ignominious confusion.

Sam Clemens, who was always partly Tom Sawyer, made his debut as a public speaker in Hannibal at Mrs. Elizabeth Horr's Dame School, or J. D. Dawson's school, or William Cross's. Perhaps, like Tom, he contended with stage fright, for he was a shy boy, yet he learned to overcome diffidence. In his *Autobiography* he says that a few bad moments of panic at the outset of his first San Francisco lecture in 1866 marked the last time he was ever

15

frightened before an audience. Still, he carefully fostered an impression of uncertain timidity. At the height of his speaking career, one newspaper critic said that on the platform his manner was "half scared . . . as though he hadn't the least idea what he was there for, and would give more money than he ever saw to get out of the scrape without serious trouble."[1] This contrived behavior provoked laughter, which was precisely what he sought. A real handicap was a wretched memory that betrayed him, despite continual rehearsal, even when he had become an experienced lecturer. This shortcoming he also turned to account, as when, once getting lost in the middle of a favorite anecdote, he took the audience into his confidence in an impromptu explanation of his forgetful lapse, and with it scored a noisy success.[2]

Over fifty years ago aged Hannibal residents, reminiscing for the *Morning Journal,* recalled "Old Man Cross" and the log schoolhouse on the site that became the public square. There were stories of festive Friday afternoons when pupils spoke pieces. Sam Clemens, Will Nash, John Robards, John Garth, and other boys fervently poured forth such favorites as, "The boy stood on the burning deck," "Strike till the last armed foe expires!" "Sink or swim, live or die, survive or perish, I give my hand and my heart to this vote!" Paine says that on these occasions Sam sometimes read his own creations, one of them being so pointed a burlesque of older classmates that he narrowly escaped a drubbing. Possibly he talked himself out of trouble. Girls, attuned to a gentler mood, recited "I met a little cottage girl," "In slumbers of midnight the sailor boy lay," and other verses languishing and tender. Since everybody knew everybody else's piece, there was no novelty about these programs except for the ingenuity of the young hellions in the audience at making life miserable for the speaker. Mark Twain, describing for the Virginia City *Enterprise* a similar afternoon in a Carson City school in 1864, said that some pupils spoke well, others in a stately, slow-moving way that suggested a seesaw: "The boy—stoo-dawn—the bur—ning deck—/ When-sawl—but *him*—

had fled—." Performances stylized, mumbling, rattling, singsong were no tribute to the beauty of language perhaps, but they were public speaking of a sort.

In the momentary glow of attention and acclaim on those Friday afternoons, young Sam may have confirmed his preference for the spoken word. His drawling "long talk" made him a fascinating story-teller, and he never stopped experimenting with devices to make the telling better. Forty years after Hannibal days he remarked that the ability to talk was invaluable, far superior to the ability to put thoughts on paper.[3] Sending Mary Rogers a part of his autobiographical manuscript in 1906, he said that he intended to go over it again aloud, for oral reading was the only sure test[4]— as it had been of the dialogue of *Huckleberry Finn* and other books. At another time he said that talking was harder work than writing, but he did not shirk the effort, and the result is that his best writing sounds more casually talkative than formal or literary. Breaks indicated by dashes, repetitions, easy informality, colloquial idiom, and rambling sentences indicate that to Mark Twain language meant speech. It was his medium.

The most admired speaker in St. Petersburg was the preacher Tom Sawyer listened to, now and then, every Sunday. Attending church only under duress, he suffered boredom through drowsy sermons, though once aroused by a vivid word picture of the millennium with its touching tableau of the lion and the lamb lying down together, his imagination nominating himself as the child to lead them—if it were a tame lion. His ear caught the studied rise and fall of the minister's voice as he lined out a hymn. The Rev. Mr. Sprague was so accomplished an elocutionist that when he read poetry at church sociables, ladies rolled their eyes in ecstasy. Tom never did, nor did he show a particle of religious zeal. Yet the church was ever in his consciousness, even in the gaudy role of Black Avenger of the Spanish Main returning from grisly conquests to swagger in and overawe the congregation. He envied the commanding position of the preacher, who rolled out sonorous phrases for the edification of a captive audience. Tom may have longed to edify, but the pulpit, like the Sunday School rostrum, was more important as an eminence for showing off. In 1902, Mark Twain told a Hannibal High School graduating class that he had wanted to be a preacher. "And often and often in those days," he said, "I desired earnestly to stand in that Presbyterian pulpit and give instruction—but I was never asked until today. My ambition of two generations ago has been satisfied at last." In a characteristic fillip he added that the ministry had appealed to him because "it never occurred to me that a preacher could be damned. It looked like a safe job."[5]

That remark may have been Twainian embroidery long postdating the early ambition, for the desire to instruct, to entertain, or, like Tom, to show off was an equally valid compulsion. To Tom Sawyer, a preacher was negligible as entertainment, but to Mark Twain the churchly craft suggested unrealized possibilities. Preachers, he believed, could be more entertaining—certainly more tolerable—if they studied the art of speaking. In *A Tramp Abroad*, contrasting the gay continental Sunday with the doleful American one, he said:

the average clergyman could not fire into his congregation with a shotgun and hit a worse reader than himself, unless the weapon scattered shamefully. . . . One would think he would at least learn how to read the Lord's Prayer . . . but it is not so. He races through it as if he thought the quicker he got it in, the sooner it would be answered. A person who does not appreciate the exceeding value of pauses, and does not know how to measure their duration judiciously, cannot render the grand simplicity and dignity of a composition like that effectively.

That Mark Twain appreciated the value and duration of pauses, also emphasis and phrasing, is borne out by plentiful testimony on his skill as story-teller and as a sensitive reader of poetry. Had he ever occupied a pulpit, he could surely have made Scripture reading a thing of beauty.

A tenuous attraction to the sacerdotal persisted for some years.

After abortive mining adventures in Nevada, he says, the offer from the Virginia City *Territorial Enterprise* came at a critical moment, when he "stood upon the verge of the ministry or the penitentiary."⁶ In 1866 the Sacramento *Union*'s assignment to the Sandwich Islands arrived opportunely, for he was "once more penniless and pointed for the ministry."⁷ When he returned from Hawaii to lecture in California, he encouraged the press to refer to him as "St. Mark," the "missionary," and during his speaking tours he often said that he intended to "preach"—i. e., lecture— at some town or other.

If he offered no uplift, exhortation, or moral suasion in the true clerical manner, the motivation for his public speaking was probably not much different from that of pulpiteers, among whom some of the most notable were as adept as Tom Sawyer at showing off. Mark Twain was not a conventional churchman, but he felt a kinship with clergymen, cultivated their society, and bragged of friendships among brethren of the cloth. In San Francisco in 1866 he said he was "thick as thieves" with the Rev. Dr. Stebbins, and he was "laying for" the Rev. Dr. Scudder and the Rev. Dr. Stone. Before he left the West Coast, he sought letters of introduction to Henry Ward Beecher, the Rev. Dr. Tyng, and other prominent eastern divines. "Whenever anybody," he said, "offers me a letter to a preacher, now I snaffle it on the spot."⁸ This interest had nothing to do with their piety or theology. During the long friendship with the Rev. Joe Twichell, neither their conversations nor their letters were pious or theological. Mark Twain probably respected successful clerics for their established position, erudition, and breadth of mind, all of which, by association, might give him a public guaranty of respectability. His parvenu side required the endorsement of intellectual and social standing. Furthermore, the best ministers were good speakers, whom he admired for a mellifluous flow of language on matters secular as well as sacred.

The Rev. Dr. Bellows was, he said, an "eloquent man—a man

of imperial intellect and matchless power . . . unquestionably a brick."[9] The fluent Beecher, one of the highest-priced attractions on the lecture circuit, readily concentrated his spellbinding rhetoric on topics social, economic, and political. Mark Twain was not slow to learn these facts. Other parsons, like E. H. Chapin, De Witt Talmage, O. H. Tiffany, Robert Collyer, and W. H. Milburn, were dependable performers on a lyceum course, whether given in the Music Hall of Boston or a village church. Although Mark Twain said that he disliked to lecture in a church because people were afraid to laugh there, he lectured in many churches. With impish delight he strove, not always successfully, to dispel the sanctimonious pall with a gale of mirth. A shrewd critic once said: "Nature seems to have designed him for a Methodist circuit preacher, but forgot to endow him with a particle of reverence."[10] He would have made a dubious preacher for a strait-laced congregation, perhaps for any congregation in a century more orthodox than ours, but he could have been a most lively one, and sensible too. There may be more sincerity than meets the eye in his facetious identification of lecturing as preaching.

Whatever the wellspring of his desire to stand and deliver before an audience, Mark Twain was a stupendous talker, who never lost his fondness for the platform. Yet to hear him tell it, he found public speaking unrewarding, detestable, infamous drudgery. Repeatedly airing his hatred of the onerous business, he raged about the hardships of lecture tours, missed connections, tiresome train rides, nondescript small towns, barren hotels and their rascally proprietors, cranky audiences, bores, obnoxious committeemen, and a multitude of irritations that touched off his explosive emotions. Nevertheless, despite violent complaints, swearing off over and over, and permanently retiring just as often, the lure was irresistible. When he was almost fifty he said to an interviewer: "I love the platform, and I would like to live on it but I cannot be traveling about all the time."[11] Five months before his death he confessed to a correspondent that after a successful lecturing career he had expected to savor the freedom of release from its exhausting demands, but that he had not enjoyed the freedom.[12] We may surmise that only poor health prevented him from responding to the urge to the last day.

His success was accidental, for beyond professed desire to give pulpit instruction, no evidence suggests that as a youth he considered a lecturing career. In early years he was apparently unaware of his own gifts as a talker, and of the gifts of others. The only consequential speaker Tom Sawyer ever heard was Senator Benton, who was a crushing disappointment because he did not come close to being twenty-five feet tall. The senator's stately language should have impressed the boy, but the story says nothing of the speech. When Madame Caprell, the New Orleans clairvoyant, told Sam in 1861, "you might have distinguished yourself as an orator," she but underlined an unconsidered potential. Around him was no shortage of examples, for lecturers flourished in the mid-century, particularly in states east of the Mississippi. The redoubtable cold-water advocate, John B. Gough, castigated the drunkard; Susan B. Anthony crusaded for woman's rights. The fiery William Lloyd Garrison inflamed his audiences, the scholarly George William Curtis enlightened them, the whimsical Oliver Wendell Holmes amused them, the benign Emerson sometimes puzzled them.[13] Divines and laymen jogged around the country discoursing on subjects literary, moral, historical, Biblical, and philosophical.

Young Sam may have seen the names of famous speakers in exchanges received by the Hannibal *Journal*, but he did not hear any prominent lecturers in his home town. In the fall of 1849 the Hannibal *Missouri Courier* announced the forthcoming appearance of Senator Benton, but since there was no later story of his speech, the Senator apparently never got there—and that may be a reason why Tom Sawyer remembered no word. The village was too small to attract wandering stars of the platform. Its apostles of culture and righteousness were homespun evangels versatile enough, like the Duke of Bridgewater in *Huckleberry Finn,* to "sling a lecture sometimes." A Professor Ryan lectured on psychology in 1850; the Rev. Mr. Snow, editor of the *Temperance Battery,* spoke in 1853. In 1848 a heavy assault on the demon rum brought forth temperance lectures by the Rev. Dr. Fitzgerald, Dr. Elliott, J. Vail, Brother Granger, and Brother Orion Clemens. Sam being then at the Tom Sawyerish age of twelve, Tom's temporary alliance with the Cadets of Temperance may have stemmed from that crusade.

Local speakers were probably too familiar to elicit wonder or a desire to emulate. When Sam visited New York in the summer of 1853, he arrived in the off-season for lecturers, but in the metropolis voices were never still. In September, several days of "The Whole World's Temperance Convention" were turbulent with sound and fury. There were rousing speeches by Miss Anthony, Thomas Wentworth Higginson, and Horace Greeley, and a heated parliamentary imbroglio involving Wendell Phillips. A few days later an Anti-Slavery Convention produced impassioned words by Garrison, Lucy Stone, and Lucretia Mott. On October 18, Peter Cooper spoke at the cornerstone-laying at Cooper Union, where Mark Twain would make his New York debut thirteen and a half years later. On October 20, the anniversary speech of the American Institute was delivered by the emergent statesman, William H. Seward.

On none of these events did seventeen-year-old Sam Clemens comment in extant letters from New York. He goggled at displays in the Crystal Palace, climbed to the top of Latting Observatory, viewed the Croton Aqueduct, remarked upon frequent military parades, and at least once went to a theater to see Edwin Forrest in *The Gladiator.* Actors were another guild of speakers. The youthful critic took in the play attentively, but he seems not to have considered that either speaking or acting—arts he mastered with great skill—were relevant to his own life.

After about a year of roaming—from New York to Philadelphia

to St. Louis to Muscatine—he landed in Keokuk. There, on January 17, 1856, he made what is generally called his maiden speech. It was an impromptu appearance and he spoke reluctantly, as befitted a lowly compositor earning mythical wages of five dollars a week in his brother Orion's Ben Franklin Book and Job Office. The occasion was a dinner celebrating the one hundred and fiftieth birthday of Benjamin Franklin, patron of printers. In the handsomely decorated dining room of the Ivins House assembled local notables of the *Evening Times* and *Gate City*, employees of printing establishments, political bigwigs, and other guests. After the principal after-dinner speeches of the Hon. J. B. Howell, A. T. Walling, Orion Clemens, and a dozen others, some wag suggested calling upon the bashful Sam. Thirty years later an eyewitness recalled that he got up slowly, blushing and stammering, but that he pulled himself together to deliver "a remarkable production of pathos and wit, the latter . . . predominating, convulsing his hearers with round after round of applause."[14] Unfortunately, no details of this talk have been preserved. The wit and pathos, however, were an early example of the combination that was to become familiar in his speaking.

After an uncertain youth, piloting days, and chasing seductive rainbows through the barren mountains of Nevada, without ever finding the pot of gold, he arrived, dusty and bedraggled, at the *Enterprise* office in Virginia City in late summer, 1862. He had come, he said, to write for the paper. Taking easily to robust western journalism, he was soon holding forth "by the grace of Cheek," in the words of an impertinent colleague, as "Monarch of Mining Items, Detailer of Events, Prince of Platitudes, Chief of Biographers, Expounder of Unwritten Laws, Puffer of Wildcat, Profaner of Divinity, Detractor of Merit, Flatterer of Power, Recorder of Stage Arrivals, Pack Trains, Hay Wagons, and Things in General."[15] He was already an experienced man when he went over to Carson City in late autumn to report the doings of the Territorial legislature.

A provocative occurrence during his stay there was the formation of the Third House, composed of legislators, newspapermen, lawyers, and others, and devoted to satirical mockery of formal legislative sessions. A memento of that body is a broadside, entitled: *Annual Message of Captain Jim, Chief of the Washoes, and Governor (de facto) of Nevada, Delivered Before the Third House of the Territorial Legislature, Friday, November Fourteenth, One Thousand Eight Hundred and Sixty-Two.* A foresighted member, named "S. Myth, of King's Canon," moved that "Five Hundred Thousand Million Copies . . . be printed and circulated throughout the fertile Realm of Sage Brush and Sand, for the better Enlightenment of the Benighted, Deluded and Heterogeneous Inhabitants thereof." One copy, at least, has survived.[16]

Several candidates for the authorship of this anonymous document have been suggested: Hal Clayton, a Carson attorney; Clement T. Rice, "The Unreliable" of the Virginia City *Union*; J. Ross Browne and Dan De Quille.[17] These nominations do not rule out the possibility that Sam Clemens may have had a hand in it. At that time he had not yet adopted his nom de plume. Captain Jim, a wily but amiable Indian and town character, known as Chief of the Washoes, was familiar enough to make his name attractive to Sam, who may have seen in it the barbed suggestion that a government of Indians would have been as intelligent as the elected legislature. If Captain Jim's Message was the first to the Third House, then its session of 1863, when Mark Twain presided, produced the second Message, and that of 1864 falls into place as the Third Annual, which it was called at the time. The text of the 1862 Message, a wordy burlesque of political claptrap, was the sort of thing Sam had tried at least once before. Earlier in the year, when Chief Justice Turner made a speech at Aurora, Sam did not hear it, but, acquainted with the judge's rococo language larded with irrelevant poetical allusions, he wrote for the *Enterprise* an imaginary account of Turner's remarks, full of platitude and bombast. It was this story, he says, that got him the job on the paper.

Captain Jim's speech resounds with orotund statements, makes ridiculous assertions, and proposes fantastic legislation. Considering national affairs, the "Governor" says that a fast mobilization of the Nevada militia could easily have quelled the "most monstrous rebellion" raging in the eastern states. Had "your most excellent Chief Magistrate" been in command of the situation, "to-day, instead of wars and rumors of wars, and the martial tread of armed soldiery to the music of the stirring fife and martial drum, reverberating throughout the length and breadth of our distracted and unhappy country, all would have been peace and quiet, and every man, woman and child would be in full enjoyment of their innate and constitutional privileges."

Turning to Territorial matters, he says that the appropriation of $750,000,000 to bribe California legislators to sell land to Nevada has proved inadequate because "the price of votes in the California legislature far exceeded the most extravagant expectations of your commission." For this purpose the Governor requests a budget of $975,865, 784. Recommending revision of the trial and jury system, he says: "I would most earnestly . . . impress upon your deluded minds the . . . necessity of . . . disregarding the inalienable rights of your fellow-citizens, by expunging from your Statute Book, the . . . writs of *Supercedeas* and *Habeas Corpus,*" thus conferring "upon your worthy Chief Executive the untrammeled right to hang whom he pleases. . . . henceforth . . . such as incur his Excellency's displeasure will be hung first and tried in the Supreme Court six months or one year thereafter, as circumstances may direct."

He recommends converting part of the Territorial Penitentiary into a lunatic asylum for "the keeping and confinement of the members of the two lower branches of the legislature"; abolishing common schools because "our people already know too much"; and an Incorporation Law hedged with enough restrictions "to render it a perfect nullity, and as now, secure to the capitalist [sic] of California all they desire." After a brief statement on the sound financial condition of the Territory—"fully able to owe as much again as her present indebtedness, and no Territory is better calculated to refuse payment"—he closes with a ringing peroration:

Gentlemen of the Third House, your constituents are looking to you with eager eyes and palpitating hearts, for . . . such laws as shall redound to . . . their best interest; and that by your united efforts, as the representatives of this great and glorious people, and the smiling providences of a great, good and beneficent Creator, they expect that our land of sage-brush and sand will continue to make her gigantic strides along the pathway of peace, prosperity and happiness, and that the day is not far distant when she, by her own effulgent rays, shall eclipse all other stars holding a place in the brilliant galaxy of the National Constellation.

In its broad satire and exaggeration, this message exemplifies the work of an apprentice humorist striving for effect. Such a one was ebullient Sam Clemens, full of self-confidence and deviltry after about three months as one of the rowdy crowd on the *Enterprise*. Whether or not he had anything to do with Captain Jim's Message, a fair surmise is that he was on hand when it was delivered to the Third House on November 14, 1862.

In late 1863 he again reported from Carson City on the Territorial legislature, as Mark Twain this time. The *Enterprise* was a political power, largely because of the sardonic stories of its red-haired correspondent, who breezily exposed incompetence and stupidity. If his acidulous pen made him a reporter to placate or to fear, he was nevertheless a favorite of solons and journalists. Unanimously they elected him President of the Third House, which convened upon adjournment of the Constitutional Convention, at 11 P.M., December 11. On December 13 he wrote an account of proceedings for the *Enterprise*.

Solemnly escorted to the chair by Messrs. Small and Hickock, "Mr. Small stepping grandly over the desks, and Mr. Hickock

walking under them," the President expressed pleasure over "the
proudest moment of my life," and pledged his "earnest endeavor
to give entire satisfaction in the high and bully position to which
you have elevated me." Then followed an incoherent session in
which legislators, riding their favorite hobbies, were rebuked for
prosy expositions of old arguments that the President said he had
been "reporting and reporting . . . for the last thirty days." Mr.
Stewart droned on and on about the woes of the poor miner; Mr.
Johnson lengthily announced that he was not a candidate for the
Senate; Mr. Sterns dilated wordily on the unwisdom of taxing
mines. When Messrs. Youngs, Ralston, Small, Larrowe, Musser,
Brosnan, and others hemmed and hawed, broached irrelevancies;
or raised stupid questions, the chairman suppressed them in a
tumult of gavel-pounding and profane reproof. "Gentlemen," he
said,

Your proceedings have been exactly similar to those of the Convention
which preceded you. You have considered a subject which you know
nothing about; spoken on every subject but the one before the House,
and voted, without knowing what you were voting for, or having any
idea what would be the general result of your action. I will adjourn
the Convention for an hour, on account of my cold, to the end that I
may apply the remedy prescribed by Dr. Tjader—the same being gin
and molasses. The Chief Page is hereby instructed to provide a spoon-
ful of molasses, and a gallon of gin for the use of the President.

In the noisy give-and-take of this session he was evidently un-
troubled by the shyness of boyhood and youth. With brazen gusto
he belabored various members: "Mr. Youngs, if you have got
anything to say . . . don't stand there and shake your head and
gasp, 'I—ah, I—ah,' as you have been in the habit of doing. . . .
You rose for information. Well, you'll not get it—sit down. . . .
when you get up here to make a speech, I don't want you to yell
at me as if you thought I were in San Francisco. . . . Plant yourself, sir—plant yourself. I don't want any more yowling out of
you now. . . . How do you suppose anybody can listen in any

comfort to your speech, when you are fumbling with your coat all the time you are talking, and trying to button it with your left hand, when you know you can't do it? . . . drop that presumptuous third person. 'The Secretary would beg leave to state!' The devil he would."

When the House reconvened after recess, it passed burlesque amendments to existing laws, changed the name of the state to Washoe, substituted "Excessive board" in the statement "Excessive bail shall not be required," and provided that "No Sheriff or other officer shall be expected to arrest any assassin or other criminal on strong presumptive evidence, merely, nor any other evidence, unless such assassin or other criminal shall insist upon his privilege of being arrested." After that flourish, reminiscent of Shakespeare's cautious Dogberry, it was time for another cold treatment.

Mark Twain headed his Third House story for the *Enterprise*: "Reported by Phonographic Short-Hand." Yet perhaps the author, like a Congressman furbishing his words for publication, may have written some of his brusque remarks into the record after the event. At any rate, the "I—ah" disease and the coat-button-fumbling were good object lessons for a prospective speaker. Learning them well, Mark Twain did not later distract audiences by fidgety mannerisms or by the hesitant ah-ing of the amateur. Sometimes he stammeringly repeated a word as if unsure of the next. But he was sure because he had written the whole thing, including repetitions artfully injected to suggest a careful search for exactly the right term. Then he came out with the preconceived *mot juste* as if he had just luckily hit upon it, and the effect was enhanced by the assumed stammer.

About this time another important contributor to his platform schooling was Artemus Ward, who arrived in Virginia City in late December, 1863. Ward and his manager, Edward P. Hingston, together with Mark Twain, Joe Goodman, Dan De Quille, and other convivial spirits, spent a rollicking ten days doing the sights, the restaurants, and the bars of the town. The famous showman of "wax figgers" from "Baldinsville, Injiany," spoke his celebrated piece, "The Babes in the Wood," at surrounding towns—Gold Hill, Silver City, Carson, Dayton, Washoe City—and at Virginia itself. As one of the audience there, Mark Twain said of the lecture:

There are perhaps fifty subjects treated in it, and . . . a passable point in every one of them, and a healthy laugh, also, for any of God's creatures who hath committed no crime, the memory of which debars him from smiling again while he lives. The man who is capable of listening to the "Babes in the Wood" from beginning to end without laughing either inwardly or outwardly must have done murder, or at least meditated it, at some time during his life.[18]

Mark Twain's laughs must have been inward, for he was reported to have listened solemnly without cracking a smile—perhaps, it was surmised, because of the *Enterprise* hoax in which he had murdered the Hopkins family. Possibly he was intently studying the technique of this man who had such a great reputation as humorist and speaker: Ward's way of shifting swiftly and incoherently from subject to subject, his audacious exaggeration, irrelevance and absurd anti-climax, pseudo-serious concentration on humor without "message." These devices, refined and elaborated upon, became part of the standard platform equipment of Mark Twain.

By 1864 the Third House was an institution, and he was its acknowledged "Governor." Assured of a spirited Third Annual Message, the trustees of the new Presbyterian Church of Carson City invited him to deliver it for the benefit of their building fund, all tickets one dollar apiece. Governor Twain replied that if the public insisted on paying to hear "a grave state paper," he was agreeable, furthermore that, "although . . . not a very dusty Christian . . . I take an absorbing interest in church affairs, and would willingly inflict my annual message upon the church itself if it

derive benefit thereby." Promising "no amusement but . . . a reasonable amount of instruction," he said that "I am responsible to
the Third House only and I hope . . . to make it exceedingly warm
for that body, without caring whether the sympathies of the public
and the Church be enlisted in their favor, and against myself, or
not."[19]

Of this occasion, on January 27, 1864, in the district courtroom
of the Ormsby County Courthouse, no extant record informs
us of attendance or receipts. Mark Twain observed, with satisfaction, that the audience was larger than Artemus Ward's, and he
later said that the proceeds were enough "to put a new roof on
the church, and everybody said that that roof would cave in, some
time or other, and mash the congregation, because I was one of
those sinful newspaper men, but it never did."[20] One listener,
Major Dallam, sketchily reported the event by saying that Governor Nye led off with a formal inaugural. Whereupon "Mark
Twain . . . delivered *his* inaugural . . . to a very large audience
of gentlemen and about all the ladies in Carson City. Mark gave
the Governor some hard hits, in a sly way, but no one enjoyed
the fun more than rotund and rubicund Nye."[21] How well the
governor enjoyed the fun at his expense may be problematical,
for he seems to have entertained no flattering opinion of the
speaker.

In a brief report written for the *Enterprise* the day after, Mark
Twain said that the courtroom was a difficult place to talk in
because it was "about seventy-five feet from floor to roof," and had
no ceiling. Hence, as an unpractised speaker, he was at first in-
audible to those in the rear rows, who jogged him with calls of
"Louder—louder" until he raised his voice. Still, he was gratified
that "Some folks heard the entire document," and that prominent
citizens "said they would travel several miles to hear that message
again."

According to Paine, the affair surrounded Mark Twain for the
first time with the accompaniments of a conventional lecture.

Members of the Third House clustered about the speaker on a stage before a mixed audience that packed the auditorium and overflowed into the aisles. Politicos, newspapermen, and townspeople, including women and children, made this group more diversified than any Mark Twain had hitherto faced. It gave him a good opportunity to test his powers. Undoubtedly the speech satisfied his hope to "make it exceedingly warm" for the Third House, as well as others. Laughter was said to be uproarious and applause loud. As a token of community favor he later received from Theodore Winters and Judge A. W. "Sandy" Baldwin a gold watch inscribed to "Governor Mark Twain."

Although the Third House resolved that 300,000 copies of the speech be printed in all languages, apparently it never was. Mark Twain's first thought was to amend and correct it for publication. Then, two months later, distinguishing as always between the written and the spoken word, he said that since the message was composed to be delivered orally, it could not be published without revision, which he was too indifferent to undertake. Hence, no text has survived, nor any first-hand account of his behavior on the platform: nothing about composure or lack of it, boldness or timidity, mannerisms, gaucherie, and most telling hits, all of which would be interesting to know.

The Virginia City *Daily Union,* chief rival of the *Enterprise,* published a sort of review by a writer who called himself "Meriden." This critic roundly condemned "The Third House and Other Burlesques." Mark Twain, said he, was a "character" like Emperor Norton of San Francisco, both being grotesque. Furthermore,

The style of the burlesque governor is. . . . like that of the literary bubble . . . "Artemus Ward". . . . The originality of the famous Artemus, and the yet unextensive Mark, is affinitive and relates chiefly to a clownishness which . . . wears out under the public taste . . . it strives to enliven, but always afflicts. . . . The burlesque Governor's originality never reaches a prouder hight [sic] than when he can add to some extravagant item the inelegant and obsolete . . . "so to speak" and "as it were." . . . His satire tends to the amusement of his publishers only, when he ornaments a church item with . . . "dusty old Christian;" or when, in describing a public school . . . mentioning "an auburn-haired juvenile, who wiped his nose with his fingers in so audible a manner as to require . . . castigation from the teacher;" or, when he intermixes through his reports of legislative . . . proceedings allusions to himself, and expresses his disapprobation of . . . measures by saying "Now that is an infernal humbug," and by . . . other familiarities equally contemptible in the literary sense, and . . . scandalizing to the reportorial profession. . . . The humor and the wit thus exhibited partake wholly of the characteristic of the monkey as he climbs.[22]

This critic revealed genuine flaws in the humor of the youthful Mark Twain. The words are damning, yet it is often hard to decide, at so remote a date, when Virginia journalists were being serious reporters and when straight-faced humorists. Still, if Meriden meant what he said, he probably did not represent the majority view.

Suffice to say that the delivery of the Third Annual Message marked the first appearance of Mark Twain before an audience that had paid to hear him. If he was as successful as fragmentary evidence attests, he may have considered possibilities latent in the speaker's profession. Not very seriously, however, for in his *Autobiography* he says that only the "accident" of the Sacramento *Union's* commission to the Sandwich Islands produced the "notoriety" that led him to the lecture platform.

2
First San Francisco Lecture

THERE WAS less of accident than of design about the trip to the Sandwich Islands, for Mark Twain himself proposed to the proprietors of the Sacramento *Union* that they send him out there as special correspondent. When they agreed, somewhat to his surprise, he embarked on the *Ajax* on March 7, 1866. Arriving in Honolulu eleven days later, he thereafter enjoyed what he calls "half a year's luxurious vagrancy." Actually, he stayed about four and a half months that were not noticeably vagrant. He liked to encourage the impression that he was a superbly indolent man, as indeed he often was, yet when anything stirred his interest and aroused his imagination, he worked hard. No writer as prolific of copy as he was at various times, particularly when he churned out thousands of words weekly during his western years, could have been lazy all the time.

An eager tourist, he jaunted among the Islands, made copious notes, and faithfully lived up to his agreement with the *Union* in twenty-five letters, of about 1800 to 3500 words each, compounded of fact, fiction, humor, and satire. The arrangement was a good stroke of business for both sides. The dispatches added to his reputation, proved popular with California readers, and justified their price of $20 per letter, in addition to which he received

$100 a column for three nonpareil columns of the scoop on the *Hornet* disaster.

He was so entranced by the casual ease and caressing atmosphere of this peaceful spot in the Pacific that he always looked upon it as an earthly paradise, which it may well have been before American frenzy bestowed the blessings of progress and commercialism. Hence, returning to the states on August 13, he found himself at loose ends and discontented: out of a job and soured on San Francisco, which seemed a cramped and ugly place compared to the dreamy carelessness of Hawaii. He was also, he says, hard up, even after collecting the tidy sum of $800 from the *Union*. Probably he was. Fond of good living and never a man to hoard money like a miser, he spent freely, and he generally conformed to the American custom of living up to and beyond his income, of whatever size. That he racked his brain for "a saving scheme of some kind" is understandable. Considering lucrative possibilities, he concluded to capitalize on the success of the *Union* letters by giving a lecture on the Sandwich Islands. The story of its inception and delivery, as he tells it in Chapter LXXVIII of *Roughing It,* has been accepted as a factual recital. Paine says that this account is "a faithful one." Yet conjecture and conflicting fact make it appear more fanciful than faithful.

Feverishly and hopefully, he says, he wrote a lecture that he proudly showed to friends, only to be dashed by their dubious head-shakings, their gloomy forebodings that no audience would show up, their fear that he would break down miserably. Evidently some did doubt his ability to carry off a public performance. One reporter later wrote: "I was fearful that Mark could not talk as he can write, and thought that he might break down when making his first appearance."[1] Still, such a unanimously cool response as he describes was cavalier treatment for a local celebrity hailed as the most piquant writer on the West Coast.

Uncertain and disconsolate, he might have given up the scheme had he not been encouraged by a San Francisco editor. As an

The Young Samuel Clemens.

From left to right: Josh Billings, Mark Twain, and Petroleum V. Nasby. Courtesy of the Mark Twain Papers, University of California, Berkeley, California.

Mark Twain in London, about 1883.
Bettmann Archive

observer told the story some years later, Mark Twain shambled into the *Call* office on a rainy night looking "as if he had just been fished out of the Dismal swamp." Tossing a sodden roll of manuscript on an editorial desk, he asked for an opinion on it. "I've been to Bowman," he said, "and I've been to Harte and Stoddard, and the rest of the fellows, and they say, 'Don't do it, Mark; it will hurt your literary reputation.'" Reading enough to see its merits, an editor asked:

"Mark . . . which do you need most at present, money or literary reputation?"

"Money, by—!" We are sorry it is necessary to blank out his full reply. Mr. Clemens could be profane, in those days, on occasion.

"Then go to Maguire, hire the Academy of Music on Pine Street, and there deliver this lecture. With the prestige of your recent letters from the Hawaiian islands, you will crowd the theater."[2]

The editor also proposed charging the audacious price of one dollar per ticket. This approval, says the would-be lecturer, stiffened his resolve to proceed. It seems strange that the veteran of two, possibly three, sessions of the Third House should have needed any impetus other than his own, or that he should have doubted his ability to make good on the platform. If the *Call* editor gave the necessary push, it was good from then on, for never again did Mark Twain question his competence as a speaker, nor was he ever again aghast at charging a dollar a head, or more when the traffic would bear it.

Having taken the decisive step, having gone into debt to set the stage for his appearance, he gloomed and fretted over possible failure. In his own words he was "the most distressed and frightened creature on the Pacific coast." His lecture, which at first he had thought amusing, grew duller with each re-reading until he regretted that he "could not bring a coffin on the stage and turn the whole thing into a funeral." Finding the box-office closed at four o'clock the day before the event, he dismally concluded that no tickets had been sold, and that he would face an empty house. If the office was closed, the probable reason was that it had already sold all its tickets to a stampede of buyers, as he surely must have known. The facts do not justify his apprehension; on the contrary, they point toward a happy outcome.

Beginning on September 27, all San Francisco papers carried advertising—"a hundred and fifty dollars' worth," bought on credit—announcing the lecture on October 2 in Maguire's Academy of Music, hired for fifty dollars, also on credit. The ads allowed an opportunity for Washoe humor by their ostensible promise, in large type, of A SPLENDID ORCHESTRA, A DEN OF FEROCIOUS WILD BEASTS, and MAGNIFICENT FIREWORKS. Small type dispelled the promise: the orchestra had not been engaged, the wild beasts were in the next block, the fireworks had been abandoned. However, "A GRAND TORCHLIGHT PROCESSION May be expected; in fact, the public are privileged to expect whatever they please." In addition to newspaper notices, huge posters were tacked up all over town. Whatever doubts beset the lecturer, they did not inhibit his advertising.

Papers made sport of their wayward fellow townsman. It was not true, said The Californian, that he intended to conclude the performance with a war dance because, although he had trained for it, he had collapsed before slimming down to the proper weight. Furthermore, the lecture would contradict absurd reports of his romantic island adventures: the mermaid story, also "the base fabrication with reference to the waterfall of the Mountain Princess and . . . other strange stories which have caused him so much annoyance since he has relinquished his missionary labors."[3] It was doubtful, said the Alta California, "whether Mark will execute the Hawaiian Hornpipe, but his friend 'Brown' will 'pipe his horn' and sing a refrain in the Kanaka tongue."[4]

Serious forecasts augured success. "We have no doubt," said the Call, "the house will be crowded. . . . many will desire to

hear and see how 'Mark' acquits himself . . . before an audience.
. . . We may rest assured the lecture will be a good one. . . ."[5]
"Those who wish to get seats," said the *Evening Bulletin,* "will do
well to go early, for the indications of a grand rush are unmistak-
able."[6] "That Mr. Mark Twain," said the *Alta California,* "will
deliver a 'high-toned' lecture, if he speaks 'loud' enough . . . none
can doubt. . . . he will succeed beyond a peradventure; and he
will have a big audience, too, and all will go in anticipation of
a rare treat."[7] These predictions were accurate, for the citizenry
besieged the several ticket offices. In the office of *The Californian*
a surging mob of buyers completely disrupted the regular routine
of editorial duties. On the day after the lecture the *Evening
Bulletin* confirmed the impression of a heavy advance sale by
reporting that "Nearly every seat in the house had been engaged
beforehand, and those who came last had to put up with the best
they could get."

In sharp contrast to this encouraging bustle, Mark Twain's
own story in *Roughing It* reads as if conceived in isolation remote from all knowledge of what was going on around him. He
does not mention glancing at a newspaper or inquiring about ticket
sales. He appears not to know that he was blessed with a host of
admirers who would assuredly flock to the theater to hear him,
nor, among many well-wishers, does he meet one who cheers him
with a hopeful word. This unreal detachment is incredible behavior for so astute an entrepreneur. The man who had ener-
getically plastered the town with advertising, and who was always
most at home where life flowed thickly, could not have been so
aloof without being out of character. It is impossible to believe
that he had not sensitively taken the pulse of affairs, that he was
oblivious of optimistic press forecasts, and unaware of the general
fanfare that had alerted the public. Another strain on credulity
is his ostensible ignorance of the rush for tickets, which began
the day the first newspaper advertisement appeared.

Hence, his alleged fear of an empty house becomes suspect,

and his professed panic unconvincing. For days, he says, he moped
around in a slough of misgiving, losing sleep, losing appetite,
losing heart—in a city that, if we believe him, must have been
close to a sterile vacuum, empty of almost everything and everybody except himself. At six o'clock on the appointed evening he
slunk into the Academy of Music by a back door, then, for an
hour and a half in the "gloomy and silent place," endured an
attack of "the horrors." At eight, the hour he had announced that
"the trouble" would begin, he wandered out upon the stage, fearful and quaking, to be greeted by thunderous applause from an
overflow audience. The press reported a sellout: "One of the
largest and most fashionable audiences . . . ever seen within . . .
the Academy of Music"; "from the footlights to the rear row of
the Family Circle . . . densely packed"; "dress circle and parquet
. . . thronged with fashionably dressed ladies, while a very large
number of gentlemen . . . ranged themselves in a standing posture
against the walls"; " 'stuffed' to repletion." Well represented were
" 'our best people,' the regular opera 'set.' " The precise number
is unknown, but if the Academy of Music was larger than Platt's
Hall, which seated 1400, a fair estimate might be somewhere between 1500 and 2000.

The size of the crowd and the tumultuous reception so un-
nerved Mark Twain that "for a full minute," he says, he could
not gain control of himself. Yet a correspondent of the Marysville
Daily Appeal discerned no sign of distress. ". . . the crowd," he
said, "had no more effect upon his nerves, than if he had been
addressing a few boys in a cellar. I felt assured the moment he
made his bow that he was all right."[8] If momentarily shaken, he
soon recovered, launched into his lecture, and assumed direction
of the claque he says his disquietude had led him to organize.

Three old friends, planted in the parquet, had agreed to laugh
lustily at the bare suggestion of a witticism, even at "jokes . . . so
dim that nobody will ever see through them." A stranger named
Sawyer, who had a laugh "hung on a hair-trigger," had become

a confederate in a scheme to be controlled by the lecturer with the aid of "the wife of a prominent citizen." Sitting "prominently in the left-hand stage box," she was to keep a steady eye on the speaker, and, when he smiled at her, respond at once with laughter as a signal to other conspirators to laugh promptly and loudly. All went well, Sawyer and others roaring so valiantly that they carried the house by storm. Then the lecturer, rounding off "a bit of serious matter with impressive unction (it was my pet)," involuntarily smiled upon the lady. Her immediate "mellow laugh . . . touched off the whole audience; and the explosion that followed was the triumph of the evening." Thus, he says sadly, "my poor little morsel of pathos was ruined."

The story of this clever plot might seem more credible—certainly more original—had not details of an almost identical plot appeared in Washington Irving's biography of Goldsmith in 1849. Irving quotes a fragment from the memoirs of Richard Cumberland, an eighteenth century playwright, who made up a highly imaginative story of a claque that insured success for the first-night performance of *She Stoops to Conquer*. The leader was Dr. Johnson. Like Mark Twain's lady, he sat in a left-hand box, and by his laughter signaled other friends of Goldsmith. Cumberland had in tow a character called Adam Drummond, who was possessed, like Sawyer, of a booming horse laugh; other allies were Edmund Burke, Sir Joshua Reynolds, and a number of Scotsmen described as "predetermined applauders." The scheme succeeded despite the raucous Drummond. After obeying signals for a time, he got out of hand by braying and snorting at every sally, whether funny or not, and thus marred Goldsmith's seriousness somewhat as mistimed laughter damaged Mark Twain's.[9]

That he found his ingenious plot in Irving's biography may be conjectured, for the similarity is close. Even so, nothing need have prevented Mark Twain from appropriating these devices of organized support, but that he put them into practise is questionable. On the untoward laughter that, he laments, spoiled his "morsel of pathos," no newspaper review commented. Perceptive reporters, and apparently the audience, recognized and respected his serious flights. "At times," said the *Alta California,* "he would soar to the sublime, and his description of the volcano of Kilauea was as graphic and magnificent a piece of word painting as we have listened to for many a day."[10] That word picture was probably his pet "bit of serious matter." "From the lecturer's reputation as a humorist," said the *Evening Bulletin,* "the audience were unprepared for the eloquent description of the volcano . . . their appreciation of which was shown by . . . continued applause."[11] Spontaneous applause, but evidently no unseemly laughter that, coming at such a wrong moment, some reviewer surely would have reprehended. San Franciscans were not so gauche that they did not know the difference between the sublime and the ridiculous.

Besides, enthusiastic newspaper accounts show that he had no need of an organized claque. The moment he sauntered upon the stage he won his audience, which cheered, clapped, and laughed before he had spoken a word. Almost unanimously papers praised "one of the most interesting and amusing lectures ever given in this city," "valuable information and eloquent description," "shrewd observation," "side-splitting similes, grotesque imagery, and fearfully ludicrous stories," "a hit, a great hit." A few critics carped mildly. The *Daily Dramatic Chronicle* complained of a voice too subdued to carry to the rear rows. Prentice Mulford, of *The Golden Era,* said that "Mark made a number of very good hits, and then he made some passes which were not hits at all." He also observed that "Mark's gestures were not the ideal of grace," and denounced the servile San Francisco dailies for their disgusting "uniformity of praise. . . . They are all afraid of you, Mark; afraid of your pen."[12] If Mark Twain knew that his satirical pen intimidated editors, he need never have doubted a triumphant reception—at least by the press.

The most judicious criticism was Bret Harte's, which turned

up as correspondence "From California" in the Springfield, Massachusetts, *Republican* on November 10. Commending the performance as "a brilliant success," Harte went on to say that Mark Twain

established his reputation as an eccentric lecturer whose humor surpassed Artemus Ward's with the advantage of being of a more legitimate quality. . . . His humor . . . is . . . of the western character of ludicrous exaggeration and audacious statement, which perhaps is more thoroughly national and American than even the Yankee delineations of Lowell. His humor has more motive than that of Artemus Ward; he is something of a satirist, although his satire is not always subtle or refined. He has shrewdness and a certain hearty abhorence [*sic*] of shams. . . . His faults are crudeness, coarseness, and an occasional Panurge-like plainness of statement.

That analysis testifies to keen perception, exercised a generation before many critics discovered that Mark Twain was more thoroughly American than Lowell or any other. Since his journalism was often eccentric, rarely subtle, and frequently crude, also coarse, he carried those characteristics to the platform. Nor did he ever entirely lose them despite intensive schooling in refinement by such tireless social mentors as Mother Fairbanks and his wife, Livy. The exaggerated and audacious, his stock in trade as a writer, stayed with him as a speaker. More than one critic made the obvious comparison with Artemus Ward, the consensus being that Mark Twain was better because his material was more solid, because it showed none of Ward's straining for effect, and because his humor was his own, not borrowed. Eschewing niceties of judgment, the San Francisco verdict was that his debut in the Academy of Music established a lecturing reputation equal to that already gained as a writer. The *News Letter* spoke for a large majority in its blessing: *Pax tuiscum, Sancte Marcus, Missionarius.*[13]

Of that lecture only uncertain fragments remain. Paine reproduces passages called "From Mark Twain's First Lecture," yet no evidence shows that he spoke about the "View From Haleakala" included there, or discussed the sugar industry. Both were in the second San Francisco lecture, but probably not in the first. Walter Frear cites a summary from the Brooklyn *Eagle* of 1873 as "One of the fullest accounts of the lecture."[14] But there was no such thing as *the* Sandwich Islands lecture, for the author revised it so many times that he lost count. One surviving manuscript page shows many changes, as if it had been often reworked. We have no assurance that Mark Twain gave this lecture—or any other, for that matter—precisely the same way each time, or exactly as reported by any newspaper. No certainty, either, of how much, if any, of the first version remained in later revisions.

After using it in one form and another for a number of years, he became tired of it, and in the eighteen nineties he said that he had long since destroyed it. Possibly the manuscript melted away because of his easy habit of sending sheets to correspondents who wrote for an autograph and a "sentiment." Hence, no full text of the first San Francisco lecture exists. Fragments and later summaries, however, make one point clear: that much, perhaps most, of the effect depended not upon matter but upon manner. Pleasantries that seem commonplace in print, flights of fancy that seem trite may well have been side-splitting and impressive when spoken by Mark Twain. The hilarity of his audience implies that he was funny to look at, and that the way he said things was funny. Deliberately he bid for laughter, then and thereafter. From the start of his speaking career, adopting the technique of Artemus Ward, he cultivated casualness and apparent artlessness, experimented with modulation, and used incongruous association, all of which he improved upon as he gained experience. Manner was the secret of his success.

He began in the Academy of Music with an ingratiating impromptu: "Ladies and gentlemen . . . this is the first time I have attempted to speak in public, and if I know myself as well when the lecture is over as I do now, it will be the last."[15] He paraphrased the Declaration of Independence to the effect that when in the course of human events he had to face an audience, it should bear the affliction patiently. Not being used "to getting up operas of this sort," he apologized for the lack of an orchestra and for the absence of the trombonist, who had been discharged because unwilling to perform alone. Then he drifted into a description of the Islands, their geographical position, climate, products, and religion. He also discussed virtues and vices of the islanders, their history, customs, and traditions. The scapegoat, Harris, came in for ridicule, and missionaries for both praise and blame. Throughout, factual information alternated with absurdity, the two sometimes disconcertingly blended.

The lecturer gave full measure by talking for an hour and a quarter, a time that nobody considered too long. At the conclusion, sustained applause brought him back to the stage for a brief epilogue in which he begged pardon for the affliction he had asked the audience to bear patiently. His only reason for tormenting the public, he said, was to make money to publish a book he was writing on the Sandwich Islands.

He did not publish the book, although he included an account of his island experience in *Roughing It* five years later, as he also included what is strongly suggestive of a tall story of the Academy of Music performance on October 2. Five years were enough to blur fact with fancy in the mind of so imaginative a man. He liked nothing better than to embroider a tale, and he had so faulty a memory that he needed the aid of his brother, Orion, to supply details of their stage journey across the plains. The satisfaction he expressed over the outcome of the lecture venture was undoubtedly genuine, even though what he calls "abundance of money" was less abundant when he had paid his bills. Gross receipts were probably about $1400, which, after deductions for advertising, hall rent, and a shadowy "manager," dwindled considerably.

Mark Twain was content. Some days later he was reported to

have asked a newsman what people were saying about the lecture. "Why," was the answer,

"the envious and jealous say it was 'a bilk' and 'a sell.' "
  "All right. It's a free country. Everybody has a right to his opinion, if he *is* an ass. Upon the whole, it's a pretty even thing. They have the consolation of abusing me, and I have the consolation of slapping my pocket and hearing the money jingle. They have their *opinions,* and I have their *dollars. I'm* satisfied."[16]

He liked the jingle of dollars, as plentiful evidence on later enterprises testifies. Not that, as a speaker, he did not give his best when returns were meager. He became a professional, who tried to satisfy his own criteria, which were more exacting than the public's. Still, as against the reward of self-satisfaction for a good performance at a small fee, a crowded house and substantial receipts were certainly preferable. After October 2 he had a valuable intangible asset, for his great success supplanted doubts and fears with bold confidence.

3

Touring Speaker

AFTER such an auspicious beginning, the obvious move was a lecture tour. Sure of himself, encouraged by the knowledge that he was the only lecturer in the locality, Mark Twain arranged an itinerary with the aid of a former *Enterprise* man, Denis Mc-Carthy. "The Orphan," as he was called, went along as friend, manager, agent, and dispenser of good will, for he was both amiable companion and competent drinker. Vinous sociability, in which Mark Twain was himself no laggard, would be taken for granted in mining camps, where the pair were bound on a five weeks' swing that touched California towns and took them back to old Nevada haunts before the return to San Francisco.

Within a week after the Academy of Music performance they set out for the first stop, Sacramento. "The City of Saloons," as Mark Twain called it, was unpleasantly warm, and the place was torn up by mountainous piles of earth on the unfinished grade of the Central Pacific Railroad. Inhabitants scrambled up and down inclined ramps that, said he, gave "infinite variety to a promenade."[1] The experience was tonic, too, for "What the people there needed was a chance for up-hill and down-hill exercise, and now they have got it." For several days he trudged about disrupted streets, repeating a pattern of pre-lecture events similar to that of

45

San Francisco. Newspaper advertisements announced his appearance, on October 11, in the Metropolitan Theater "For Only One Night! And Only a Portion of That!" There was a new set of misleading remarks: "THE CELEBRATED BEARDED WOMAN! Is not with this Circus"; "THE WONDERFUL COW WITH SIX LEGS! Is not attached to this Menagerie"; "THE IRISH GIANT! Who stands 9 feet 6 inches . . . and who has been the pet of kings . . . will not be present and need not be expected." On the other hand, "THE KING OF THE ISLANDS!" who "Failed to arrive . . . for the Lecture in San Francisco . . . may be . . . expected on this occasion." He had failed to arrive on October 2, and possibly he was expected in Sacramento, but that he ever reached there does not appear.

Posters, praising Shakespeare's *Richard III*, "replete with thrilling incidents and startling situations," announced that this sensational drama "would have been produced on this occasion but for the much regretted absence of America's Great Tragedian, EDWIN FORREST!" High words about Richelieu, as "felicitously set forth in Bulwer's well-known Drama," led up to the statement that this "noble play" would also have been on the program "save that circumstances . . . compelled the continued presence of the Renowned Tragedian, EDWIN BOOTH, in New York." This broad humor backfired with a man-in-the-street in Sacramento. Invited to hear the lecture, he replied with an emphatic "No, sir . . . you can't humbug me that way. I've heard Mark Twain and I know he can't play 'Richard the Third' or 'Richelieu' either. You can't get me there to-night."[2]

The Sacramento *Union* indulgently observed that the visitor's "toils and sufferings as a missionary have not . . . sicklied him over with the pale cast of thought. . . . Familiar as he is with the Kanaka tongue, he will . . . tell his story in his best California English, and it is . . . hoped he will make as many converts to his creed of mixing amusement with instruction as he did among the serious people at the Bay."[3] Converts were pleased and alert.

To an audience containing "a liberal share of the beauty, intelligence and fine clothes of Sacramento," the speaker talked nonchalantly, as he had to San Franciscans. Next day's *Union* remarked upon "an easy colloquial style" that seasoned "a large dish of genuine information with spicy anecdote," the whole being "sufficiently racy and bristling with points to enliven the gravest audience." The *Bee* said that "It was pleasant to listen to a lecturer who . . . talked so wisely," the change from pathetic to humorous being "so sudden that before a tear had time to gather head enough to fall, the laughing came in. Occasionally . . . tears came from the overflow of laughter."

Thus early did Mark Twain practice mixing the solemn and the gay. When both were in the same sentence, the abrupt shift momentarily stalled the emotional machinery of his audience. A statement that began seriously slid off to an absurd conclusion so unobtrusively that the explosive response came only after a confused delay. He brought to perfection the anti-climactic climax, borrowed from Artemus Ward, and delivered in a subdued tone as an inconsequential afterthought. Although he was at first put to it not to chuckle at his own jokes, he learned to put on an expression of pained surprise when his hearers belatedly burst into laughter. On this tour he experimented with tricks of manner and voice, probably exaggerating the drawl for humorous effect. Throughout his career he never stopped experimenting, for as a student of speaking he was a perfectionist.

Embarking on the steamer *Flora,* the troupers sailed up the Sacramento River to Marysville for an engagement on October 15. The voyage was the first leg on a journey to interior mining camps, once booming in flush times, now prey to depopulation and decay. In a remote town a lecture was a rare event, often staged in a barnlike schoolhouse or church, or a town hall built in more prosperous days, now down-at-heel with weathered frame and broken windows. Some keeper of the keys a mile or two up the canyon generally had to be routed out at the last moment to open the building. Tallow candles sputtering in tin sockets only intensified the gloom. The audience, neither fashionable nor prompt, ignored the scheduled hour, and sometimes had to be summoned by the village tavern dinner bell. A few stragglers might show up early, but others, as if afraid of entering too soon, clustered around the door and inquired what was going on. Some wandered off to the nearest saloon. When the lecturer was well past his opening "Ladies and gentlemen," in tramped the late ones, boots thudding as they settled down noisily in a clatter of knocked-over benches and a buzz of beery whispers. The speaker survived this hubbub as best he might, and resumed his discourse with whatever aplomb he could muster.

Mark Twain sometimes had to put up with a primitive setting, but Marysville was far from decrepit. He complimented it as "the most generally well built town in California—nothing in it, hardly, but fine, substantial brick houses." Yet subsiding gold fever forecast deterioration. "It is a pity," he said, "to see such a town as this go down." He and the Orphan, having "passed all the 'bars' on the 'raging Feather,'" according to the local *Daily Appeal,* arrived two days early. "Mark," said the paper, "was soon 'taken in' by a few citizens who seemed anxious to cultivate by inoculation a crop of his peculiar and odd type of fruit."[4] A reasonable guess is that this party did not pass all the bars in Marysville. McCarthy was such an able toper that Mark Twain said he mistook the whole trip "for a spree."

Mark Twain was also a willing reveler, so much at home in a hard-living, hard-drinking society that he later felt the need, particularly during his courting days, of stern reform. Indeed, in sagebrush country he was regarded as an authority on drinks. A Como brewery boasted that its lager was "the best in the Territory, as we can prove by 'Mark Twain,' who has sat in the brewery and drank 'gallons and gallons' of it without arising from his seat."[5] Mike McClusky's Gold Hill bar advertised "Reporter's drink"—guaranteed to cool off a man in hot weather and warm him in cold—that likewise carried Twain's connoisseur's endorsement. A story current in the gold country was that his *nom de plume* came from his habit of treating friends, on tick, in John Piper's Virginia City saloon, and singing out "Mark twain" to the bartender, who chalked the score on the wall. If not a Coal Oil Tommy, as one reporter said, he had a fondness for "the ardent." Yet he appears to have been somewhat fussy about his tipple. "Mark don't drink," said a contemporary, "—except when his spirits are properly amalgamated with sugar, glass, lime, ice and a teaspoon."[6]

A forehanded arrival allowed time for leisurely amenities, engaging a hall, publishing notices, and stirring up interest. Without an advance agent or central bureau, a speaker made his own arrangements as he went along. Another job, delegated to McCarthy, was to find a man to introduce the speaker. The process was so offhand that this functionary might be a conscript chosen at random from an audience and cajoled into accepting the assignment. The vagaries of this system, together with the later discomfort of enduring labored introductions on the lyceum circuit, led Mark Twain to discard the ancient custom and to introduce himself.

On the Marysville performance, the *Appeal's* reporter, who walked out after a half hour, produced only a short and feeble summary. The next port was Grass Valley, a famous camp in the early days of the great rush, and still producing gold in 1866. It had other distinctions, having been the temporary haven of the international siren, Lola Montez, and the birthplace of the popular comedienne, Lotta Crabtree. A native son of pioneers destined to bring honor to the town was an eleven-year-old inhabitant named Josiah Royce.

The two travelers jogged by stage thirty-five miles east over a road so dusty and dreary that at the end of it Mark Twain was delighted to find the oasis of a good hotel, probably the International. The town, he said, reminded him somewhat "of Virginia

City in her palmy days" because of its mines run by Comstock
veterans, and a few new buildings that suggested an upswing.
Describing mines and quartz mills, and fascinated by sums of six
figures, he seemed himself back in the palmy days of his own
imagination, when fancy had conjured mythical fortunes out of
promising leads. The editor of the *Daily Union* had warned the
lecturer not to bypass Grass Valley, "a 'pretty smart chance of a
place,'" with "plenty of coin, lots of people who are capable of
appreciating 'good doings.'" The speaker, said he, would do well
to stop there, not only to garner some of the coin, but also to
"shake some of the foot-hill dust off . . . and take a drink. . . .
Let us hope we are understood."[7] He was. Mark Twain shook off
the dust and took restoratives.

On the evening of the 20th the *Union*'s reporter did his stint
by writing that "Crowds are flocking into Hamilton Hall . . . to
hear Mark Twain's lecture on the Sandwich Islands." He also
said that he had seen the lecturer "preparing himself for a clear
voice with a copious dose of gin and gum, after which he started
for the Hall with the irregular movement of a stern wheel boat
in a heavy wind."[8] After the performance a mob of friends closed
in on Mark Twain and bore him off to Stokes' Oyster Parlor, then
went on to Ed McSorley's saloon—"Winks understood at the
bar"—where the hot whiskey punches were acknowledged to be
the best "spiritual" consolation in town. Dawn found the hardy
ones sprawled about his hotel room, Mark Twain still talking and
fogging the air with great clouds of rank smoke.

On they went to nearby Nevada City. Mark Twain observed
that the inhabitants were "a notably refined and intelligent society," in which he enjoyed himself "rather too well to bother
much about statistics." Perhaps the enjoyment lay in more of
those eating-drinking-talking gatherings where he was the main
attraction. He relished all three, especially talking, telling story
after story. No doubt at such times he noted the effect of the
drawl, and filed away in his mind anecdotes that brought the

heartiest laughter. They would later become part of his extensive platform repertoire.

To publicize his lecture on the 23d, he devised another variety of exaggerated advertising. Announcing a program of sleight-of-hand, he promised "At a given signal" to "go out with any gentleman and take a drink. If desired, he will repeat this unique . . . feat . . . until the audience are satisfied that there is no deception in it." He promised "At a moment's warning" to "depart out of town and leave his hotel bill unsettled," an amusing trick that, "performed . . . many hundreds of times, in San Francisco and elsewhere . . . has always elicited the most enthusiastic comments." Furthermore, "At any hour of the night, after 10," he would "go through any house in the city; no matter how dark . . . and not miss as many of the articles as the owner will in the morning."9

In a scanty report of the lecture, the *Transcript* could pump up nothing better than a string of lukewarm cliches. The interior press was cognizant of Mark Twain, but not exuberant. Such apathy makes one wonder whether, even in the breezy West, his foolery was entirely acceptable. Presumably people liked humor, but some were troubled by it as a commodity for the public rostrum—as Artemus Ward had discovered on his western tour. Highlighting this point, the *Transcript* later published long dithyrambic stories—taking many times the space given to Mark Twain—about the readings of Eliza A. Pittsinger, touted as a poetess of surpassing genius. Her manner was sentimental, trite, gushing, ornate, and solemn. In some quarters these qualities were evidently considered more worthy than wit, satire, and plain fun. Throughout his speaking career Mark Twain suffered from the strange paradox of a people supposedly responsive to humor, yet afraid of it, even offended by it.

Using Nevada City as a base, the tourists jogged on horseback to Red Dog and You Bet, about nine miles distant. Once lively camps in rich placer diggings, these towns were now only small places of about a hundred inhabitants each. The two were so close together that the audience was probably more or less composed of the same people in both. Two stories have come down about the introduction at Red Dog. In his *Autobiography* Mark Twain tells of dragooning from the audience "a slouching and awkward big miner," who said: "I don't know anything about this man. At least I know only two things; one is, he hasn't been in the penitentiary, and the other is [after a pause, and almost sadly], *I don't know why*."[10] These words—which Paine suggests that Mark Twain himself supplied—so pleased him that he later used them to introduce himself. Another story is of a less skillful amateur, who could only say: "Ladies and gentlemen, this is the celebrated Mark Twain from the celebrated city of San Francisco, with his celebrated lecture about the celebrated Sandwich Islands."[11] Thirty-nine years later Mark Twain, thinking back over many lectures and many dinners, recalling chairmen urbane and clumsy, cited his five perfect introductions, and by contrast noted as one of the worst the bald words of the hapless fellow at Red Dog.[12] Perhaps both stories are true. One or the other of these introductions may have been spoken at You Bet.

Returning to Nevada City at night, the two horsemen gave their mounts their heads in a villainously dark forest because, said Mark Twain, "by many romantic books we had been taught a wild and absurd admiration for the instinct of that species. . . ." The instinct of these steeds, he complained, was "to hunt for places where there wasn't any road, and . . . it never failed them," the while vagrant branches scraped and buffeted the riders. Horses, he concluded, "never throw away a chance to go lame, and . . . in all respects they are well meaning and unreliable animals." Evidently he was not at ease in the saddle, for he never expressed any exhilaration about riding or admiration for horses. In Hawaii and Palestine he was always stuck, so he said, with a sorry nag, spavined, wind-broken, blind, and contrary. The most ludicrous equestrian experience he ever described was the disruptive encounter with the Mexican plug in Carson City: bounced, jounced, jolted, and bucked off. That story served him well, for he told it over and over, delighting audiences around the world.

The troupers were ready to descend upon Virginia City, over seventy miles east. Taking off by stage over a rough but scenic road that wound through mountains, they ended their first day's journey at Meadow Lake, which Mark Twain called "the wildest exemplar of the spirit of speculation I have ever stumbled upon." In 1866 it was a town of a few hundred people, yet neatly laid out with wide streets on which were buildings enough to accommodate several thousand, who never arrived. There were two-story frame houses and one elaborate mansion of cut stone, a Bank Exchange, a Metropolitan Hotel, printing shops, stores, restaurants, billiard parlors—nearly all empty. It was a ghost town, but a well-dressed wraith: "bright, new, pretty," said the visitor, "all melancholy and deserted, and yet showing not one sign of decay or dilapidation! I never saw the like before."

The next day brought another long trip on an overcrowded stage. According to Mark Twain's report, it carried fourteen passengers squeezed into space meant for nine, and was piled high with baggage enough for 150: carpet bags, valises, trunks, blanket rolls, chairs, and joints of stovepipe. Passengers scrambled out on upgrades and walked a good deal on all grades to spare the horses. The animals were a sad lot: "a weird-looking, bow-legged crow-bait . . . a thoughtful Senator-looking skeleton . . . a horse with only one ear," another with a "curb-stone backbone," and one, "the wheel horse on the port side, which had been staging some 28 years, it was said." Nevertheless, plenty of talk, plenty of chaff about their slow progress made "a right jolly trip of it."

Although Virginia City, like other towns, had passed the peak of flush times, Mark Twain said that it "bore quite a business-like aspect, and it was said that she was enjoying a very fair . . . prosperity." The spirit there was still about as vigorous as that of four years before, when the tousled Sam Clemens had drifted in to enliven the *Enterprise* with outrageous humor. Flippantly and seriously the press welcomed "the wandering Bohemian," who was Virginia's best-known citizen.

To know that he is in town, said the *Daily Union*, "is to note . . . articles that are missing . . . silver spoons, old stoves, worn out amalgamating pans . . . anything smaller than a 40-stamp quartz mill."[13] After the forthcoming lecture, said the paper, "a grand tableau of the murdered Hopkins family will be given. Mark will also perform . . . interesting feats such as eating three fried eggs, one cup of coffee and a number of rolls—all without speaking a word." An extraordinary feat, indeed, for him. "We have heard," concluded the *Union*, "of Bohemians falling so low as to become candidates for Governor, Congress or U. S. Senator, but when one condescends to turn lecturer we—well, Mark, we are glad to see you at your old home after so long an absence."[14] Extravagantly, the *Enterprise* saluted him:

The enthusiasm with which his lecture was . . . greeted is . . . ringing throughout California . . . in his native heath we may expect to see the very mountains shake with a tempest of approval. Our State can justly claim Mark Twain. . . . he has . . . warmed his fancy in tropical climes, and expanded his thought by ocean pilgrimages . . . these rest upon . . . foundations laid in our native alkali and sage brush. . . . he will receive an ovation seldom if ever equalled in our city.[15]

The event, in Piper's Opera House on October 31, confirmed that forecast by a house jammed to the doors with about eight hundred people, all seats and standing room one dollar each. The ovation was vociferous. Long after, Steve Gillis said that "when he appeared on the platform he was greeted with a hurricane of applause."[16] But neither Gillis nor others mentioned the ingenious introduction suggested, according to Paine, by Joe Goodman: that when the curtain rose, Mark Twain be discovered at a piano picking out and singing one of his favorite songs, "I had an old horse whose name was Methusalem." As if oblivious that the curtain was up, he should suddenly discover that it was, then begin the lecture. Paine says that he used this method with happy effect, but there is no contemporary report of it.

In its review the *Enterprise*, as if exhausted by its prelecture flight, fell back upon the ordinary: "immense success," "fashionable audience," "drollest humor," "inimitable style," "lofty flights of descriptive eloquence." Such comments were to become the hackneyed observations of many critics. It is a pity that so few had enough acumen to say anything more specific. Still, the stereotypes represented Virginia opinion, which was that he might have lectured a week to a full house every night. With great pride he reported that "Sandy Baldwin says I have made the most sweeping success of any man he knows of."[17] Yet he resisted importunate friends who urged a second performance. Later he did occasionally repeat a lecture in large cities, once for a number of days in London, but if he spoke twice in any town during a season he preferred for the second appearance something different from the first. Depending upon the eccentric, surprises, and tricks of manner, he knew that repetition vitiated charm.

A letter from over a hundred citizens of Carson City invited him to speak there, promising a large and friendly attendance. As "Ex-Governor Third House and late Independent Opposition Missionary to the Sandwich Islands," he thanked them for "generous toleration . . . of one who has shamefully deserted the high office of Governor of the Third House of Nevada . . . thus leaving you to the mercy of scheming politicians. . . ." Gladly accepting the invitation, he said that he would appear on November 3 in the Carson Theater to "disgorge a few lies and as much truth as I can pump out without damaging my constitution."[18] Then came Dayton on November 8, Silver City on the 9th, Gold Hill on the 10th. He said that he also intended to speak at Washoe City. Possibly he did, probably between November 3 and 8, for he commented on the quartz mills of Washoe and its several good mines. But there is no account of a lecture in that town, no extant story of the Carson performance, and only the barest notices of stops in Dayton and Silver City.

At one or other of these Comstock camps he inserted in his talk, probably as an introduction, the Hank Monk—Horace Greeley story: " 'Keep your seat, Horace, and I'll get you there on time'—and you bet he did, too, what was left of him." This anecdote was an old chestnut on the West Coast. Artemus Ward had elaborated upon it, with much absurd detail, as "Horace Greeley's Ride to Placerville." Mark Twain, using a pedestrian version similar to that in *Roughing It,* perversely took up the story as a means of breaking the barrier of reserve at the beginning of a lecture, repeating the dreary story in a colorless voice until the audience laughed. In his next San Francisco performance he told it three times before his listeners, sensing the humor of repetitive dullness, broke down. Paine says that Mark Twain would have been hysterical if the audience had held out longer. Probably not, for he deliberately used that unfunny story later, once telling it five times before fetching the house. Of that occasion he said that he was prepared to go on repeating it indefinitely because he had to make the crowd laugh.[19]

At Gold Hill, receipts of about $100 meant a house too small to be profitable. Other news from there had little chance against the exciting story of the fake robbery on the Divide. There, as Mark Twain and McCarthy were hiking back to Virginia late at night, they were set upon by "Stonewall Jackson," "Beauregard," and accomplices, who relieved the pair of their money and the cherished gold watch presented by Sandy Baldwin. Accepted by some as a report of a bona fide robbery, the news produced stern reaction. "This is no joke," said the Oakland *Daily News,* "but it is downright sober earnest. There should be a little hanging done among the rascals."[20] The Virginia City *Union* was not fooled. The robbers, it said, were "the departed spirits of the

Hopkins family, whom Mark murdered (on paper) . . . a short distance from Dutch Nicks. . . . Mark, we will relate 'a pleasing little incident.' When Hank Monk drove Horace Greely [*sic*] over the mountains . . . he didn't lose his watch."[21]

According to newspaper stories, McCarthy had been one of the conspirators who arranged the joke, but Mark Twain was apparently taken in to the point of offering a reward, no questions asked, for the return of the watch. The adventure gave him plenty to talk about when he took "a run with the boys" for the rest of the night in Virginia—a pleasant social custom in which everybody spent all his money buying drinks for everybody else. To recoup the loss by holdup, he scheduled a second lecture in Virginia, engaged the Opera House, and revamped his manuscript. Then, when he discovered that he had been hoaxed, he was in a splendid rage. In a huff he cancelled the engagement and set out for San Francisco, receiving the stolen goods on the stage as he was about to depart.

"Sans Souci," an impudent columnist of *The Golden Era,* said that the Divide episode was a put-up job arranged by Mark Twain. The story ran that this "man of mark," planning to go East, hoped to get travel money from another performance in San Francisco. He needed $1000 because "Whisky on the steamship is two bits a glass, and there are some trifling expenses beside." Advertising being costly, he and McCarthy discussed possibilities of free publicity. " 'Listen,' said Mark, 'we must meet an adventure. We must get ourselves murdered, only we must not be murdered in fact. Perhaps . . . as murder is attended with risk it will do to be robbed.' " Let us bury gold and watch, they said, then say we have been held up, and "the affair will make a sensation." So it turned out. Mark Twain wrote a humorous "Card to the Highwaymen," which, printed in many papers, made him "more famous than ever." Having consulted "two or three friends," the pair had planned "a friendly robbery" that occurred only "in the imagination of the parties interested." Playing his part, "The humorist grew wrathy, and swore more than a gentleman ought to swear. But this, too, was a part of the programme." When the news leaked out that he had been robbed "only as all men are daily robbed—by their friends," people laughed again, and his fame grew. So, having received money and watch, "Mark turned his face toward San Francisco, where a golden harvest awaited him."[22]

That engaging narrative is at odds with all other accounts of the affair. Sans Souci appears to be romancing. Yet Mark Twain's own story at the time, later furbished for *Roughing It*, conveys no impression of fright over the holdup—almost as if he knew it was a fake. But when he learned of the hoax, his violent distemper seemed genuine, especially to those confederates who bore the brunt of his profane displeasure. Cancellation of the second Virginia performance, with consequent loss of a goodly sum, looks like the summary action of a thoroughly annoyed man who was not pretending. Still, it is unwise to reject out of hand any tale about Mark Twain. Sans Souci may have spun his yarn from a thread of truth, or half-truth.

Mark Twain raised no fuss about the widespread free advertising. He put the incident into his second San Francisco lecture and implied that the robbers were the same ones who had earlier held up the stage on the Geiger grade, blown open the Wells, Fargo box, and taken $5000. Advance notices, announcing a "farewell benefit," said that "The wisdom will begin to flow at 8" in Platt's Hall on November 16. Putting all 1400 seats in the reserved category, he "sold them all," he said, "in 5 hours, & closed the box office at 3 P.M.—but did not charge extra—being a fool—simply charged a dollar a ticket."[23] That quick sale was probably like the rush that had preceded the first performance in October, when his story was of shakes and shivers in a land of oblivion. This time he was so conversant with the hourly demand that he could chide himself for not having boosted the price. Alertness in November makes more questionable alleged apathy six weeks earlier.

He added new Sandwich Islands items: Haleakala, the House of the Sun, boohoo fever, elephantiasis, cannibalism. Otherwise he talked ramblingly of climate, sugar and cotton, peculiarities of the natives, missionaries, and so forth. Humorously savage about international hypochondriacs who flocked to Hawaii, he also blasted Bishop Staley for attempting to establish a state church, and approved of manifest destiny by asserting that America must eventually own this territory. Recalled to the stage at the end, he told the only original joke heard in the Islands during the year: to the question, what scriptural injunction applied if he were asked to walk a mile with a friend, the answer was: "If thy friend ask thee to go one mile, go with him Twain." If that quip was original, it soon lost its newness, for in after years he heard it often enough from toastmasters to become weary of it.

Press opinion next day was more divided than it had been in October. The *Call* said: "whether . . . owing to . . . native bashfulness, or the effect exercised upon his nerves by the late robbery in Nevada, (whose people appear to be, as 'Mark' says, 'on the *Divide*,') the lecture became . . . confused, facts and facetiae . . . intermixed. . . . Comparing the weather in Sacramento with that in Honolulu, he has known it to be so hot in the former . . . that green-backs went up to 126 in the shade." The *Alta California* provocatively remarked:

The lecturer treated the audience to two gorgeous pieces of word-painting, but with unexampled diffidence pretended to forget a word, so as to break the spell in which he held the audience and prevent that tempest of applause which would surely have followed had he continued his eloquent passage to the close without interruption.

That observation suggests that his serious moments in October had cast a spell then, and that they had not been damaged by laughter. This time, to insure a fitting response of impressive silence, he pretended to forget. Or by that pretense was he asking for the laughter that had not been forthcoming before? Perhaps, for Mark Twain was a paradoxical man who wanted it both ways: a reputation for eloquent seriousness and for humor—all at once. On the eastern lecture circuit he sometimes ended the serious volcano description with the *sotto voce* comment: "There, I'm glad I've got that volcano off my mind"; or "There, I call that rather neat." These remarks were obvious bids for laughter. After a purple passage he might pause expectantly, then say that applause should come at that point. It generally did. Appeals more crass were applauding himself, and the gesture he used on at least one platform of clasping his hands over his head like a heavyweight champion acknowledging the cheers of a prizefight crowd. As he became older he fretted over being considered merely a funny man. Nevertheless, as if uncertain of his own seriousness, as if embarrassed by a public expression of beauty and emotion, he could rarely resist the flippant jibe of the jester. To the end of his career he measured an audience by the frequency and volume of its laughter.

Most San Francisco critics treated the performance ungently. The *Chronicle* said that he had apparently been "alkalied . . . in the savage wilds of Washoe, and . . . had become a little demoralized. He was . . . too familiar with his audience." Some jokes were "so nearly improper—not to say coarse—that they could not be heartily laughed at by ladies." The *Evening Bulletin*, troubled by "audacious humor, sometimes verging on coarseness," complained of "irrelevancies pardonable only to a popular humorist talking among his neighbors." Harshest of all was the *Daily Times*, which observed that "Mark Twain . . . fulfilled his promise of perpetrating a robbery." People growled when the lecture "spun itself out at an early hour," but "the gas was turned out, and the grumblers went home. Mark pocketed the cash and went to the Occidental."

This rough treatment was salutary. Probably he had been overconfident, mistakenly assuming that the careless fare favored in mining camps was suitable for the metropolitan Bay city. No doubt he heeded sharp complaints of shoddy workmanship. When he set out on the eastern circuit, he was meticulous about details, spending hours writing and memorizing a manuscript, composing transition sentences to give a semblance of unity, and rehearsing varieties of phrasing and inflection. Seldom did he give any critic the chance to say, as *The Golden Era* said, that he had not done his best.

Having given the lecture on Friday, he expected to sail for the East on Monday, November 19, but he did not get off then. Paine offers no explanation of the postponement, and Walter Frear says only that "for some reason or other Twain deferred his sailing."[24] Two items in Nevada papers may give the reason. On November 21 the Washoe *Evening Slope* carried this squib:

> The proceeds of "Mark Twain's" benefit in San Francisco, was [*sic*] attached for the benefit of one of his creditors. In future it will be well for Mark to hypothecate his evenings in advance . . . to protect himself from his natural enemies the police. Between the highwaymen and the police, Mark seems to be getting the worst of it . . . these . . . days.

On the 23d the Gold Hill *Daily News* said, more vaguely, that he had "a very severe attack of impecuniosity, owing to another meeting with fellows 'not on the divide;' so he did not get off on the last steamer. . . ." San Francisco papers did not enlarge upon this item, and Mark Twain himself neither confirmed nor denied the story.

Yet the debt and unknown creditor are plausible, for the upshot was an extension of the lecture tour to three other towns, as if forced by "impecuniosity." Down the peninsula he went for an engagement at San Jose on November 21. Arriving at Armory Hall some time after the scheduled hour, he found his audience of three hundred grumpy and frigid. Making the mistake of starting timidly, he did not dispel the frosty antagonism. Then, glimpsing an eager and friendly eighteen-year-old girl, he began to talk directly to her, and the crowd thawed. Consistently he later used that technique of speaking to one responsive-looking listener, and thus gradually winning the approval of everybody. In a copy of *The Autocrat of the Breakfast Table,* beside Holmes's advice to a lecturer to choose the brightest face and talk at it, he entered the marginal comment: "I always do *that.*"[25] As a clever lawyer sizes up a jury, he learned to judge the temper of an audience. Then, like a courtroom artist, he played upon sensibilities near the surface, and strove to rouse them when they were dormant.

In San Jose he put into his lecture, evidently for the first time, the offer to illustrate cannibalism by devouring a child if some lady would be so good as to furnish an infant. Used frequently thereafter, that bizarre proposal startled, not to say shocked, eastern audiences. Years later, commenting on the humorist's license to exaggerate, he said there was no certainty that distortion would be understood, for in any crowd, simple or sophisticated, was sure to be at least one dense auditor who could never see the joke.[26]

Next day's *Mercury* praised "beautiful . . . description" when he laid aside the role of humorist. . . . To use the expression of a wrapt listener . . . 'He's lightenin.' " The less complimentary *Evening Patriot* acknowledged "beauty of imagery" and "a great deal of . . . wit at which the audance [sic] laughed immoderately," but reprehended "too much buffoonery . . . almost as hard to digest as the old missionary was to the cannibal." Mark Twain, pleased at having won over a hostile audience, called San Jose one of his favorite stops. Yet he did not test that opinion further, for this occasion was his only appearance there. Its people might be genial, but they were too few for his taste, and receipts too small.

He journeyed back up the peninsula and across the Bay to Petaluma for a lecture on November 24. Of that performance the most diverting memento is a blast by the local *Journal and Argus.* Having been overlooked in the distribution of complimentary tickets, the editor penned a strong editorial entitled "Reprehensible." Mark Twain, he said, was a clever writer, but "as a lecturer he falls below mediocrity." He condemned San Francisco editors for "the reprehensible practice of disguising the truth in reference to qualifications . . . of persons who sell their talents . . . and too frequently 'sell' those who go to hear them." Interior towns having been often deceived by such misleading propaganda, people had become so wary that "lecturers of real merit are frequently mortified by finding themselves facing an audience that would be a discredit to the attractions of a hand-organ."[27]

The Santa Rosa *Democrat* published a satirical answer. Citing Mark Twain's platform success in California and Nevada, this editorialist lamented disaster in Petaluma:

Alas! . . . He failed—miserably failed . . . to satisfy our contemporary. . . . How sad . . . to find all his bright hopes dashed to earth! It won't do for some weak admirer . . . to suggest that Mark was not bound to furnish the Editor of the Petaluma paper with brains to appreciate his ability. . . . The *Journal and Argus* has spoken and Mark Twain is ruined forever.[28]

The Grass Valley *Union* also rallied to the defense with an editorial about "Unfortunate Clemens!" who had blighted his prospects "by attempting to pass the ordeal of the corn and spud producers of the Russian River country."[29] Mark Twain himself rarely made the error of quarreling with critics. Like all other men, he relished praise, and he was most pleased with favorable, even fulsome, criticism. The unfavorable was naturally distasteful, but he usually took it in silence. Of derogation like that in Petaluma, he was shrewd enough to know that, far from being harmful, it made friends speak up for him and increased his popularity.

Back down the coast he went to Oakland for an engagement in College Hall on November 27. Because of a misunderstanding about the time, only a small crowd of about two hundred turned out. As a prelude the College School brass band noisily rendered a program of national airs, to the acute distress of the speaker. In notebooks and letters of following years he recorded his sufferings during a band concert or several numbers by a soloist, the while he fidgeted in the wings, impatient to get on with his lecture. After thirty years' experience with that sort of thing, he said that he wanted no help on the platform, wanted nobody but himself to have the chance to exhaust an audience.[30]

The short tour ended without having yielded much to relieve impecuniosity. But San Francisco promised a rich harvest, for an imposing array of governors, generals, clergymen, and others invited him, "as a testimony of esteem," to repeat the Sandwich Islands lecture before leaving for the East. Gratefully accepting, Mark Twain said that "whether I have deserved this further generosity or not, I shall none the less industriously endeavor to persuade strangers that I have, anyhow."[31] Naming December 10 in Congress Hall as time and place, he promised to do his best.

Advertisements, announcing "positively the last 'farewell benefit,' " said that "Much entertaining information will be furnished, and many uncommonly bad jokes indulged in," also that the performance would conclude with an "IMPROMPTU FAREWELL ADDRESS, gotten up last week, especially for this occasion." Placards tacked up everywhere asked: "Where is Congress Hall?" That, said the *Daily Times*, "is one of Mark Twain's jokes; for he is a funny man . . . superior to a dozen Orpheus C. Kerrs,"[32] then obligingly informed readers that Congress Hall was on Bush Street above Montgomery.

Mark Twain did his bit by writing for the *Alta California* a long letter in which he professed distraction over dispatches about the troubled relations between the United States and Mexico. Trying to understand them had so unsettled his mind that he wished he had not agreed to "preach." He said he was all tangled up in diplomatic correspondence involving Austria, Ambassador Bigelow, the Marquis de Montholon, Almonte, "Mike Hidalgo," Princess Carlotta, and "the policy of the French government as pointing to ultimate repudiation of Enclosure No. 3, and the resumption of the principles set forth in Enclosure No. 1." According to Drouyn de Lhuys, Bigelow had been spending time at Ems. "I don't know who Em is, and I don't care—she is probably not any better than she ought to be, though, I expect—but I do know that Bigelow might be in better business." The most troublesome document was Secretary Seward's communication to the Emperor Maximilian:

the Austrian volunteers being only a contingent, and not a necessary interregnum within the meaning of international law, and the violation of treaty stipulations not virtually depending upon the acceptance or dismissal of a proposition so fraught with vital consequences to both nations, whether of the Old World or the New, he does not so consider it.[33]

Thus he happily reverted to the snarled syntax that had served him on the *Enterprise*.

To a crowded house he delivered the "old original" Sandwich Islands lecture, then said good-bye in a set piece charged with overblown rhetoric alien to his customary style. Thanking fellow-citizens and the press for many kindnesses, he spoke of his return

to that . . . home we all tenderly remember in our waking hours and fondly revisit in dreams . . . familiar to my recollection, but . . . an unknown land to my unaccustomed eyes. I shall share the fate of many another longing exile who wanders back . . . to find gray hairs where he expected youth, graves where he looked for firesides, grief where he had pictured joy . . . remorseless change where he had heedlessly dreamed that desolating Time had stood still!—to find his cherished anticipations a mockery, and to drink the lees of disappointment instead of the beaded wine of a hope . . . crowned with its fruition!

Wishing San Franciscans peace and prosperity, he predicted a great future for the city:

From the opulent lands of the Orient . . . from tributary regions that stretch from the Artic [sic] circle to the equator, is about to pour in upon her the princely commerce of four hundred and fifty million souls. . . . waste places shall blossom like the rose and your deserted hills and valleys shall yield bread and wine for unnumbered thousands.

He bade them "a kind, but not a sad farewell."[34] In that finale, which his hearers found moving, he showed that he was capable of the serious without bidding for laughs. If the flourishes were ornate and trite, they were at least free from buffoonery.

After a heartfelt leave-taking and a gracious salute to the press, next day's San Francisco papers could hardly be less than kind. The lecturer, said the *Evening Bulletin*, "departs with a brilliant reputation. . . . Men of this sort . . . never overstock the market, and Mark will find room for an honorable career in the field to which he is going." "This popular lecturer," said the *Daily Times*, "has struck a new lead in . . . literary research, and his multitudinous friends all hope that his 'prospects' will 'pan out rich.'"

How Mark Twain had panned out in California and Nevada is uncertain. A few years later he said that he had lost money in small towns like Marysville, San Jose, Grass Valley, Nevada City, and Carson. Sacramento and Virginia were good for one or two nights each. "But six nights in Platt's Hall, San Francisco," he said,

are the only ones . . . I would give you my old boots for—but they are worth close onto $8,000 gold, clean profit—more than that, if you charge 50 cents extra for reserved seats (which ought to be done—& you'll have from 500 to 1,000 $1.50 seats, that way.)[35]

Forty years after the 1866 tour he said that on it he "amassed twelve or fifteen hundred dollars," which "was about half—the doorkeeper got the rest. He was an old circus man and knew how to keep door."[36] Mark Twain's memory being unreliable, the accuracy of that reminiscence can hardly be determined. Yet perhaps twelve hundred was not far off, for he had enough for passage money and a modest stake besides.

On December 15 he sailed on the *America*. Early in the year newspaper rumors had said that he intended to return to the river to resume piloting, but that plan had been discarded sometime since. Bound, as he thought, for a trip around the world, he carried the *Alta California's* commission as Traveling Correspondent to Europe and the Orient. In New York he signed up instead for the Grand Holy Land Pleasure Excursion aboard the *Quaker City*. From the tour would come fresh material for new lectures with which he expected to assault the cultural bastions' of the eastern seaboard.

4

Westerner in the East

ARRIVING in New York in January, 1867, he found himself well enough known to be approached with proposals to publish "The Jumping Frog" and other sketches, and to receive offers from newspapers. Between March 14 and June 27 he published in the *New York Weekly* five letters on "The Sandwich Islands as Seen by Mark Twain." They improved his reputation in the East, and the first three were good advance publicity for his New York lecture in May. Possibly he wrote them deliberately as an advertisement, for, like Walt Whitman, he was not a man to stand by modestly while waiting for attention to wander his way. He went after it with great energy, as if determined to compel recognition.

During the voyage from San Francisco and after, he had been steadily sending travel letters back to the *Alta California*. He wrote about the sea journey, the ship and its passengers, crossing the Isthmus, Key West, and the many sights and sounds of New York. On this visit he seemed more alert to the passing show in the feverish city than he had been as a youth fourteen years before. He commented on the fatiguing size of the place, and he was shocked, or pretended to be, by theatrical leg-shows, which he nevertheless inspected thoroughly, like a deacon determined to see the worst and enjoying every moment of it. After several months of sensation and hubbub he concluded that New York was "a splendid desert—a domed and steepled solitude, where the stranger is lonely in the midst of a million of his race."[1] True, but this former inhabitant of tumultuous San Francisco and of raucous Virginia City gave the extraordinary explanation that he missed the "provincial quietness" he was used to!

In one letter, dated February 23, he spoke of hearing a lecture in Cooper Union by the stormy Anna Dickinson. This fiery speaker, only twenty-five, attracted large crowds whom she impressed by vehement emotionalism, if not by logic, and by an abounding self-confidence that concealed a woeful ignorance of history and politics. Sometimes called "an oratorical Joan of Arc," and likened also to such varied heroines as Portia, Juliet, Evangeline, and Cassandra, she had taken to public speaking at the age of nineteen after having been discharged from the Philadelphia mint for accusing General McClellan of treason at the battle of Ball's Bluff. Stumping for abolition, women's rights, anti-trade unionism, and violently waving the bloody shirt, she was a favorite of radical Republicans. In 1867 her bitter invective and her opposition to General Grant were alienating some of her friends; partisan editors called her "political witch," "parrot," and "crowing hen." Yet her earnestness and determination made her a compelling speaker, much in demand for lyceum courses.

Mark Twain observed her with the eye of a student hoping to learn a thing or two. He noted the full house of 2500, a larger audience than he had ever faced, Peter Cooper escorting her to the stage, Horace Greeley introducing her. He described her: deep-set eyes, "thick, straight hair" cut short, "a heavy cherry-colored silk dress, cut very plainly, and lace cravat and cuffs." Striding about the platform, eyes flashing and voice strong, she spoke rapidly and without notes on the subject, "Something to Do," denouncing humanity in general and men in particular for restricting women to few employments when the sex was capable of better things than kitchen and factory. "Her vim, her energy, her determined look," said Mark Twain, "would compel the respect and attention of an audience, even if she spoke in Chinese —would convince a third of them, too, even though she used arguments that would not stand analysis." He noticed one defect, characteristic of female speakers: working the audience up to a pitch of enthusiasm, then, instead of springing the climax, dragging toward it "so slowly that by the time she reaches it they are nearly cooled down . . . again." Still, he found the speech "worth listening to," commendable for its "grim humor" and biting sarcasm that was "her best card." It made him conclude that "She will make a right venomous old maid some day, I am afraid."

Whether or not she lost her venom, she did remain a spinster, though courted by many admirers, including, so Mark Twain said, another well-known lecturer, Petroleum V. Nasby (David Ross Locke), and the famous editor and diplomat, Whitelaw Reid. Her later life showed symptoms of frustration. When her platform popularity waned, she tried the stage without success, and in late middle age narrowly escaped being committed for insanity. After living as a recluse for forty years, she died, aged ninety, in 1932. Mark Twain eventually met her, but the two were never easy with each other. When she visited Hartford, one observer, Hattie Lewis, said that the pair "seemed to be always trying to test each other's right to be famous."[2] Both being voluble talkers and soloists, perhaps neither was happy when forced to listen to the other.

Mark Twain respected her ability enough to listen to a second lecture by her, but that he learned much either time is questionable. Vim, energy, a rapid-fire delivery, and her kind of biting sarcasm were all alien to him. His method was to win hearers softly and casually, to put them at ease with drawling slowness, not to assault them. Self-confidence he had, but not her sort of assertiveness: rather, an assumed diffidence that was the opposite of bluster. Yet he was impressed with her "message" and probably envious of her power to hold the attention of a large audience. That evening in Cooper Union may have intensified the thoughts that had been in his mind before leaving San Fransciso: of himself

Culver Pictures, Inc.

Cartoon from New York magazine.

From the *Sunday Oregonian*, August 11, 1895.

COOPER INSTITUTE

The Sandwich Islands.

By Invitation of a large number of prominent Californians and Citizens of New York,

MARK TWAIN

WILL DELIVER A

Serio-Humorous Lecture

CONCERNING

KANAKADOM

OR,

THE SANDWICH ISLANDS,

AT

COOPER INSTITUTE,

On Monday Evening, May 6, 1867.

TICKETS FIFTY CENTS.

For Sale at OMMERMERG & SONS, 652 Broadway, and at the Principal Hotels.

Doors open at 7 o'clock.   The Wisdom will begin to flow at 8.

standing in a New York auditorium and addressing a similar crowd.

He signed on for the *Quaker City* excursion, then took off in early March for a visit with the home folks. After fifty-two haggard hours of railroading—contending with continual jolts and stops, cramping efforts to sleep, cold, stove frugally locked to prevent using too much coal (a precaution followed, according to a fellow-traveler, "on all them d—d Jersey monopoler roads")—he arrived in St. Louis. There he began a short lecture tour by giving the first two of five Sandwich Islands talks in the Middle West. Invited to speak on behalf of the South St. Louis Mission Sunday School, he appeared in Mercantile Hall on March 25 and 26.

Not being well known in St. Louis, he aroused interest by a long letter in the *Missouri Republican* of the 24th. "I wish you would mention it in your paper," he said, "that I am going to lecture for the benefit of a Sunday School, so that they will see it in California, because . . . if I were merely to say it myself, without any endorsement, they would copper it." Hoping to make the benefit a success he had adopted the popular custom of offering prizes. For the best conundrum, a handsome elephant, "a little cadaverous now," but if stuffed with hay capable of becoming "a favorite at the fireside, and the pet of the household." For the best poem on Summer or Summer Complaint, "eighteen hundred Auger Holes. . . . Competitors . . . may call around and look through them free of charge. . . . They will be found to possess as many virtues as any auger holes." For the most convincing essay on female suffrage, "that splendid piece of property known as Lafayette Park," complete with "walks, and bridges, and holes in the ground, and piles of dirt, and . . . neat legible signs to tell you where the grass is when there is any there." The winner's attempt to gain possession of the property "must be a fortune in itself, and will afford him the liveliest entertainment as long as he lives." The humor seems labored, but perhaps it served its purpose.

About the same time he wrote for the *Missouri Democrat* three articles ridiculing female suffrage, including letters from such imaginary feminists as Mrs. Zeb Leavenworth, "Originator and President of the Association for the Establishment of a Female College in Kamchatka," and Mrs. Mark Twain, "Secretary of the Society for Introducing the Gospel into New Jersey." This raillery, at least, let readers know that Mark Twain was in town. He even went to church twice and to Sunday School three times, possibly not so much to advertise as to indulge nostalgia, like Tom Sawyer returning from a cruise on the Spanish Main. At one session he entertained teachers and scholars with the story of Jim Smiley and his jumping frog, telling it through to the end despite the efforts of a scandalized deacon to stop him. The hearty laughter that violated godly proprieties delighted Mark Twain. ". . . you know," he said, "you cannot help but respect a man who makes speeches to Sunday schools, and devotes his time to instructing youth."[3] Undoubtedly he could have done much to relieve the austerity of religion had any elders had the hardihood to turn him loose in a church.

For an enthusiastic house on the 25th he began with the Hank Monk-Greeley story, proposed to lead the crowd in singing the missionary hymn, "From Greenland's icy mountains" (but no one piped up), then slid into the text by way of geography, native customs, and so on. There were jokes about the abundance of "office-holders and office-seekers . . . plenty of such noble patriots"; boohoo fever, accompanied by "severe headache, backache and bellyache"; poi, which "smells a good deal worse than it tastes, and . . . tastes a good deal worse than it looks"; and "the long green swell of the Pacific," an ode that insulted a California country editor who wore such flashy clothes that he looked like "a plagiarism of the rainbow." The lecturer was so well pleased that in an *Alta California* letter he praised St. Louis as one of those places "where audiences are jolly, and where they snap up a joke before you can fairly get it out of your mouth."[4]

The next night stormy weather greatly diminished the audience.

In an interview twenty-eight years later Mark Twain said that in a hall seating one thousand he had about eighty people and "a vast acreage of chair backs." When he induced everybody to move forward, the little cluster was lost in emptiness: "It was like lecturing to the disciples on the edge of the Sahara."[5] Yet he became so comradely with this small crowd that he rambled on for more than two hours. He proved that he was not yet a professional when, at the end of the poetic passage on the volcano of "Kee-law-ay-oh," he applauded himself until the audience joined in. He did it again after describing a tropical flower, and offered to repeat this choice bit if requested. These sideshow antics he was slow to give up.

On April 2 he spoke in Hannibal at Brittingham Hall, the largest in town, but no extant story tells of the acclaim that probably greeted him in the old home place. Then he went on to Keokuk, preceded by advertising of the circus variety. As if boasting of the largest elephant in captivity, posters informed the city that "Sam. Clemens, the greatest humorist in America," was to lecture in the Chatham Square M. E. Church on April 8. That claim was a fair one, even though an immodest display of self-aggrandizement. More skillfully masked later, it was evident to the end in the white suits, the scarlet gown of Oxford, and the dreary dictations about all the fashionable functions he attended and the important people he met on his last trip to England. Mark Twain was Tom Sawyer, the show-off. "Youth," Livy's pet name for him, could not have been better chosen.

The Keokuk *Daily Constitution* of April 7 outdid the posters by saying that he was "the most extraordinary delineator of human character in America or upon the continent of Europe." That was a handsome puff, relegating to inferior positions such Europeans as Victor Hugo, Flaubert, Daudet, Ibsen, and the de Goncourt brothers. Not even ardent West Coast admirers had been so prodigal of praise. The *Gate City* of the same date remarked that, although his "funny stories . . . are not so well known here as in

California," the performance should be a rare treat for "lovers of genial humor," who would "find nothing coarse or vulgar in Mark Twain's lecture. He also sometimes (by mistake, he says) indulges in beautiful flights of fancy and eloquence." Deprecating his own eloquence, he was still trying to get credit for it without frightening the lowbrows. There was a little of the mucker pose in Mark Twain.

It is interesting to note that he was less well known in his home territory than he was on the Pacific Coast, and perhaps also in the East. Fame penetrated slowly. Five years later the Hannibal printer, T. "Pet" McMurray, said that the name "Mark Twain" meant nothing in the hinterland of Knox County, Missouri.[6] In 1867 he did not look like a man of distinction. Eighteen years later an observer recalled him as he appeared in an off-guard moment at the lunch counter of the Keokuk C. B. and Q. Railroad station:

a form, evidently that of a man, perched upon a high stool. . . . its heels recklessly clinched on the top rung, which caused the knees to come in almost immediate contact with the chin. . . . heavy arctics covered his feet . . . a slouch hat, pulled carelessly out of shape, protected his head. From under the brim peered out a few curly locks. Between this and a high collared overcoat was a face. The expression compared favorably with the growling emissions, so we knew that they came from none other than Mark Twain.[7]

Possibly his sourness was the result of putting up at the rundown Heming House. Always enraged by a shabby hotel, he said that this one was too bad even for perdition.

When he arrived in Washington later in the year, Senator William M. Stewart described him as "a very disreputable-looking person," who "slouched into the room" dressed in "a seedy suit, which hung upon his frame in bunches with no style worth mentioning. A sheaf of scraggy black hair leaked out of a battered old slouch hat, like stuffing from an ancient Colonial sofa, and an evil-smelling cigar butt . . . much frazzled, protruded from the corner of his mouth." Altogether, "He had a very sinister appearance."[8]

Since the senator wrote that when he and Mark Twain were not on the best of terms, animus may have accented the unflattering portrait. Yet there was truth in it, for even friendly contemporaries testified that he was a sloppy dresser. Small wonder that this shaggy westerner startled the conventional parents of his beloved Olivia Langdon by showing up in yellow duster and dirty straw hat, his large head topped by that unruly shock of reddish hair, or that in staid New England he must have seemed like a rampant buffalo in fur coat and cap. Until domesticity loomed, and both Mrs. Fairbanks and Olivia Langdon pitched in to spruce him up, Mark Twain was no model of sartorial elegance, and he was a perplexing riddle to those who measured character in terms of haberdashery. Even after marriage he distressed his wife by careless indifference to clothes. Once he casually called on Harriet Beecher Stowe without putting on a tie, then, when reproved, sent it over to her. For years he clung to the unfashionable string tie he said that Livy handled only with tongs, and dismayed her by donning those white cowskin slippers with the hair out.

To his audiences he did not seem sinister, as Senator Stewart called him, nor did he growl, as he did at the Keokuk lunch counter, but his face generally wore a melancholy look, once described as that of "a man who is about to preach his own funeral sermon." Matching the countenance was a voice that made another reporter think of "a little buzz-saw slowly grinding inside a corpse."

On the day after the Keokuk lecture, both local papers praised briefly, although the *Gate City* remarked that "his style of speaking, and his manner generally is too quiet . . . to please a popular audience," and called for "a little more voice and a little more nerve in . . . delivery." The quietness disconcerted listeners accustomed to the declamatory style. People who liked a roaring show were most happy when thundered at by the equivalent of a hellfire-and-brimstone preacher. If he gestured vigorously, shook a fist now and then, or pounded the lectern, so much the better. Mark Twain did not shout, did not stride about the platform, did not wave his arms. Chatting conversationally, wrinkling up his nose and half closing his eyes, he lounged loosely upon and around the desk, occasionally marching and counter-marching for a short space, once in awhile vaguely gesturing with one hand, or quizzically pulling his mustache. In these ways he varied so much from the conventional that critics called him eccentric.

The next stop was Quincy, Illinois, where he spoke under the auspices of the Encore Club for the benefit of the Quincy Library, at Hamilton Hall, on April 9. The Quincy *Herald* of the 7th guaranteed "original, quaint, irresistible humor—refined enough for the most fastidious and pointed enough for the most obtuse." The emphasis on refinement becomes oppressive. It was probably Mark Twain's own doing, for one of the first things he did in a town was to call on its newsmen to brief them on his performance and to jolly them into good will. San Francisco complaints of coarseness may have made him sensitive to the assumed genteel taste of the midwest. If so, he had already begun to work himself over before Mrs. Fairbanks began to remodel him. It is to be hoped, however, that he did not reform so far as to cater to the most fastidious in the cornbelt. That attempt might have reduced his lecture to the colorless and commonplace.

Ever his own best publicity man, he wrote for the Quincy *Whig* of April 6 a letter to an imaginary John Smith. Professing surprise at finding John in Quincy after having met him in San Francisco, New Orleans, New York, and elsewhere, he cautioned against roving too freely because

a rolling Smith never gathers any moss. There is no real use in anybody's gathering moss, John, because it isn't worth any more in market than sawdust is, and hardly even as much—but . . . the world has a foolish prejudice in favor of a man's gathering moss. So you had better locate, John, and go to gathering some.

Expressing warmest feelings for Smith, "moss or no moss," he invited him to the lecture, also some of his relatives: "I would say bring *all* of them, John, and say it with all my heart, too, but the hall only covers one acre of ground and your Smith family is a large one, John."

Bad weather kept down the house, yet the lecturer was "in full gushing vein," and as promised "gentlemanly and refined." This performance rounded out the brief tour. Probably it did not mean much financially, since three engagements were benefits. The middle-western lectures appear to have been a busman's holiday taken in a spirit of pleasure rather than a hope of gain. Eighteen years later he said that speaking "ought always to be pastime, recreation, solid enjoyment."[9] Apparently he found it so on this short swing.

Then he was back in New York, and by the end of the month deep in preparations for his lecture there in Cooper Union on May 6. Paine says that the prime mover in this affair was Frank Fuller, former Governor of Utah, but Fuller's own story says otherwise. Reminiscing over forty years afterward, he remembered that while he was one day idling in his Broadway office, in slouched the rumpled Mark Twain. He drawled:

"Frank, I want to preach right here in New York, and it must be in the biggest hall to be found. I find it is the Cooper Union, and that it costs $70 for one evening, and I have got just $7." [Later owning up to having had $700 in a hotel safe, he said: "Well, maybe I didn't bring out the second syllable quite plainly."][10]

Mark Twain's recollection was of a spontaneous uprising of former Californians and other friends, who had demanded his appearance. Whoever proposed the lecture, Fuller was precisely the man to abet the scheme. Both plunged into planning with furious zeal. Fertile in the invention of publicity, they devised posters, a pamphlet, handbills for omnibuses, and newspaper advertising, all of which, together with hiring the hall and other expenses, ran up a bill of more than $600. Fuller paid for everything. Newspaper ads, without any of the exaggerated humor of California, announced merely a "serio-humorous lecture on the Sandwich Islands," to be given "By invitation of the residents of the Pacific Coast now sojourning here, and many citizens of New York."

On the pamphlet, Mark Twain let himself go somewhat in the western manner. Borrowing a device used by Artemus Ward and Josh Billings, he listed thirty-eight lecture topics. Beginning with the Hank Monk-Greeley story, they ranged through geography, native dress, taboos, missionaries, native hospitality and rascality, volcanic eruption—a powerful description because "it has got so many long words in it"—boohoo fever, climatic conditions, and so forth, to the conclusion: "a joke which cannot fail to amuse such persons as may chance to be amused by it." Following the list of topics was the promise of "Carefully Elaborated Jokes" for all items, "some of them fearfully and wonderfully made," also "Some little pathos . . . and persons who are overcome by it may go out for a few minutes; but no weeping will be allowed on the premises." This cautious joviality was more restrained than Washoe burlesque. Mark Twain was carefully feeling his way in sophisticated New York.

Fuller even journeyed to Washington to enlist Governor Nye as introducer, and returned with the governor's fulsome letter praising the lecture for its wit and humor. This letter was added to the advertising, together with the announcement that Nye would preside. But his promise was only political blarney, for he did not appear, nor did he offer any explanation for his absence. Years later he said that he had never intended to show up, for he did not care to do a favor for Mark Twain, who was nothing but "a damned Secessionist."

The speaker was in a feverish state, alternately exhilarated by the prospect of his first New York lecture, and depressed by competition with numerous other attractions. On the same night Schuyler Colfax was scheduled for a speech in Irving Hall; at the French Theatre was one of the farewell performances of the famous singer, Adelaide Ristori; at the Academy of Music, McGuire and Risley's "Imperial Troupe of Wonderful Japanese." "The Black Crook" was showing at Niblo's Garden—"Palmer's Celebrated Parisienne Ballet troupe and the Gorgeous Transformation Scene"; Tony Pastor's Opera House offered Miss Naomi Porter in "The Quaker's Temptations." There were other plays and minstrel shows. In the face of all that, "everything," he said, "looks shady, at least, if not dark," but "I have taken the largest house in New York and cannot back water. Let her slide! If nobody else cares I don't."[11] Although he had had a clear field in California, he seems not to have considered that in a metropolis like New York he could hardly avoid entertainment competition on any date.

He did care enough to ride omnibuses to see how many people looked at the handbills (none did), and to worry over slow sales of tickets. There was no stampede to buy, as in San Francisco. The New York public went about its nervous business with a vast unconcern for this man hailed as the greatest humorist in America. When it became plain that the audience would be insignificant, he and Fuller papered the house by sending many complimentaries to bankers, teachers, and others in Manhattan and Brooklyn. The device worked, for they flocked in to fill the hall, if not the cash box.

In a ferment up to the moment of going on stage, Mark Twain rehearsed his lecture in Fuller's office, battled with a stiff collar and dress tie, and struggled into the first clawhammer coat he had ever worn—donned only because Fuller had insisted that a baggy sack suit was not the thing for New York. Failing to find Nye at the Astor House a half hour before lecture time, Mark Twain went on to Cooper Union damning the governor and damning all tailors who sewed up the buttonholes of dress coats. But he forgot his irritation when, approaching the hall, he found a crush of traffic and people swarming in. His joy was complete when he confronted that packed house, every seat taken, aisles full, and a crowd on the stage. "I was happy," he said, "and I was excited beyond expression."[12] Peering around as if looking for the missing Nye, he introduced himself, then took revenge on the unmannerly governor by a lampoon that delighted all westerners present. Swinging into his discourse, he "poured the Sandwich Islands lecture out on those people," he said,

with a free hand, and they laughed and shouted to my entire content. For an hour and fifteen minutes I was in Paradise. From every pore I exuded a divine content—and when we came to count up we had thirty-five dollars in the house.[13]

A big audience that laughed easily and often was indeed heavenly to him. Nor were receipts quite so meager as he remembered them forty years after. Fuller says that ticket sales amounted to "not quite $300," which seems reasonable considering the support of transplanted Californians and those "many" citizens. Mark Twain called the evening a "first-rate success." So it was in terms of appeal, of making himself known as a candidate for the lecture circuit.

Press previews were favorable but not extensive. Whereas well-known speakers like Wendell Phillips, Beecher, and Garrison were good for one to three columns, Mark Twain got but a small fraction of that space. There were about ten lines in the *Sun,* twenty in the *Herald,* thirty-eight in the *Times*, a quarter of a column in the *World.* The *Tribune* did better with a half column written by Edward H. House, a star reporter with whom Mark Twain had struck up a promising friendship. Papers remarked upon the speaker's comical expression, quaintness of manner, comfortable way of lounging that established "a sort of button-hole relationship with the audience," and a delivery so slow that the Sandwich Islanders called him "the lazy man with the long talk." If not wildly enthusiastic, critics civilly implied that the debut was encouraging. At the moment, however, he was far from being a celebrity in New York.

Yet the Cooper Union appearance was valuable, for when he went over to Brooklyn on May 10, its people had got the word, and they gave him a good, paying house. Venturing further into western humor, he had devised a printed program, which announced: "This lecture is considered to be the best one the lecturer ever wrote. It is also the only one he ever wrote. . . . This lecture is an infallible cure for all bronchial affections, sore eyes, fever and ague, and warts"; and added the endorsement, in invented Japanese, of Ho-Klang-Fo, Chief of the Japanese Embassy.[14] Next day the Brooklyn *Eagle* complimented "a gentleman who observes keenly, describes fully, thinks practically, and interests people in spite of themselves." The more critical *Union,* comparing him in voice and manner to "one of the staid old missionaries," said that laughing people "looked as jolly as Bacchus over a mug of the most fragrant Falernian," but that afterwards "they stoutly protested that they had found nothing funny nor worth laughing at in what they had heard." As a criticism that would recur during Mark Twain's lecture tours, that comment testifies to the effect of manner rather than substance, to a way of speaking that interested listeners "in spite of themselves." The *Union,* observing that not all of his jokes were good, complained that he "fairly rode down" one joke "about his trials in speaking the truth." Ten or fifteen repetitions were permissible but when he returned to it "the twentieth and so on to the thirtieth time, more or less, it began to grow rather stale." He probably listened to such criticism; to be dull or stale was no part of his intention.

After another performance in Irving Hall, New York, on May 16—this one barely noticed by metropolitan papers—he said that he "came out handsomely." The several appearances brought him many invitations to lecture for literary societies. One interesting proposal came from the cartoonist, Thomas Nast, who suggested that they barnstorm together, he to draw pictures while Mark Twain talked about them. But all invitations had to be declined because he was behind schedule on his *Alta California* letters, and he was too busy preparing to sail on the *Quaker City*—"laying in cider and other supplies for the Mediterranean," he said.[15] Still, the flattering shower of requests bolstered his self-esteem and went far to dispel lingering doubts of his ability to entertain exacting eastern audiences.

He sailed away to foreign parts, from which he sent back to the *Alta* many letters that would furnish the material for his first book, *The Innocents Abroad*. When he returned from the cruise to live briefly in Washington, D. C., Frank Fuller urged a lecture tour in the far west. Still out of pocket for the Cooper Union affair, he wanted some return for his generous advance of cash, and he knew Mark Twain well enough to take him to task roughly on that score. The strong language made the culprit squirm, but he mustered a battery of reasons for not making the tour. Winter travel, he said, was hard in the West. Fifty lectures at fifty dollars each would net them only $750 apiece, although he conceded that San Francisco, Sacramento, and Virginia City should each be worth two or three thousand. He needed the winter to build up a reputation so that he could make a new start in lecturing, and not have to talk in out-of-the-way places. He dreaded the thought of appearing before miners and Mormons of Salt Lake City. Still, the tour might pay if made in the spring of the following year. For the present, he preferred his steady six dollars a day in Washington.[16]

He might have added that, despite non-success as the secretary of Senator Stewart, he found social life there more lively and agreeable than struggling through mountain snow. His foreign travel letters having made his name better known, he was in demand for receptions and banquets, where he began his long career as after-dinner speaker. By early December he was composing what he called a "lecture" to be given "for the benefit of the widows & orphans of the Correspondents' Club here a month hence."[17]

That was his response to the toast to "Woman" at a press dinner on January 11, 1868, a brilliant occasion attended by senators, congressmen, and members of the diplomatic corps. One reporter, Ben Perley Poore, got into such an altercation with General Boynton that in the House reporters' gallery next day there was talk of a duel, but Poore apologized. "It is a great pity," said Mark Twain. "I never have seen a dead reporter."[18] When the Sabbath began at midnight, the fifteen toasts yet unfinished, they solved the dilemma by turning the clock back to San Francisco time. Then, said Mark Twain,

when we had used up all the San Francisco time, and got to crowding Sunday again, we took another vote and adopted Hongkong time. I suppose we would have been going west yet, if the champagne had not given out.[19]

His toast, hilariously received with frequent "[Laughter]" and "[Applause]," was serious, humorous, and mildly risqué. Woman, said he, mends our clothes, relays gossip about the neighbors, and "bears our children—ours as a general thing." Look, he went on, at the illustrious women of history. Look at Joan of Arc, look at Cleopatra, look at Lucretia Borgia, "look at Mother Eve! . . . You need not look at her unless you want to, but . . . Eve was ornamental, sir,—particularly before the fashions changed!" Schuyler Colfax said that it was the best after-dinner speech ever given. The speaker later remarked that he had done his best to elevate women

in the respect and esteem of the newspaper people. I think the women of San Francisco ought to send me a medal, or a doughnut, or something, because I had them chiefly in mind in this eulogy.[20]

Indecorous allusions brought sharp reproof from his most vigilant social and literary mentor, Mrs. Mary Mason Fairbanks. Having been on the *Quaker City* cruise as correspondent for the Cleveland *Herald,* she had undertaken to tutor the wild westerner in taste and manners. He found her so friendly and her tutelage so acceptable that he freely confided in her and called her "Mother" Fairbanks. To her reprimand about the "Woman" speech he pleaded guilty, blaming the papers for reporting "so *verbatimly.*" Promising reform, he yet had doubts, for "Every time," he said, "I reform in one direction, I go overboard in another."[21] Precisely. There was no telling what Mark Twain was likely to do or say, how he might shock the easily shockable by bawdy humor, profanity, or some robust turn of phrase that offended hypersensitive ears. Violating the mores was not difficult in a society hag-ridden by the prudish and genteel, ripe for comstockery. It is remarkable that so Rabelaisian a character should have existed, and eventually have achieved fame, in such an airless milieu. Still, if his *Quaker City* censor was quick to school his taste, it was probably a good thing. He was uninhibited enough to stand some toning down without serious damage to his gusty nature. Wisely he hearkened to her. When he gave the toast to "Woman" at another banquet on February 18, he said that it was "frigidly proper in language and sentiment." It may have been proper, but not frigid, for one reporter said that "all that banqueting crew laid down with laughter."

Meanwhile he had heard Charles Dickens read in Steinway Hall, New York—in the company, he said, of "a beautiful young lady . . . a highly respectable young white woman." He described Dickens as

a tall, "spry" . . . thin-legged old gentleman, gotten up regardless of expense, especially as to shirt-front and diamonds, with a bright red flower in his button-hole, gray beard and moustache, bald head, and with side hair brushed fiercely and tempestuously forward, as if its owner were sweeping down before a gale of wind. . . .[22]

He thought that the performance was only fair because the reader did not enunciate clearly, and his British accent was confusing, as in the pronunciation of "Steerforth" as "St'*yaw*-futh." Yet he was impressed by the animation of this clever actor, who made the process look easy. But when Mark Twain casually tried to imitate it some years later, he was amazed to discover that the apparently simple pastime of reading from a book required careful preparation.

In the midst of goings and comings he had, on short notice, prepared a lecture called "The Frozen Truth," which he delivered in Metzerott Hall, Washington, on January 10. He said that he had worked "like sin all night" to write it, yet it was mainly a transcription of *Alta California* material on the *Quaker City* excursion: preliminaries to the voyage, sociability and peculiarities of the pilgrims, groans and retchings of seasickness, and other familiar items. Excoriating the Turks, he admitted that their government was something like ours, citing a Turkish office-holder who had built himself a palace after three years in office. Imitating Artemus Ward's "A Visit to Brigham Young," he told of a confidential chat with the Sultan. This autocrat, unhappy despite 900 wives, spoke plaintively of the expense and discord of his large household: trouble with wife No. 642 who wanted jewelry; the hair-pulling fight between Nos. 422 and 764; the gigantic bed needed to accommodate the harem.[23] That story was a forerunner of the Brigham Young yarn in *Roughing It*. Such romancing made Mark Twain surmise that the discourse was "a little top-heavy . . . because there is more truth in the title than there is in the lecture."[24]

The performance was not well advertised, the manager became ill, Mark Twain was not informed until late in the day. After rounding up a doorkeeper, he went on stage in such a muddled state that he scarcely knew what he was going to say. Fortunately a good house showed up, and he managed to get through the "infernal" thing in "splendid style." Scheduled for a second performance on the 11th, he begged off because of the illness of the manager. "I had been reading my lecture to him," said Mark Twain, "but upon my sacred honor I did not think it would be so severe on him as all that. He is sick yet. . . . I will give him a chance, though—I will not read the lecture to him any more."[25]

On February 22 he celebrated Washington's birthday by delivering a Sandwich Islands lecture to a full house in Forrest Hall, Georgetown, for the benefit of the Ladies' Union Benevolent Society. This time he was entirely at ease. Walking on in what was described as "his usual cautious and deliberate manner," he apologized for the absence of an introducer. The young man delegated for the job, he said, had fallen down and broken his heart or his neck, he wasn't sure which. Referring to his talk as a benefit for the poor, he said that he had always had a grudge against the poor, and was therefore glad of the chance to inflict a lecture upon them. In honor of the date he told the cherry tree story, with adornments, then remarked that, although a newspaper man, he was like George Washington because he could not tell a lie.

The Sandwich Islands talk contained standard items of previous versions and some new ones, like the Honolulu gas company that collected only thirteen dollars and a half in one month because everybody went to bed at nine o'clock. The Washington *Morning Chronicle* of the 24th said that the audience, "including many of the most prominent persons of Georgetown and this city," was "in almost continuous roars of laughter," the amusing effect heightened by "his peculiarly slow and inimitable drawl."

5

Return to California

IN A SWIRL of action, Mark Twain was a busy contributor to Washington, New York, and California papers. Becoming bored with routine reporting, he reverted to satire in stories like that in the New York *Tribune* of February 13, "The Facts Concerning the Recent Important Resignation," a two-column burlesque of proceedings in the House, written with all the extravagant audacity of the old days on the *Enterprise*. He turned down lecturing invitations, and revised his foreign travel letters for publication. When the *Alta* seemed reluctant to release his correspondence, he embarked for California on March 11, 1868, to thresh the matter out, and arrived in San Francisco on April 2. He stayed three months, preparing copy for the *Innocents*, and spending two weeks on a lecture tour. With a new talk made from the *Quaker City* junket, he retraced the route of 1866, except for the least profitable stops. Within ten days of his arrival in San Francisco, papers announced his appearance on April 14 in Platt's Hall, where he would speak on "Pilgrim Life. Being a sketch of his notorious voyage to Europe, Palestine, etc."

Free and easy western slanging reasserted itself. "The *High Muck-a-Muck* of . . . fun and fancy," jeered *The Golden Era*,

has summoned a conclave of his braves, and the Kuklux Klan of Mark Twain-ites will promptly respond in force. . . . His reliquary gathered from every clime will be opened to the unbelievers . . . giving all an opportunity to repent. He announces his intention to enter . . . into the scandal of the *Quaker City*, tell with what facility he belted Orion, as well as all the male passengers . . . and how his innate morality was unsuccessfully assailed during his perilous career. His affections are still unengaged.[1]

The last statement was an error, for he had lost his heart to Olivia Langdon, the semi-invalid daughter of a wealthy coal dealer of Elmira, New York. From the moment he had glimpsed her portrait in her brother's stateroom on shipboard, he had been swept by an irresistible attraction that became intensified when he met her, and never wavered during an ardent courtship and thirty-four years of marriage.

The *Era*'s predicted response "in force" was a fact; the house was sold out within a few hours. Stopping the sale, said Mark Twain, "made a large number of people mad. . . . But *I* couldn't help that. I didn't want them standing up & bothering me."[2] Nevertheless, a mob of standees squeezed in. According to one reporter:

People . . . became suspended from hooks, clung tenaciously to the walls, grouped upon window sills, grappled at gas fixtures, mounted the plug hats and well covered shoulders of strangers, crushed and ruined a legion of waterfalls, chignons and curls.[3]

The wealth, beauty, fashion, and intellect of San Francisco jammed the hall, and Mark Twain pocketed over $1600 in gold and silver.

He began by saying that he would not discuss the Holy Land because he had already been well scolded for remarks on that subject. Then, telling a long story about falling in love with a Russian girl who weighed 252 pounds, he said he hoped to get her off his mind. Having her on his conscience was no matter because it could easily bear the weight. He spoke of the inquiry into the moral character of prospective excursionists—he having given as references General Grant, President Johnson, and Emperor Norton—idiosyncrasies of the pilgrims, the visit to the Emperor of Russia, ancient Mediterranean cities, Jerusalem, and the Sultan with his 800 wives (one hundred fewer than in Washington). Closing with a tribute to America, he praised the country of energy, freedom, beautiful women, cheap accident policies, incorruptible politicians, and Congressmen who showed their patriotism by prompt collection of their salaries.

The audience laughed at the Sultan and the pilgrims—relishing as a special tidbit the bellyaches and pukings of seasickness— and applauded ruined Rome and Pompeii, but next day's press was critical. The lecture, said the *Evening Bulletin,* "was not as completely prepared . . . as his first on the Hawaiian Islands . . . there was . . . regret that he had not said more about Palestine . . . and less about the bald-headed, spectacled and sedate old pilgrims. . . ." Mark Twain, said the *Call,* seemed like an indignant crusader, for he "battered the casques of friends and foes. . . . working himself into a grotesque rage over dulness, carving the sconces of proper folk, and making it lively for . . . respectability." Graphic passages contrasted sharply with "more slipshod doubtful jokes." On the 19th the *California Weekly Mercury* fired a shattering broadside:

That it was a . . . palpable failure may be surmised, when it is known that the truculent ass who writes the criticisms for the *Alta* and *Times* pronounced it a "perfect success." . . . the discourse . . . was foul with sacrilegious allusions, impotent humor, and malignant distortion of history and truth. . . . a man so lost to every sense of decency and shame should better be allowed to expire in obscurity. . . . There are indeed persons with whom this . . . riff-raff passes for wit, but we give God thanks that they are not of our kidney.

The San Rafael *Marin County Journal,* condemning the whole proceedings as "Sickening," denounced "This miserable scribbler, whose letters in the *Alta,* sickened everyone who read them, and of which the proprietors of that paper were heartily ashamed," yet who "has the audacity and impudence to attempt to lecture to an intelligent people."[4] This writer was outraged, as many others were, over impious reports from the Holy Land: the comment, for instance, on the impossibility of a Second Advent in Palestine because the Savior, having once been there, would assuredly never return to so dismal a country. From the pulpit a San Francisco clergyman thundered against "this son of the devil, Mark Twain." Pointed reprobation made him take to dodging around corners when he saw a preacher on the street. Once, when he mustered the nerve to go to church, he heard himself reproved by a young Baptist minister who reprimanded the small-minded sin of ridicule in "the letters of this person, Mark Twain, who visits the Holy Land and ridicules sacred scenes and things."[5] The sinner was man enough to shake hands with the preacher, thank him for the dressing-down, and acknowledge that he might have taken the wrong tack on the Holy Land, "but not altogether." We may agree. From our less reverent vantage point, his earthy story of barren Palestine and its starving, disease-ridden populace seems more genuine than the mawkish sentiment and inhumane piety of his fellow-travelers, the pilgrims.

Still, the censure is a refreshing reminder that even among his most devoted admirers Mark Twain was not universally approved. Sacrosanct least of all to himself, he joined the adverse chorus by admitting that his performance was "miserably poor." Repeating the lecture the next night, he made a better showing. The *Alta* said that this time he " 'got the hang of the sermon' " with "that confidential tone that breaks down . . . barriers between the man on the stage and people occupying the seats."[6]

At Sacramento another crowded house greeted him on April 17 in the Metropolitan Theater. He began by apologizing for the absence of Elder Knapp—a revivalist down on theaters, dancing, popery, Unitarianism, Universalism, and sprinkling—who, he said, had written the lecture, but was unable to deliver it in person. Then he went on as in San Francisco, alternately making fun of the pilgrims and reflecting solemnly on once proud cities now ruined and desolate. On the day after, the Sacramento *Union* observed that the first five minutes "sounded extremely frivolous," and remarked that "his address is not very good and his voice is low and sometimes aggravating to listeners." The paper complimented him for his "use of adjectives . . . something marvelous, especially in piling up invective," and pointedly commented on sentence structure: "The listener fears at first that the sentence is going to be weakened or lost in the confusion of polysyllables, but to his amazement out plumps the exact and fitting substantive at last."

These remarks tell something of Mark Twain's speaking style, which was similar to his written. He did pile up adjectives. His long sentences grew less by multiple parentheses—he was no Henry James—than by phrases and clauses introduced by "and." The loose, conversational structure, at the opposite extreme from conventional oratory, puzzled listeners throughout his career. Puzzling also was his negligent "address," as unconcerned as a loafer's on the courthouse square. No front, no starchiness, but an assumed air of seriousness, even of sanctimony. The low voice was a handicap, but it was so natural that apparently he never tried very hard to change it. Added to these eccentricities was a slow delivery, once described as words "separated as if there were a two-em quad between them."[7] His lecturing technique was so unorthodox that it sometimes provoked querulous vexation.

In one way his method was first-rate, for he had learned to dispense with a manuscript, and to rely only on brief notes jotted on small slips of paper. From the start he adopted an admirable rule: a lecture should be spoken, as if spontaneously, not read. So he memorized a manuscript, then gave it so artfully that more than one critic believed he was speaking impromptu. As a reporter once said: "The jokes are uttered as if he had just thought of them a minute before, and didn't perceive the point of them quite as soon as the audience."[8] Furthermore, having rehearsed orally, he knew the speaking time to the minute, hence never made the common mistake of taking twice as much time as he had been allotted. In these ways he was a model speaker.

He went on to Marysville and Nevada City. The Nevada *Daily Gazette* of April 20 greeted him as "This desperate joker," who would "preach on the Quaker (City) religion. . . . Those who expect a buffoon will be disappointed. He is a refined humorist and a scholar." Not always refined, and not exactly a scholar, he was not continually a buffoon either, yet in less happy moments distressingly addicted to buffoonery. He played the jester's role before a small house in Grass Valley. For some prankish reason he induced two well-known citizens to sit on the stage: one, an ardent bald-headed Republican, a banker and total abstainer; the other, an ardent bald-headed Democrat, a hard-up newspaperman and whiskey drinker. Possibly, considering the furore over the Holy Land letters, it was Mark Twain's way of suggesting that he was endorsed by both the respectable and the raffish. " 'Mark,' " said the waggish *Daily Union* of the 23d, "arose between these two thorns, got behind his mustache and started in." The first two stories were ancient: about the man who was twenty-four thousand, nine hundred and ninety-two miles from Marysville the way he was going, but only eight miles if he turned around; and about the boy who wanted a little devil to play with. "We *always* liked these stories," said the editor wistfully. "Our grandfather used to tell them. . . . they have stood the test of time." Fresher anecdotes accompanied "graphic description of the arid wastes of Palestine, and the misshapen waists of the Turkish ladies," and of "Damascus, the pearl of the East; (besides Damascus, he mentioned unfavorably several other cusses)."

After dashing over to Dutch Flat, he returned by steamboat to Sacramento, enjoying peach blossoms and roses blooming in the balmy air. Entraining for Virginia City, he rode to the summit of mountains where hundred-foot snowdrifts gripped the heights in the clutch of winter, yet where the sun beat down with blistering heat. He took a six-horse sleigh to Donner Lake, changed there to a mail coach for a stretch to Coburn's, took another train, changed again to a coach, and finally reached Virginia after an exhausting day of hard travel. It was good training for the rigors he would encounter in making one-night stands on the eastern circuit. "Sam," said the Virginia *Daily Trespass,*

is looking a little lean to what he used to, but we suppose that comes of eating in Turkish restaurants and joining the Eye Owe Gee Tease. He still talks as rapidly as ever—gets out a word every three minutes.[9]

The I. O. G. T., Independent Order of Good Templars, was a temperance organization of which Mark Twain was not a member. The sly dig of the *Trespass* was probably the result of a brief encounter with Ned Buntline (E. Z. C. Judson) aboard the river steamer *Capital.* This dime-novel writer, jack-of-all-trades, and shifty character had capped a lurid past—dishonorable discharge from the Union Army, four marriages, a narrow escape from lynching—by turning temperance exhorter for the Templars. Some said he was a bilk at everything except lying. His story, in the Sacramento *Weekly Rescue,* of meeting Mark Twain was no doubt enough for a scoffing reporter to seize upon.

Presumably the returned wanderer met a royal reception in Virginia and enjoyed convivial reunion with old friends, but neither he nor others have left us any story of this homecoming. The Webb sisters, current attraction at Piper's Opera House, graciously suspended their show to allow him to appear there twice. On the second night an assayer named Conrad Wiegand presented a forty-dollar bar of silver bearing the inscription: "Mark Twain—Matthew, V: 41—Pilgrim." That Bible verse is the if-asked-to-go-a-mile-go-with-him-twain admonition. "Twain," jeered the *Enterprise,*

would never object to going even farther, if sure of getting a fellow to the bar presented . . . and provided he was furnished a seat in a good, easy-going and softly-cushioned carriage.[10]

He went over to Carson City for an engagement on the 29th. There is a plausible story of that occasion, reported by an eyewitness many years later. After making his bow, Mark Twain was said to have unrolled a great sheaf of brown wrapping paper, on which the lecture was written in large letters with a grocer's marking brush. To read it he turned away from the audience, held the sheets high toward the light, and craned his neck upward as if he could not read in any other posture.[11] That he used this device is conjectural. Still, as a pointed criticism of the dim lights of small town auditoriums—of which he had had much experience —the stunt seems in keeping with his fertile inventiveness.

Prevailed upon to remain over a day to repeat the Sandwich Islands lecture, he gave it to a very small house of about one hundred. He called this performance "the last will and testament" of that talk, having dug it up from the grave of his memory. It was not quite the last, for within three weeks he was again revising it, and during the next five years he often used it for eastern and British audiences.

Going back to San Francisco, he enjoyed sleighing through a snowstorm; bowling along at ten miles an hour was more exciting, he said, than anything in Palestine. In the city he worked on the *Innocents,* composed a new lecture on Venice, wined and dined at the Lick House, and in spare time kept his name in the papers. Entering the controversy over the authorship of "Rock me to sleep," he demolished the claims of an aspirant named Ball:

O Bally, come back from the echoing shore! Cease for a season the public to bore with your infamous rhymes and your stupid complaint, for you know you are claiming to be what you ain't. Oh, drivel no more—don't snuffle, don't weep—hang up your lyre, Ball—I'll rock you to sleep.[12]

Receiving from San Andreas friends the corpse of a jumping frog, he responded with a eulogy, "Another Old Californian Gone." That heading, he said, was always used by newspapers for "a person of no particular consequence" because it "gives the deceased a sort of fictitious consequence, and prevents him going out of the world a complete and perfect nobody. It also insures him against making an unnoticed entrance into the next world." But since this frog "could not have been flatter if he had lain on some level surface a fortnight, with the United States on top of him," he believed it was not the celebrated jumping frog of Calaveras County because "that frog was not susceptible of flattery."[13]

Planning to sail from California on the last day of June, he waited over, he said, "to lecture & so persecute the public for their lasting benefit & my profit."[14] For this one he published in San Francisco papers an elaborate preliminary of manufactured letters. The first, signed by prominent citizens, the board of aldermen, fraternal organizations, "Various Benevolent Societies, Citizens on Foot, and 1500 in the Steerage," beseeched him not to lecture. "There is a limit," they said, "to human endurance." Mark Twain, affecting indignation, replied that the request was "entirely unprecedented," and that he was bound to torment the people once more because he wanted to tell them all about Venice, "what it achieved in twelve hundred years, and what it cost me in two hundred." Other notes, from clubs and banks, the clergy, and the chief of police, advised his speedy departure. Mark Twain had the last word, announcing that the lecture would be given on July 2, also that "public displays and ceremonies projected to give fitting eclat to this occasion" would be deferred until the Fourth. On that day there would be "a gorgeous display of fireworks . . . which I have ordered at my sole expense, the cost amounting to eighty thousand dollars."

The full title of this lecture was "The Oldest of the Republics, Venice, Past and Present," and the auditorium was the Mercantile Library. Seats went so fast that he soon rescinded the "children under one year, half price" rule to make room for more adults at full price. The speaker began by expressing appreciation for the full attendance, especially gratifying because "there was such a wide-spread, such a furious, such a determined opposition to my lecturing on this occasion. [Laughter.] . . . I never had such a unanimous call to—to—to leave, before. [Great laughter.]" Proposing to inform, he said that the lecture might be "somewhat didactic. I don't know what didactic means [Laughter] but it is a good high sounding word, and I wish to use it, meaning no harm whatever."[15]

Giving a concise history of Venice, he talked about his experience there, caprices of the gondola and gondoliers, and the universality of human nature, now and then digressing to cathedrals, monks, and contemptible Americans who ape foreigners. All of that was similar to his treatment of these topics in *The Innocents Abroad*. "After the lecturer had done his historic detail," said *The Californian*, "he began to do his audience . . . he sprang all kinds of concealed jokes, drolleries, flashes of humor . . . till the hall echoed with their cachinnations."[16] Mark Twain said that he felt "some inches taller" because of the hearty reception, yet he had doubts about the lecture. What was considered good by friends in San Francisco might be, he thought, a flat failure in the East, and he was sure that "Venice" would be "roughly criticized" there. Evidently he felt strongly about its inadequacy, for he never repeated it, although he incorporated parts in the lecture composed for the first eastern tour. Still, he was proud to report to Mother Fairbanks that "there is no slang, & no inelegancies in it—& I never swore once, never once was guilty of profanity."[17]

In 1866 both he and the press had made much of his farewell to California, but in 1868 there were no remarks about an affecting leave-taking. Yet this farewell was final. He did not so consider it then, for several times in later years he planned western tours. They did not materialize, and he never returned to California. He had finished with the Pacific Coast, as he had also finished his lecturing apprenticeship preparatory to the professional circuit.

8

The Lecture Circuit

MARK TWAIN's fear that his "Venice" lecture might fail before an "unbiased" eastern audience suggests that he was somewhat apprehensive about a circuit tour. If so, he had reason. This time he could not count on the advantage, as in the West, of friendly listeners predisposed to approve. He would have to show these strangers. Nor would he be the sole performer at large, as in California. Many seasoned competitors allowed comparative judgments by equally seasoned audiences.

Since the 1820's the lecturing business had flourished in the East, and had gradually extended its range until a hamlet in Illinois was likely to be as conversant with speakers, and as critical, as a long-established community in Massachusetts. A town was small indeed that did not boast a literary society or lyceum association devoted to uplift and enlightenment. To inform and improve, these organizations invited lecturers to discuss topics timely and perennial. Six or eight speakers made a "course," which might vary from the African travelogues of Paul B. Du Chaillu, to Civil War reminiscences of literate generals to the acrimony of Wendell Phillips or the emphatic feminism of Susan B. Anthony.

A very popular speaker lectured two hundred nights or more a year, and scarcely any was so inept that he could not find a few engagements. P. T. Barnum lectured, Clara Barton, Julia Ward Howe, General O. O. Howard, General Kilpatrick, Robert Ingersoll, Frederick Douglass, George Francis Train, Horace Greeley, Bayard Taylor, Theodore Tilton—and a host of others. Women, perhaps hoping to emulate Anna Dickinson, stormed the rostrum to charm, to instruct, and to assail masculine stupidity that oppressed women. Elizabeth Cady Stanton, Jane Swisshelm, Kate Field, Mary Livermore, Mrs. E. Oakes Smith, Lillie Peckham: they were part of a variegated sisterhood that cooed, cajoled, and berated. Then, as now, a notable name like Emerson, or a notorious one, like Victoria Woodhull, had drawing power. Yet the less prominent also had their day of transitory attention: Lillian Edgarton, "The Pearl of the Platform"; Mrs. Susannah Evans, "celebrated temperance oratress"; Waterhouse Hawkins, "the eminent palaeontologist"; and others long forgotten. As the modern American listens, entranced, to the interminable gabble of TV and radio, so by the hour nineteenth century audiences happily wallowed in billows of rhetoric rolling out from hundreds of platforms. During the "season," from about October to March, an army of pundits, prophets, reformers, preachers, and professors took to the road, bustling from town to town, crossing each other's trails and occasionally meeting to swap yarns about missed trains and missed dinners, cold halls and cold audiences, absurdities and satisfactions.

The prevailing tone of a course was serious, for the word "lecture" had a formal connotation allied to learning and culture: pedagogical, wholesome, grave, exhortatory. Adept performers rang the changes on all meanings by tricks of voice and gesture, and by unashamed showmanship. Beecher was a compelling spectacle, his full pink face like a well-fed cherub's, frock coat and long flaxen locks making him look like a Pre-Raphaelite version of a Congressman. A worldly man with a strain of coarseness, something of a cynic only superficially spiritual, he moved in a golden aura of his own creation. Skillfully he plucked the heartstrings. His emotional liberalism identified the common people with God, his stock of unoriginal ideas did not tax the mind, vague but musical metaphor charmed the ear, and rapt listeners, hypnotized by presence and voice, felt en rapport with a great man. Shrewdly sensing the popular side of any question, he seldom failed to move his auditors. An accomplished actor and revivalist, he thundered and thumped and told stories funny and pathetic—with tears when needed—to make an audience shudder, laugh, and weep. On Sundays the ferries, called Beecher's boats, hauled mobs of worshipers over to Brooklyn's Plymouth Church. New York papers reported the annual pew-renting as if it were a stock market transaction, listing high prices paid by wealthy parishioners. The fluttery idol-worship of Beecher was like the hysteria over twentieth century crooners who have made adolescents twitch and scream and swoon.

John B. Gough, a bearded, portly man without grace of manner or voice, mesmerized an audience for two hours, roaring against liquor and staging a vaudeville show of frenzied acrobatics. Himself a reformed sot who had once gone on wild ten-day sprees, he graphically illustrated the drunkard's progress. Frantically he waved his arms, staggered about the stage, reeled and fell in violent contortions that left him dripping. After a perspiring evening he donned two overcoats to ward off the chill outer air, then immediately returned to his hotel for a brisk rubdown. "Ye moldering victims!" he shouted, "wipe the grave dust crumbling from your brow; stalk forth in your tattered shrouds and bony whiteness to testify against drink!"[1] As crusader and comedian, he was as entertaining as a variety show, as scarifying as a revival, and so much in demand that he was deluged with lucrative offers. A British promoter offered him $1200 in gold per lecture for one appearance a week for a year in London, besides a furnished house rent-free. Gough was the most sought-after and, with an annual income that reached $30,000 or more, the most affluent speaker in America.

Mark Twain heard him once; in one of his notebooks is a burlesque tale illustrating the power of the Gough influence. It is the story of a drunkard who brained his family with a bottle. Sobered and remorseful, he signed the pledge, remarried, reared another family, backslid into drunkenness, and in a fit of boozy pique wiped out wife and progeny with the same bottle. Again he sobered and repented, again remarried, again got drunk and liquidated the family with the identical sturdy bottle. Then he heard Gough lecture. Frightened into genuine reform, he gave up the bottle both as solace and bludgeon. Whereupon widespread hosannahs, the multiple killings being ironically written off as inconsequential.[2]

Josiah Holland, editor of *Scribner's Monthly*, forerunner of the *Century*, had a severe manner and an Indian-like way of stalking about the platform. Yet his message was sweetness and light. Hear him on the theme of "Work and Play": "Weave on, in glad content, industrious worker of the mill, for thou art weaving cloth of gold, though thou mark not its lustre."[3] That must have been surprising news to underpaid men, women, and children laboring in textile mills sixty to seventy hours a week without ever having discovered that cloth of gold was legal tender. Mark Twain called Holland "a remorseless intellectual cholera . . . the very incarnation of the Commonplace."[4] He was, but the commonplace paid when delivered with unction. Still, if an audience enjoyed soothing syrup, it could also swallow the acid of an agitator like Wendell Phillips. This perennial objector and storm-center of bitter controversy—"an unsafe pilot," one critic called him, "but a mighty useful fog-whistle"—spoke with an eloquence that made his words flash with color and crackle with flame.

De Witt Talmage, a popular preacher with a flair for the sensational, relied upon posture and modulation. Exploiting strong clear-cut features, erect carriage, and startling gestures, he made the ordinary seem impressive. One device was to hurl a question in a low, intense voice. Then, after striding wordlessly about the stage, he suddenly faced his audience, crossed his arms, stamped his feet, repeated the question in a loud voice, and roared the answer. The effect was terrific. Mark Twain once expressed an unflattering opinion of Talmage when he asked Howells:

Do you forget that Heaven is packed with a multitude of all nations . . . all on the most familiar how-the-hell-are-you footing with Talmage swinging around the circle to all eternity hugging the saints and patriarchs and archangels, and forcing you to do the same unless you choose to make yourself an object of remark if you refrain? Then why do you try to get to Heaven? Be warned in time.[5]

Olive Logan, "The Lily of the Lyceum," depended upon fashionable clothes and a theatrical manner, which made the press shower extravagant compliments. She "dresses wisdom in the robes of wit," said the New York *Tribune,* "quickens all that is fine . . . imparts to life that glow of enjoyment which burns up . . . the chaff of the commonplace."[6] Mark Twain considered her prominence only "manufactured notoriety," built up by press-agentry probably similar to the propaganda machinery of Madison Avenue, and he dismissed her as "merely a name and some rich and costly clothes."[7] That estimate was correct, yet for several years her pronounced femininity and stylish ensembles—smart velvets, gold band encircling the brow, cascade of curls, chignon—attracted large crowds and made her an implausible celebrity in the papers. Olive Logan's disapproval of the short skirt, Olive Logan's views on marriage and divorce, Olive Logan's remarks on the theater and nudity in art: for awhile such stuff put her name in headlines from coast to coast. Forty years later, when her star had long since set and her glamor had given way to white-haired age clouded by insanity, when she was faded, tottery, deaf, and broke, Mark Twain softened his earlier disdain to magnanimous pity.[8]

Although seriousness was the rule among lecturers, polite jocosity was permissible. Large doses of humor relieved solemnity when the immensely popular Nasby was on the program, or Josh

Billings, Brock McVicker, or De Cordova. There were signs that the frivolous was gaining favor as a respite from earnest sermonizing. But the strait-laced frowned upon frivolity. In *Scribner's Monthly* the platitudinous Holland reprehended the admission of "triflers and buffoons to the lecture platform . . . men . . . who have no better motive and no higher mission than the stage-clown and negro-minstrel."[9] Mark Twain, taking that remark as a personal insult, not only excoriated Holland, but also emphasized the great success of various so-called triflers and buffoons.

Until 1868 the loose lecture system required a lecturer to make his own arrangements with each society and to bargain for a price, which was generally so low that $100 was phenomenal. Forty to fifty dollars was a rough average. Emerson once lectured in Waltham for five dollars and four quarts of oats for his horse. Wendell Phillips often lectured for $25; on the subject of abolition he had frequently and gladly spoken for nothing. Gough, who made 383 talks his first season, received a total of $1059, out of which he paid his own expenses. His plan was never to ask a fee, but to allow the local committee to decide how much he deserved. Since the natural tendency is to avoid imputation of miserliness, that scheme eventually netted more perhaps than a stipulated price.

Finances were so precarious in a small town lyceum society that public-spirited supporters had to underwrite deficits. If a course made money on popular speakers who filled the house, it lost on what Mark Twain called "house emptiers." Money troubles often made a society short-lived, but when it died a new one was likely to be born elsewhere. Thus, a continuing demand gave full employment to lecturers. They published their own ads and hoped for takers. Thus:

Rev. Professor Richards, A. M., will lecture on "Thomas Hood" for $50 and expenses. . . . Z. R. Sanford, Esq., will read his original poem, "Fringes," for $50, with modifications. . . . Mr. L. Bradford Prince . . . will discourse about "Fashion" or "Rienzi" for $25 and traveling expenses. . . . J. O. Miller—The eloquent Orange County Farmer, a highly reputed humorist. Terms, $50, with modifications.[10]

In 1868 James Clark Redpath and George L. Fall systematized the business by founding the Boston Lyceum Bureau. It assisted local committees to arrange dates, gave them more balanced programs, and even offered cut rates for successive engagements close together. Besides, it relieved lecturers of the drudgery of making out schedules, looking up transportation, and haggling over price. Standardizing fees, the Bureau, for a ten percent commission, took care of all details. The advantages were so obvious that most of the leading speakers in the country immediately flocked to Redpath. His array of talent encouraged the development of the "Star Course" in large cities, which engaged en masse the best of the Bureau's performers, and sharply increased fees. The average went up to about $100, a figure that Mark Twain said denoted "second-class stars," and for top attractions—Beecher, Gough, Nasby, Phillips, Anna Dickinson—the price was $200 to $400. Editors grumbled over prohibitive fees. The Chicago *Times* complained because a speaker "must be recompensed by the modest sum of $150 or thereabouts for merely reading an hour and a half from a manuscript!"[11] The rising cost of culture irritated consumers. In the familiar American way they considered of no consequence the time spent in preparing a manuscript, and they were strong for uplift provided it was cheap. For small lyceums Redpath booked the best attractions they could afford, but only on condition that a course also take one or two low-priced third-raters. Thus the agency worked equitably for lecturers, though it disgruntled audiences that had to put up with the pipings of a little-known "fair authoress" or "lectress" when they wanted the booming of heavy oratorical guns.

In the early fall of 1868 Mark Twain enlisted the aid of Redpath, who took him on as a hundred-dollar man, and scheduled about forty engagements. As tours went, this one was short and poorly arranged for economical travel. Belatedly signing up with the Bureau, he found many courses filled, hence had to accept a miscellany of towns, a third of which were scarcely more than villages, on a tortuous route. He started at Cleveland in mid-November, then for three and a half months hopped back and forth between the East and Middle West on a weird itinerary of zigzags and redoublings upon itself. Gaps of days between performances ran up hotel bills; unscheduled trips to Cleveland to see Mrs. Fairbanks and to Elmira to see Olivia Langdon added to expenses that consumed half the income. Reproving himself for delay, he lamented that, whereas he might have made $10,000, he expected to clear not over two thousand. Possibly the net return was even less, and he earned it the hard way.

In late summer, having tentatively thought of either Venice or California as his subject, he discarded both in favor of a new lecture called "The American Vandal Abroad," which he wrote in one day. That speed was only a feat of transcription, for, as he said, he "smouched" most of it from his forthcoming book, *The Innocents Abroad.* Since a lecture subject was merely a label, necessary but not binding, there was something in this one of "The Frozen Truth," "Venice," and "Pilgrim Life." The foreignized American and his fractured French, Versailles, the Milan cathedral and sacred relics, the assumed stupidity that made life miserable for European guides, Venetian canals and gondoliers, the Parthenon by moonlight, the call upon the Emperor of Russia: all went into the "Vandal" in much the same form and same order that they appear in the book. He lifted verbatim the description of the Sphinx, the ridicule of "M'sieu Gor-r-*dong,*" and the concluding summary, called "fireworks," of imposing sights like Gibraltar, Damascus, and St. Peter's.

As usual, serious passages blended with humor about duplication of churchly relics, shopping by scow in Venice, and the upstart behavior of the vandal. He broke specimens from the tomb of Romeo and Juliet, strutted down Parisian boulevards, derided the old masters, remarked that "The atmosphere of Greece is as clear as the nose of a man with a cold in his head," sneered that the Arabian desert "ain't a patchin' on the Overland route to Califoriny," and carried everywhere his outlandish blue cotton umbrella. Still, said Mark Twain, "I treat him gently & good-naturedly, except that I give him *one* savage blast for aping foreign ways."[12] That was a proper touch for patriots. The vandal flattered the complacent nationalism of many audiences, who saw him less as an object of ridicule than as a praiseworthy symbol of American swagger, making the eagle scream in foreign parts, and noisily asserting his provincialism even as Mark Twain did in the *Innocents.* '

Starting in Cleveland on November 17, he prefaced his appearance by a story in the *Herald* about his Double, who had lectured in various places under his name, then left without paying his bills, which were duly forwarded to Mark Twain. "It (the Double)," he said, "delivered a lecture in Satan's Delight, Idaho, on 'The Moral Impossibility of Doughnuts'—a subject in which I *never* took the slightest interest in my life." In Ohio and Wisconsin,

It advertised Itself to lecture and didn't; It got supernaturally drunk at other people's expense; It continued Its relentless war upon helpless and unoffending boarding-houses.[13]

Slippery impostors—there were probably more than one—were not imaginary. They plagued him off and on, and they were so elusive that he never managed to suppress them. Twenty-seven years later, in Sydney, Australia, watching an elaborate funeral procession, he asked the name of the honored dead, and was told that the deceased was Mark Twain. Possibly he was one of those frauds who had long evaded the police. Mark Twain said that he cheerfully joined the mourners because it was the first time to his knowledge that anybody had ever had a chance to attend his own funeral.

The Cleveland debut was strategic, since it assured him charitable treatment by the Fairbanks paper, the *Herald*, and subjected his lecture to the watchful eye and ear of Mother Fairbanks. She was squeamish about the story of the skinned man and the gory episode of the stabbed man, but evidently not severe, for in the *Herald* next day she praised

brilliant entertainment. . . . We congratulate Mr. Twain upon having . . . conclusively proved that a man may be a humorist without being a clown. He has elevated the profession by his graceful delivery and by recognizing in his audience something higher than merely a desire to laugh.

Nevertheless, he worked for laughs in Cleveland, as he did in every other town. A Chicago critic later in the tour said: "There is nothing in his lectures, for he very properly sacrifices everything to make his audience roar, and they do."[14] At the end of his most poetic passage, the much-admired apostrophe to the Sphinx, he could not resist tacking on a few words about the vandal carelessly whistling in the shadow of the ancient monument. This flippant touch crumbled beauty in a crash of guffaws. In Mark Twain the clown was generally within easy hail. Akin to the humorous muse of Rabelais and Shakespeare, it was a clown of facets, witty, given to low comedy, and not above inflating the self-satisfaction of the groundlings.

Twelve hundred people braved the rain and slush of a stormy night to fill Case Hall. Disposed to be critical of this neophyte, they soon succumbed to his humor, his drawl, and his nonchalance, though some were annoyed by the low voice. The "buttonhole relationship" remarked upon at Cooper Union was in evidence here. Sixteen years later Mark Twain recalled that at one point, losing his place, he asked the audience to help him out. When people only laughed, he repeated his request, and they laughed harder. Finally Solon Severance, a *Quaker City* shipmate, arose to say that "if he was really in earnest he would remind him what lie he was telling when the interruption occurred."[15] The camaraderie of an old home week pleased the speaker. "Made a *splendid* hit last night," he said jubilantly, "& am the 'lion' to-day. . . . I captured them, if I *do* say it myself."[16]

Thus the tour began auspiciously, and success went with him to Pittsburgh. With justifiable pride he reported that, playing there against the famous actress, Fanny Kemble, he drew a crowd of 1500, whereas she had only a meager 200. The *Gazette* of the 20th commended dignified bearing, choice diction, humor that was funny but not extravagant, and the refreshing absence of facial contortions.

As calm, self-possessed, graceful and easy . . . as Wendell Phillips, his rival as a humorist, but of another school . . . Mark Twain, with no . . . unbecoming effort to excite . . . risibility . . . succeeds . . . in convulsing with laughter the veriest cynic before him.

The *Dispatch*, on the other hand, came out with blistering dispraise. Mark Twain, unruffled, said that since he liked to express his opinions in print, the paper had the same privilege, and he was not disposed to quarrel. This professional attitude was one of his best traits. He would have been more or less than human not to have been hurt by damning criticism, but it never knocked him out.

At Elmira, on November 23, the success story hit a snag, or at least he thought so. The *Daily Advertiser* printed conventional compliments, but he failed to satisfy his own standards. It was a "lame delivery," he said, a "botch of a lecture," so poor that at the end he apologized to the audience. That must have been humiliating because one listener was Olivia Langdon, for whom he had hoped to shine. Undoubtedly she had disturbed his aplomb and distracted his mind; he was so deeply in love that the wooer had overwhelmed the lecturer. Involved in an impetuous courtship, he brought to bear all the forces of promised reform, of church-going and Bible-reading, assuming a frightening sanctimony and an unnatural abstemiousness to win the favor of Livy and her hesitant family. He was so earnest that he told Mother Fairbanks he had resolved to give up strong drink, to do nothing that might pain her and Livy, to associate only with good companions: in short, to become a Christian.[17] For the time being, resolution held firm. A middle western reporter made the remarkable statement, which would have astounded California and Nevada cronies: "Drink never crosses the threshold of his humorous mouth."[18]

When Livy came close to capitulation after a several days' siege, and when he had left Elmira after a week's stay, he tried to get down to business. Yet on the train to New York, attempting to memorize his manuscript, he confessed that "It was Livy, Livy, Livy, Livy, all the way through! . . . one sentence of Vandal to ten sentences about *you.*"[19] The rosy haze still befogged him when he spoke in the small town of Rondout on December 2. A week later the *Kingston Argus* disposed of him in one sentence: "The lecture of Mark Twain . . . did not give . . . satisfaction, many being disappointed."

By the time he reached Newark, the lecturer had temporarily won over the lover. He was a noisy success for the Clayonian Society with the "Vandal" under the title of "Brother Jonathan Abroad." In a sketch entitled "A Wicked Fraud," written for the Newark *Express,* he purported to reveal how he had been taken in by one of the Clayonians. The young man, lamenting the sad state of an uncle who never showed any emotion, said that he longed to see him laugh or weep once more. "My son," said Mark Twain,

bring the old party around. I have got some jokes in this lecture that will make him laugh if there is any laugh in him—and if they miss fire I have got some others that'll make him cry or kill him, one or the other.

So there he was in the second row. The lecturer bombarded him with mild jokes; then with severe ones . . . dosed him with bad jokes and riddled him with good ones . . . fired old stale jokes into him, and peppered him fore and aft with red-hot new ones . . . assaulted him on the right and left, in front and behind . . . fumed and sweated, and charged and routed. . . .

Finally he hurled "a joke of supernatural atrocity full at him," without ever starting the ghost of a smile or the glint of a tear. Then he sat down, hoarse, exhausted, and bewildered, only to learn that "that confounded old fool in the second row" was "deaf and dumb, and as blind as a badger."[20] This story, similar to Artemus Ward's "How the Napoleon of Sellers Was Sold," is no doubt one of those tall tales.

From Newark he journeyed 150 miles north to Norwich, New York, dropped down to Scranton, then backtracked to Fort Plain, stopping a day at Elmira en route. Before the tour was well under way he had traveled over 2000 miles, and had weathered some of the ups and downs of trouping. At Newark he had been without sleep for thirty-six hours, he said, then got thoroughly chilled waiting twenty minutes for a carriage at midnight. At Norwich he relaxed for two days in the home of Judge Mason. The lady of the house won his gratitude by allowing him to smoke, strew clothes around his room, sleep late, eat at any hour, and track snow over the carpet. She must have been a forbearing woman, for Mark Twain was not an easy person to have around the house. Neither placid nor orderly, he could disrupt domestic routine and fray the nerves of the precise housekeeper. The *Enterprise* had once reported him as saying:

It is irksome to me to behave myself. . . . I had rather call on people who know me and will kindly leave me entirely unrestrained, and simply employ themselves in looking out for the spoons.[21]

Aware of his own careless habits and love of comfort, he learned that, as a rule, a touring lecturer had more freedom at a hotel than in a private home, where he might be subjected to a frigid room, unreasonable demands upon him as conversationalist, a prohibition against smoking, and, as he put it, "unholy breakfast hours." "When I am ill-natured," he once said,

I so enjoy the freedom of a hotel—where I can ring up a domestic and give him a quarter and then break furniture over him—then I go to bed calmed and soothed and sleep as peacefully as a child.[22]

As somebody's guest, he might be shown the dreary sights of the town, or taken around to meet the mayor, the wealthiest man, and the town wit, who never failed to crack mossgrown jokes. From a hotel retreat he could decline these dubious pleasures. Occasionally, when he could not politely reject the hospitality of a local clergyman or tycoon, he suspended the hotel rule. Then, if he had a rough time in the family of some well-meaning but inconsiderate parson, he expressed violent irritation to his favorite correspondents, Livy and Mother Fairbanks.

Such a place was the home of the Rev. Mr. Nevins in Stuyvesant, New York, where he landed late in February. All afternoon he had to sit in a parlor and talk. Tea time brought an irruption of young ladies and a bedlam of chatter. By lecture time he was fatigued. After the performance company stayed till midnight, after which three young ladies asked him questions for another hour, and when they turned in kept up a loud bedroom giggling and jabbering long after. To add to his troubles, the stove smoked.[23] Man's inhumanity to lecturers made him endorse the rules proposed by Josh Billings for lyceum managers. "Let the lekturer alone during the day," said he,

don't call on him, don't let enny body else call on him. . . . Never offer to take a lekturer to a private house, unless your hotel burnt up last night. . . . All lecturers are to a certain degree Bohemians, they are not ekonomists at home, in the way of law, and household order.[24]

Taking off on a long, slow trip westward, Mark Twain arrived in Detroit on December 21 for a lecture the next night. The *Free Press* of the 23d was not entirely pleased. The performance, it said, was droll and at times brilliant, but the speaker's "capabilities as a writer are far in advance of his powers as a lecturer," and his delivery "was not what might have been expected, an assumed drawl . . . spoiling the effect of many of the finest sentences." That comment is unusual, for the drawl was attractive to many, both in public speaking and conversation. Possibly the sharp contrast with the hard, flat locutions of the Middle West subtly unsettled this critic. Mark Twain was sensitive about his languorous speech, and quick to resent any suggestion of ridicule. Yet he made fun of it himself in his essay, "The Facts Concerning the Recent Carnival of Crime in Connecticut," when Conscience says: "I shall always address you henceforth in your o-w-n s-n-i-v-e-l-i-n-g d-r-a-w-l—baby!" A puzzled old man once asked after a lecture: "Be them your natural tones of eloquence?" The answer should have been yes, for slow speech was natural to Mark Twain, not assumed. Perhaps he exaggerated the drawl on the platform, where it was well suited to those long-drawn-out anecdotes full of detail and suspense. The exalted flights, the word painting, may have needed more acceleration and vigor.

He went on to Lansing and Tecumseh, then rushed over to Cleveland, missing an engagement at Fort Wayne, Indiana. He had to discuss with Mother Fairbanks and her amiable but footling husband, Abel, the possibilities of settling in Cleveland as part owner of the *Herald,* and, more important, he had to talk about Livy. Mrs. Fairbanks was not only literary and social mentor, but also confidante to whom he revealed his aspirations and his love. He made a sortie to Akron, then dashed back to Cleveland to celebrate the New Year in a round of social gatherings during which he reluctantly yielded to his hosts' desire to show him off as parlor entertainer, but let them know he wanted no more of that.

Beginning on January 2, 1869, in Charlotte, Michigan, he embarked on the most intensive part of the tour, making twenty-one appearances during the month on a nervous itinerary that shuttled back and forth among Michigan, Illinois, Indiana, Iowa, and Ohio. His text varied as he incorporated new and absurd adventures of the vandal. In Detroit he had gone to the Paris opera without knowing the difference between dialogue and scenery. In Chicago he was trout-fishing on Lake Como, selling the fish on the Rialto, dining with the resident mummy of a pyramid, inspecting the wall where St. Paul was let down in a basket that was sold for firewood, and inviting the Czar to call on him in San Francisco. Another Chicago story was of a sailor afflicted with "horizontal paralax," who was dosed with four shovelsful of laudanum and a huge mustard plaster, the laudanum to put him to sleep, the plaster to wake him up. In Peoria the vandal was unconcernedly picking his teeth in the shadow of the Sphinx. In Davenport he was exploring the secrets of the harem in Damascus. This impudent upstart tickled the fancy of audiences, who thought he was a delightful fellow. Newspapers stories said that crowds were large, eminently respectable, highly intelligent, and invariably well-dressed. As one reporter boasted:

Broadcloths and silks were in the ascendant, and the rowdy or "fast" element congenial to negro minstrel exhibitions was but slimly represented.[25]

The humorist, said another, did not depend upon "local vernacular," and told his jokes "without a single low or ungrammatical phrase." That spoke well for the schooling of Mother Fairbanks' cub, who made a point of sending her some of these notices of a rise toward propriety of the former wild humorist of the Pacific slope.

Like the vandal, Mark Twain also had new adventures: in small town hotels, where dim gaslights taught him to carry a stock of candles; in the slowness of trains, jolting all day from Chicago to Indianapolis, then rattling for another day west to Rockford, Illinois. He saw himself described contradictorily and condescendingly: at Chicago as "Blessed with long legs . . . tall . . . head round and set on considerable neck, and feet of no size within the ken of a shoemaker"; at Peoria as a "well-built, trim-looking little gentleman"; at Davenport, strangely, as "an original yankee."

Ottawa, Illinois, produced a series of mishaps. When he arrived there, he had lost the baggage containing his platform claw-hammer, hence had to appear in what he called his "bob-tail coat," which made him ill at ease. (A remarkable change, that, from the careless indifference to clothes of a few years before. Love had wrought wonders.) The auditorium was a church, "harder to speak in," he said, "than an empty barrel would have been." The "idiot president" of the local society began to introduce him while people were still finding their seats, and they kept on clattering in until the lecture was well under way. Mark Twain became so exasperated that he ordered the doorkeeper to lock all doors. Then, his poise shattered, he stumbled through, making in his own estimation such a miserable failure that he apologized to the audience, as he had in Elmira. He "bade the house good-night," he said, "& then gave the President a piece of my mind, without any butter or sugar on it."[26] Unfortunately, we have no verbatim transcript of one of his wrathful explosions. No doubt at such a time all the painfully learned precepts of Mother Fairbanks vanished in a hurricane of earthy metaphor and hearty profanity that would have made her shudder. Committeemen tried to cheer him with praise, but he was unconvinced, and the Ottawa *Republican* of January 21 partially supported his judgment in the equivocal statement:

One man said it was "very funny and at times eloquent." Another, equally as well prepared to judge, thought "the lecture was mostly nonsense and stale at that."

Indicative of comparative values, when Olive Logan appeared in Ottawa shortly afterwards, the same paper gave her a story over twice as long as it had given Mark Twain.

In Iowa City three days later he blew up again, loudly, at the Clinton House. When the landlord, trying to be of service, waked him at nine o'clock, the temperamental visitor erupted in a storm of rebuke. Then, unable to go to sleep again, he thought of coffee, but could find no bell to summon it. So he slammed the door until the landlord came up again to be met with another violent outburst. The Iowa City *Republican* made quite a story of these tantrums, calling Mark Twain "a splendid species of the Vandal and all his works," and remarking upon "a terrible racket . . . and unearthly screams, which frightened the women of the house." The landlord confronted "the veritable animal, with his skin on, at least, but not much else, in a towering rage," having "kicked the fastenings from the door, not deigning to open it the usual way. (That would have been too much like other folks.)," and greeting the poor man with a "torrent of curses, impudence, and abuse."[27] Possibly the paper embroidered the facts. Yet Mark Twain was later enough ashamed of his part in these noisy proceedings to write the landlord a letter of apology.

The hotel uproar probably colored the story of the performance in the *Republican*, which said that "As a lecture, it was a humbug. As an occasion for laughter on a . . . small capital of wit or ideas, it was a success." Admitting merit in passages on the Sphinx and Parthenon, the paper complained that "it was impossible to know when he was talking in earnest, and when in burlesque." Although people laughed, "half of them were ashamed that they were laughing at such . . . small witticisms. . . . We would not give two cents to hear him again." A final crusher was the observation that of all the lecturers in the season's Y. M. C. A. course, Mark Twain was "the only one . . . whose personal character was unknown."[28] And that, was the implication, had been clearly revealed by the oafish behavior at the Clinton House. The criticism was the most unfavorable meted out to him on this tour. Next day, as a last literal blow, he lamed himself badly by falling on the ice. The Iowa City engagement left no happy memories for him nor for the town either perhaps, for he never lectured there again.

It was time now for another trip to Cleveland, and he set out for the Fairbanks home, cancelling a performance at Sparta, Wisconsin. Last-minute cancellations caused ruffled feelings particularly of country people who might have spent half a day struggling into town over bad roads to hear the celebrated humorist. He soothed them as best he might, the most effective method being to appear in person on a later date. When, in late January, he filled the Fort Wayne engagement missed in December, he faced a grim audience, indignant at having been once put off, but he was pleased to report that he broke down its hostility in ten minutes. Missing engagements was not good policy for a newcomer in a competitive enterprise, but an excuse was the compulsive power of love. With one eye on Elmira and another on Cleveland, he needed a third eye to oversee policy. Nevertheless, despite a somewhat erratic concern for obligations, a flood of speaking invitations confirmed a popularity that was almost universal. Exhilarated by success, he planned a California tour soon after the close of the 1868-69 season.

Using Cleveland as a base, he journeyed to Toledo and Norwalk, then returned to the city to appear in Case Hall for the benefit of the Protestant Orphan Asylum. Concluding with a plea for donations, he admitted that to have charged a dollar for the performance would have been "a most gigantic fraud. . . . But you pay your dollar to the orphan asylum and have the lecture thrown in!" A skating rink proprietor having offered to contribute the proceeds of one evening, Mark Twain urged everyone to skate. "If you break your necks," he said, "it will be no matter; it will be to help the orphans." He dwelt upon the labor of washing all sixty orphans in a single wash tub:

They have to be washed in the most elaborate detail, and by the time they get through with the sixty, the original orphan has to be washed again. Orphans won't stay washed! I've been an orphan myself for twenty-five years and I know this to be true.[29]

The audience was not so large as that of his Cleveland debut in November, but it was a good-natured crowd that contributed $807 to the orphanage.

On January 25 he set out for a short, compact run, beginning that night at Marshall, Michigan, twenty-five miles from the town he had lectured in three weeks before. That retracing of steps was typical of the whole tour. Batavia and Freeport followed, then Waterloo, Galena, Fort Wayne, and Jacksonville: all on successive days without untoward incident. Then occurred a break of eleven days, most of which, from February 3 to 11, he was in Elmira. On the 4th he became formally engaged to Olivia Langdon, and immediately dispatched an exultant missive to Mother Fairbanks.

After eight blissful days the lover again reluctantly yielded to the lecturer. Departing for Ravenna, Ohio, he naturally paused in Cleveland. His greeting there was a telegram from aggrieved citizens of Alliance: "Splendid audience assembled—where is Mark Twain?—Somebody will be responsible for this."[30] Fumbling Abel Fairbanks, having made an engagement for him in that town on February 13, had been unsuccessfully chasing him, by letter around the cornbelt, but had absently failed to forward the news to Elmira. In a fit of temper, Mark Twain chided the dodderer for not having used the telegraph, calling him an "astonishing old aggregation of nonsense," and carrying on until Mother Fairbanks, he said, "threatened to take a broomstick to me." When his irritation had blown itself out, he was contrite and apologetic, even pleased that no telegram had arrived in Elmira to tear him away from Livy.

He got to Alliance by the 15th, knocking $20 off his fee, and paying the lyceum association extra expenses of $10. But that rearrangement of schedule threw subsequent dates out of order. He had to postpone Franklin, Pennsylvania, for two days and pay another forfeit. To get to Titusville on the 16th, he sat up after the Alliance lecture until two A. M., then caught a coal train for a leisurely two-hour jog back to Ravenna, slept there for an hour and a half, then started for Titusville about 5:30. At Corry, early in the afternoon, he waited four hours, which he put in sleeping at a hotel, and finally arrived in Titusville, dog-tired but ready, in time for the lecture. Like a general in the field, a trouper commandeered all sorts of transportation, and since he was likely to go into action at any hour, he was blest if he could snatch a little sleep, any time, anywhere.

Because he could not make Geneseo, New York, on the 18th he postponed another date and disappointed society members there who had arranged an "elegant entertainment" in his honor at the American Hotel. (Undaunted, they had their ten P. M. dinner without him.) The Alliance snarl and its attendant dislocations cost him, he said, more than a hundred dollars and "gave a power of dissatisfaction." But "nobody can say a word against Mr. Fairbanks & me, *now*—for we have fulfilled our contracts & done our duty."[31] Yet immediately after Franklin there was another cancellation at Auburn, and Mark Twain set off at once for Elmira to spend two days with Livy. This tour was an inseparable mixture of lecturing and love.

In late February he appeared at Trenton, then at the village of Stuyvesant, New York. Billed for the 27th at Lockport, he found the town moribund in the grip of sub-zero weather. So little was stirring that when lecture time came, only a few brave people had straggled into Arcade Hall. Promising to speak four days later, he dismissed them with a joke about getting their money back, although he considered that doubtful because the treasurer had been called out to see a man.

At Geneseo to fill the postponed date, he had a royal reception. Entertainment was so persistent that at one point, when his hotel room was overrun by eager young men of the town and the Methodist college at Lima, Mark Twain, pleading weariness, asked them rather brusquely to leave. Their abashed looks as they stumbled out, bumping into each other in their hurry, so smote his conscience that he could not sleep. In a typical reaction of regret, he got up and invited them all back again to be sumptuously entertained until midnight with talk, songs, piano playing, cigars, and drinks. He said that he drank nothing himself, merely "played sedate old gentleman" beaming on high-spirited youth. Such was his charm that when the crowd left they assembled in the street, Methodists and all, and gave him three vinous cheers.

On March 3 he ended the tour at Lockport before an audience puzzled by his offhand manner of springing a joke. This habit, said the *Journal* next day, made his "momentous flashes of humor . . . not always button-bursting." People "would have enjoyed his lecture much more if he had told them when to laugh." In this part of the country he must have met a good deal of that sort of slow-witted response, for he once observed that "New York State audiences are much duller and stupider than any other."[32]

Long jumps, spur-of-the-moment trips to Cleveland and Elmira, and forfeits for postponed engagements made the season no great financial success. In January he had told his sister that he had saved "about a thousand dollars," and hoped to lay by another thousand. Six months later he wrote his mother that he had made "eight or nine thousand," despite expenses that were "something frightful." Yet forty lectures "at $100 a pop," as he put it, could not have yielded that sum. Perhaps he was counting intangible assets, for he remarked that the money was only half the pay— "the rest was jolly experience."

If not all experiences had been jolly, if some episodes had ruffled the touchy Twainian temper, he had, in the main, enjoyed himself, and in about 7000 miles of hard travel he had proved his stamina as an itinerant performer. He had also so ingratiated himself with audiences that none might question his right to take a prominent place among veterans of the circuit. He had improved his lecturing reputation, and he had learned much. Still not a consistently accomplished speaker, he was more polished than the rough-and-ready story-teller of California mining camps. Mother Fairbanks need no longer be quite so apprehensive.

The tour over, he made a half-hearted show of preparation for the trip to California. The more he thought about the long journey the less attractive it became. By the end of March he was still procrastinating, still arguing to himself that he should go, but countering with disinclination to move. He could not face the prospect of several dismal months without a glimpse of Livy, and she, too, was unhappy over the possibility of separation. The result was that no western tour occurred, although the idea revived in a different form when he heard Nasby lecture in Boston.

Lecturers were generally too busy to listen to each other. John B. Gough had such a full schedule that he never heard any of his colleagues, and Mark Twain seems not to have attended more than half a dozen lectures in his entire career. But Nasby was always an event. A speaker of long experience, he filled over two hundred engagements a year, always with the same lecture, "Cussed be Canaan." A devotee of the bottle, he was sometimes too drunk to see the audience. An unfeeling editor said that to appear in Brooklyn, where puritanism was rife, Nasby had to train down to eleven drinks a day. Mark Twain went to the Music Hall with a critical chip on his shoulder, prepared to carp, but he was completely won by this unpretentious man.

Thirty years later he recalled the burly figure, "uncouthly and provincially clothed" like "a simple old farmer." Striding upon the stage without a bow to acknowledge applause, he spread his manuscript upon the lectern, and immediately bellowed the opening line: "We are all descended from grandfathers." His manner was devoid of appeal, his posture fixed: body bent over the desk and supported by the left arm, the right held across his back and swung forward every two or three minutes to turn a page. The action, said Mark Twain, was like a machine, "regular, recurrent, prompt, exact. You might imagine you heard it *clash*." Unable to remember a line of his lecture, despite hundreds of repetitions,

Nasby read steadily and loudly, "roaring to the end," Mark Twain said, "tearing his ruthless way through the continuous applause, and taking no sort of account of it."[33] That technique might seem to be the worst, yet he was one of the most popular speakers in Redpath's collection, and one of the most highly-paid.

Afterwards the two men met and discovered such a wealth of common interests that they talked all night. Mark Twain said, "I took a strong liking to this fellow, who has some very noble qualities."[34] Nasby was an elemental man of large body and expansive talk, often ribald and profane, that must have appealed to the former Bohemian of Virginia City. Indeed, Mark Twain, no inferior talker himself, confessed that, come six o'clock in the morning, he was the one who had to give up. Either then or soon after, he proposed a joint lecture tour of California in the fall of 1869. After thinking it over, Nasby declined on the grounds that his lecture was too old. Perhaps diffidence and inertia also held him back. Thus the joint tour plan came to nothing, yet for a number of years Mark Twain's thoughts perennially revolved about a return to the West Coast.

7

Second Eastern Tour

DURING the spring and summer of 1869 Mark Twain's attitude toward lecturing swung around like a weathervane in contrary winds. In April he was uncertain about facing the trials of another season. By May, having decided to go on the road again, he instructed Redpath to schedule a few small towns before Boston as tryout spots, and announced that his fee was $100, but that he would require more for long trips to the Middle West. In June, regretting his decision, he told his family that he "most cordially" hated lecturing, and shuddered to think that he—like those "old stagers," Gough, Nasby, Oliver Wendell Holmes, and Wendell Phillips—might never get out of it. Yet in July he was hard at work on a lecture, writing every day and promising Mother Fairbanks that she should see it "in almost no time, maybe less." He was also explaining to Nasby the glowing possibilities of a joint California tour, which, as already noted, did not materialize. In August, concluding that duties on the Buffalo *Express* would prevent touring, he advised Redpath to cancel all speaking engagements. In September, finding that he could not be released "from Boston & 2 or 3 other places," he authorized Redpath to farm him out "to lyceums far & near, & for half the winter or all of it."[1]

No doubt the uncertainty, the hate and the shudders were all genuine, yet, as Mark Twain observed of Shelley's love lyrics, they were "good for this day and train only." Distaste probably centered on the duller side of touring: rumbling along for hours in dirty and uncomfortable day coaches, drab rooms of small town hotels, sodden small town dinners—"spread . . . around your plate," as he once said, "in a mass-meeting of soap-dishes"[2]— village bores and the gloom of villages in winter, when they were either frozen up or deep in sticky mud. There was not much to cheer the spirit in these things. "All towns," he said, "are alike— all have the same stupid trivialities to show, & all demand an impossible interest at the suffering stranger's hands."[3] Nevertheless, he could not resist the pull of the platform. A confirmed talker who relished the speaker's spotlight, he was, after only one season, almost an old stager himself. If the public's clamorous demand made him shudder, it was also a gratifying reminder of popularity.

The contention, advanced by Paine and others, that he traveled the lecture circuit only because he needed the money may be discounted. During his absence from the *Express* office, he said, the paper would probably lose as much as he made on the tour. Modest returns from the 1868-69 season indicated that lecturing was not a bonanza. Spending freely, living well, preferring the best hotels, taking sleepers and chair cars when available, he cut heavily into gross income. Besides, the success of *The Innocents Abroad*, published in late July and bringing in about $1400 a month, suggested a method of making more money than by lecturing, and making it with less ravishment of body and spirit. One reporter wondered why "any man with such a reputation as he has acquired should barter it away on the platform for, comparatively, a mere pittance."[4] Mark Twain said in November that he was swamped "with high-priced invitations to write for magazines and papers, and publishers besiege me to write books."[5] These offers he turned down because he was touring. He talked not for the pittance merely, but chiefly for pleasure, which outweighed all objections.

In late summer Redpath issued to lyceums, mainly in New England, a four-page brochure stating that the Boston Bureau was ready to make engagements for Mark Twain, reprinting good press notices, and announcing that throughout the season he would use only one lecture, "The Curiosities of California." Paradoxically, Mark Twain had protested against this advertising because he thought it was too much like quackery. The complaint was a strange one for a man who so well understood the uses of publicity that he had widely advertised himself by all sorts of means, including exaggeration and hoax. He was never reluctant to propagandize for his own books, and when he found that one of his lectures had been poorly advertised, somebody was sure to be singed by his displeasure. His objection to Redpath's publicity may have evolved from a special regard for New England as a blue-ribbon region, symbol of national culture and respectability. Having not yet lectured there, he may have been loath to prejudice its people by any pushing gesture that could be interpreted as an affront to decorum. Sometimes described as a Yankee, perhaps he wanted to be one. A reporter once described his platform humor as of "the quaint, close, dry order of the New Englander," as if he were consciously identifying himself with the region. As a resident of Hartford he did identify himself physically, though emotionally he was remote from the spirit of New England. Yet his living there says something about the psyche of Mark Twain. If a rebel, he was also a conformist seeking approval by the culturally approved.

Actually, the Bureau's advertising was unnecessary, for a stream of Mark Twain requests had been pouring in for months. By accident, he had stepped into a circuit career at a time receptive to his talents. Audiences, tiring of the concentrated solemnity of lyceum courses, were veering toward lighter fare. One editor reflected the change by the sorrowful admission that "the majority

. . . desire humorous lectures, and will not turn out to hear a sound . . . exposition of ideas. Nonsense and not sense is what they want."[6] Mark Twain was not devoid of sense, but he gave them plenty of nonsense, and he did not furrow the brain with closely-reasoned development of perplexing ideas. With more requests than he could use, Redpath arranged a season of forty-seven performances extending over twelve weeks. The time was shorter than that of the previous tour and the route more compact. Except for a few trips into Pennsylvania, all engagements were in or near New England; most of the stops were in Connecticut, Massachusetts, and New York. This time there was on the schedule a greater proportion of substantial cities, one of them being the nation's cultural mecca, Boston.

Mark Twain did not complicate this tour by rushing off headlong to Elmira or Cleveland. As an affianced man with a job on the Buffalo *Express,* he was easier in mind than the unsettled suitor of the year before. No longer, as he said, rent by "the frenzy, the lunacy of love," he was in better condition to attend to his professional career. His letters to Livy were more relaxed now, more like himself because he was learning, he said, "to contemplate her critically as a human being instead of an angel."[7] Tender, playful, loving, often warm with exasperation over some annoying experience, they said less now of Bible-reading and church-going. Gone was the unnatural consecration of his courting days. The sterling effort of the lover to assume a saintly character pleasing to his beloved had been touching, yet to a detached observer it also seems acutely disturbing, too unreal for comfort. It is a relief to observe the reappearance of a Mark Twain more credible than the sanctimonious pietist he had tried to be.

Still, in some ways, under pressure from Mother Fairbanks and Livy, he had changed, having, so he said, given up tobacco-chewing as well as strong drink and "all other liquors." No doubt he did swear off for awhile. But at a Boston press dinner in

November he was bored by a dull evening without stimulants, and remarked upon the difference between the inspiration of cold water and that of champagne. When the wine went around at those many banquets he attended, nobody ever noted that he refused it. Teetotalism did not endure, but after he came under the eye of Livy he was much more temperate than the roisterer of the Washoe sagebrush. He was also trying, he said, to keep his hands out of his pockets, and not to sprawl full length in easy chairs. He thought, too, that he had "ceased from profanity." On that point he must surely, and fortunately, have been mistaken. Smoking he refused to give up, even for Livy. If not a shining model of Victorian propriety, he had made concessions. Whether or not they were inhibiting, he had relished the heckling and bullying of his feminine mentors, and had willingly yielded a point or two —temporarily anyhow.

The lecture entitled "The Curiosities of California" was stillborn. Nothing is left of it except a probable fragment published in *Mark Twain in Three Moods*. It describes the 1868 experience of climbing from "the roses and mosquitoes" of Sacramento to the deep snow of Donner Lake, and the twenty-mile sleigh-ride under a sweltering sun. Following that is a long, lyrical description of Lake Tahoe, of its varied blues and noble surrounding scenery, all of it similar to Tahoe passages in *Roughing It*. Other curiosities must be left to conjecture. The subject should have been close to the heart of the author, yet the result evidently did not please him. Perhaps he was further removed from California than he thought, or had forgotten too much. He did not once use this lecture during the tour. Instead, beginning at Pittsburgh on November 1, he fell back upon "Our Fellow Savages of the Sandwich Islands," and stayed with it throughout the season.

The most fluid of his lectures, it underwent continual change. Although he did not give it precisely the same way each time, it had a fairly constant core made from the original letters in the Sacramento *Union*. By 1869 he was so well acquainted with the subject that he could introduce thematic variations and irrelevant digressions. On this tour he generally began with a series of unpleasant memories, some of them lifted from other lectures: an advanced case of Oriental leprosy, the picture of the skinned man in the Milan cathedral, the boyhood corpse in his father's office and the swift departure via the window, taking the sash along— all of which allowed him to say that unpleasantness naturally directed his thoughts toward his lecture. In it was much of previous Islands material about geography, the Kilauae eruption, "the long green swell of the Pacific," native dress, dogs, customs, plurality of mothers, and so forth. Frequently he offered to illustrate cannibalism if furnished an infant, pausing expectantly, then saying, "I know that children have become scarce and high of late, having been thinned out by neglect since the woman movement began." He interpolated tall stories: of Morgan, the champion liar, who claimed that his fast horse outran a thunderstorm for eighteen miles while his dog was swimming behind the wagon all the way; of the incorporated company of mean men who docked a workman for time lost when he spent fifteen minutes in the air after being blown up. Both stories would appear in *Roughing It*.

Arriving in Pittsburgh two days before the performance, he had a festive time. Thirty newspaper men treated him to an oyster supper, minus wine and toasts, and a full evening of talk. Next day he had a stream of callers, and dutifully went to church. The preacher amused him by delivering a sermon in a manner called "frozen, monotonous, precise & inflectionless." His tentative gestures were not impressive, only scared and funny. The exhibition was a good negative demonstration of the lesson Mark Twain's experience had taught him: that the art of speaking lay in varying inflection and manipulating pauses, and making humorous sallies take an audience by surprise. He took such pains with his own unique style that one reporter said of the current Sandwich Islands lecture: "Written or spoken by another it would lose half its point and value."[8]

After the second engagement, at Providence on November 9, he abruptly faced on the following night the speaker's most severe test, Boston. The Hub, the Athens of America, was a place of such exacting standards, real and fancied, that it shook the confidence of the most stout-hearted. Boston frightened them all, even an old hand like Nasby, who quailed at the thought of standing before an audience in the Music Hall. Mark Twain said that a full house there was composed of "4,000 critics," and he believed that "on the success of this matter depends my future success in New England. But I am not distressed."[9]

He did not have a full house, but it was larger than the usual Boston lecture audience, and that was a tribute. As one reporter wrote: "who that breathes the vital air of America has not heard of the jumping frog of Calaveras County, California?"[10] For this important occasion Redpath himself walked on with the speaker and introduced him. According to accounts, Mark Twain was at ease, neither awed nor flustered by the exalted surroundings and by the task of assaulting New England reserve in its most formidable stronghold. No stage fright, untoward lapses, or fumbling marred his performance. Yet making a joke out of the high-flown Kilauae passage by one of those stage whispers—"There, I'm glad I've got that volcano off my mind"—was tawdry for Boston or anywhere else. A Springfield *Republican* correspondent said that, primed to applaud genuine eloquence, he felt himself "a little misused" by this trick, and it probably offended others. Possibly Mark Twain did it in a spirit of bravado to test the Boston reflexes, but it was time to give over such clowning. The audience must have forgiven him, for it was a genial crowd that laughed often enough to convince him that he had done well. Scouting the popular belief that Boston people were cold, he said that, once stiffness had been broken down, they could be as merry and noisy as any.

Press reviews next day were on the whole favorable, but they varied in length and tone. The *Transcript,* guardian of Boston dignity, did not unbend very far. A short fourteen lines called Mark Twain "truly an original lecturer . . . dry and droll, serious and even pathetic," and said that the first third of the talk was disappointing, but that the remainder was "richly enjoyed." The *Journal* did better: twenty-nine lines described him as "very deliberate and self-possessed," and in manner and elocution "peculiar." In a somewhat more enthusiastic account, the *Post* said that his remarks were "always amusing, frequently uncontrollably laughable, and continuously applauded."

The *Advertiser* exceeded its contemporaries in almost a full column by an attentive critic. Calling the speaker "a very good looking man," the paper commented on behavior so calm and slow that "you feel it to be an impossibility that he should ever be in a hurry or ever be out of temper." (Little did the *Advertiser* know how easily this calm man could get out of temper!) Noticeable were the "utter indifference" of delivery, the nasal voice "remarkably light and remarkably dry,—like some German wines," the rising inflection at the beginning, middle, and end of a sentence. "An air of half seriousness in the joke itself" put the audience into a "queer state" of not knowing "what to trust . . . where the fun will come in." Perhaps, said the critic, "he is not a great humorist, but he is a genuine humorist," and concluded with the generous statement: "If Mr. Clemens can please everyone as he pleased in Boston . . . he will be sure to make his fortune."

A good part of the *Advertiser's* column consisted of a detailed synopsis, with exposure of cherished jokes. This thoughtless gesture aroused the ire of Mark Twain. Taking the good points out of a lecture, he once said, was "the same as taking the raisins out of a fruit cake—it left but a *pretense* of something it was *not,* for such as came after," and synopses "do harm, because they travel ahead of the lecturer & give people a despicable opinion of him & his production."[11] In a draft of a later talk he put the story, probably imaginary, of speaking in a village and noting a farmer in the front row diligently comparing the lecture with a printed version in a city paper. Mark Twain said that this checking up made him so nervous that he lost his place; whereupon the farmer reproved him for skipping.[12] Whenever he could he pleaded with newsmen in advance not to publish his remarks, but the annoying synopsis periodically angered him.

After Boston engagements in nearby towns allowed him to retain a city base at Young's Hotel, from which he sallied forth in the afternoon to Norwich, Clinton, Jamaica Plain, Newton, and others, sometimes remaining away over night. In Boston he spent his days loafing at the Bureau office, having such a sociable time that thirty years later he recalled the good old days of Nasby, Redpath, and Anna Dickinson, lazy hours of hobnobbing with other lecturers, "smoking and talking shop." He also remembered the sad Music Hall experience of a colleague, De Cordova, the humorist, whom he heard in the company of Nasby and Josh Billings. Starting bravely, De Cordova was rewarded by bursts of laughter, which became less loud and less frequent as he went along, until the silence grew oppressive and an ominous chill settled upon the house. The poor fellow was in distress, which his three confreres in the gallery richly enjoyed. "We drew a deep sigh," said Mark Twain;

it ought to have been a sigh of pity for a defeated fellow craftsman, but it was not—for we were mean and selfish, like all the human race, and it was a sigh of satisfaction to see our unoffending brother fail.

At five minutes to nine, to catch the last suburban train, twelve hundred people walked out. Not having been forewarned of this deadline, the beaten lecturer

was like a person stricken with a paralysis; he stood choking and gasping for a few minutes, gazing in a white horror at that retreat, then he turned drearily away and wandered from the stage with the groping and uncertain step of one who walks in his sleep.[13]

In New England towns Mark Twain was received more formally than heretofore. A silk-hatted committee met his train, escorted him to the lecture hall, and sat in a row on the stage like blackface comedians in a minstrel show. The chairman, characterized as "almost always an ass," discomfited the speaker by an introduction of extravagant compliment and melancholy attempts to be funny. To relieve his embarrassment, he tried going the chairman one better in additional preposterous remarks, announcing that he, Mark Twain, was "a gentleman whose eloquence, reliability and veracity are surpassed only by his personal comeliness and native modesty."[14] By the time he reached Pawtucket in mid-December, he had suppressed officious chairmen. Adopting the custom of Artemus Ward, he introduced himself with a burlesque of the usual flattery:

Ladies and gentlemen: The next lecture in this course will be delivered this evening, by Samuel L. Clemens, a gentleman whose high character and unimpeachable integrity are only equalled by his comeliness of person and grace of manner. And I am the man!

The chairman, he said, had been excused because "no chairman can introduce me as I ought to be introduced."[15] With rare exceptions, he used various forms of the self-introduction thereafter.

In New England, citizens did not always respect the rule to let the speaker alone when off-duty. At Norwich in November, he grumbled that he "had to submit to the customary & exasperating drive around town in a freezing open buggy" to see the houses of the mayor, ex-mayor, ex-governor, state senator, and former member of Congress, the public school "with its infernal architecture," the court house, female seminary, paper mill, and bare trees "where the park is going to be." Not only that, but to meet "other inanimated wonders with dull faces, but with legs to them to show them to be human": mayor, richest man in town, editor, town wit with a stock of venerable jokes, "& a lot more of people I take no possible interest in & don't want to see." Why, he moaned, "*won't* these insane persecutors believe me when I protest pleadingly that I *don't* care two cents for all the thrilling wonders the village can boast."[16]

When he stayed overnight, he risked having the blessings of strict New England homes "inflicted" upon him. Householders' notions of hospitality there, he concluded, were to make themselves comfortable first, then let the guest worry along as best he might. At Canton his host, a Mr. Ames, allowed no smoking on the premises, a sore restriction for an inveterate smoker. Mark Twain, fulminating against "peculiar self-righteous ideas of virtue," said, "I hate Mr. Ames with all my heart."[17] Dr. Sanborn, leading physician of Rockford, asked his guest to reduce his fee by ten dollars, a request promptly refused, then compounded error by calling him for breakfast at seven o'clock. For his night's lodging and "New England hospitality," minus breakfast, Mark Twain ironically offered ten dollars, which the doctor obsequiously accepted. He was labeled "the dog at whose house I staid [*sic*]."[18]

Sometimes he was left to shift for himself, and then, as likely as not, the hotel was a hovel. The Clinton House, he said, was a "villainous" hostelry of feeble lights and threadbare furniture, "everything shabby and disagreeable." Fussy about hotels, critical of rundown furnishings and indifferent service, he wanted the best. Some years later, making a reservation at the Palmer House in Chicago, he accurately defined his tastes by saying: "I'm as fond of a good room as any old maid you ever saw."[19]

Other things made him wrathful. At New Britain, Connecticut, a man who kept his hat on throughout the performance so annoyed the speaker that he was several times on the point of reading the offender a brisk sermon on manners. Afterward his pent-up irritation escaped, and the item got into the local *Record*. "Mark," said the editor shrewdly, "will be even with that man sometime."[20] He suffered, as he put it, "ten thousand petty annoyances & vexations" in unlovely towns more countrified than urban. Yet he gave them grudging respect as testing grounds. "A country audience," he said,

is the difficult audience; a passage which it will approve with a ripple will bring a crash in the city. A fair success in the country means a triumph in the city.[21]

On this tour small towns were an anticlimax. Since he had already satisfied Boston, he need fear no other audience, city or rural.

If vexations fretted him, there were compensations in agreeable village experiences. At West Meriden, Connecticut, he had a jolly time experimenting with a new way of telling a story that made him and the audience laugh together. "I got to one particular point in it," he said,

3 different times before I could get by it & go on. Every time I lifted my hand aloft & took up the thread of the narrative in the same old place the audience exploded again & so did I.[22]

Albany pleased him. "It is hard," he said, "to make Albany Dutchmen laugh & applaud, but the subscriber did it."[23] At Fredonia he called the crowd "most delightful," and remarked that he was "just as happy as a lord from the first word . . . to the last. I thought it was just about as good a lecture as I ever listened to."[24] Thus the pleasures of touring, offsetting its trials, made his volatile spirits dance up and down the scale of emotion.

Occasionally he had what he called "a mild little adventure." Arriving in some town just before lecture time and finding no reception committee, he drifted with the crowd toward the hall. Trying to press in he was stopped by the ticket-taker, to whom he explained: "It's all right. I am the lecturer." With a sardonic wink the ticket man said, "No you don't. Three of you have got in, up to now, but the next lecturer that goes in to-night *pays*."[25] Mark Twain paid. At Cambridge, New York, the auditorium caught fire shortly before lecture time, blazing away with a vigor that seemed to preclude a performance that night. Mark Twain's feeling was one of relief, coupled with a wish that the editor of the Troy *Times,* which had published a synopsis and a humorous attempt to illustrate the drawl, had been "locked up in that burning building." But the fire was put out, and he had a full house, although, he said, "a mighty wet and smoky one."

After the performance there he talked with committeemen and drank cider till midnight. Next morning, the porter failing to rouse him, he did not wake up until fourteen minutes to eight, and he had to catch a train to Utica at eight five. No transportation in sight, and the railroad station blocks away. The landlord fluttered about, "crazy as a loon in 5 seconds," said Mark Twain,

—darted this way & that—yelled for a coach—tore his hair—swore at the porter, & was in despair—said the jig was up, & the best he could do was to take a buggy & drive me to Troy—30 miles—thermometer already below zero & growing steadily colder.[26]

With six minutes left, they ran for the station, each carrying a bag, Mark Twain winning the race and swinging aboard as the train was about to pull out. That sprint brings to the mind's eye a remarkable picture of one of the very few times when this unhurried man was in a hurry.

Talking mostly in Massachusetts towns during November, he also made his first appearance in Hartford. The *Evening Post* commented briefly on a pleased audience that responded with "a great deal of hearty laughter and frequent . . . applause." Evidently his future home town gave him a cordial welcome, yet he never had anything good to say of Hartford as a stop for lecturers. Years later he observed that houses there were small, applause thin, and indifference marked regardless of the speaker's fame, merit, sex, or nationality.[27] Dropping down to Brooklyn, he spoke twice, on December 1 and 6. The first performance, for the Brooklyn Library Society, attracted such a small crowd that he reproved Redpath for putting on the schedule "an infernal mite

society, a pure charity speculation." The second, at Beecher's Plymouth Church, came off better perhaps because Beecher's prestige, reflecting upon the speaker, made loyal idol-worshipers
automatically turn out. Between these two appearances he journeyed to Poughkeepsie. The *Daily Press* there, failing to block a
metaphor, said: "Mark is a brick, fire proof, we should think.
Long may he wave."[28]

Then he was ready for Philadelphia. A city of cultural preten-
sions like those of Boston, it gave him no qualms, and he had a
hilarious evening with an overflow audience in the Academy of
Music. In a lively story, reminiscent of the unrestraint of western
journalism, the *Bulletin* remarked that "Mr. Twain's real name
is Wam-pau-telh-macglaherty. He was converted by a Bohemian
priest named O'Callahan." Then followed a rigmarole about Mark
Twain's belief that "George Washington was an Irishman who
discovered America and was rescued by Pocahontas from an awful
death on Plymouth Rock, after a perilous voyage in the Spanish
Armada," which he saved

by cutting down a mast with a little hatchet which had been given
him by his father, who perished in the storm, and so could not give
his son permission to leave his post which the heroic boy firmly refused to forsake without his father's orders.[29]

The more conventional *Press,* of December 8, said that the
lecturer was "not riotous with his fancy," but "tenderly poetical
and discreet." Uncertain whether he was wit or humorist, this
critic concluded that "If it were not for Twain we should set him
down as a wit, but the inevitable presence causes us to classify
him with the humorists." That was a perceptive comment. Assidu-
ously he cultivated the actor's mannerisms that preceded and accompanied his performance. Believing that a speaker should
capture his audience before he utters a word, he once said that he
would risk much to gain approval at the outset. So he shuffled on
stage with stiff-legged awkwardness—"like a ready made cripple,"
one reporter said—pretended to be scared, assumed an expression

of solemn imbecility, vacantly looked around, behaved like a be-wildered bumpkin, or, as one observer said, "like a small boy who has forgotten his 'piece.' " At this dumb show the crowd laughed, and from that moment it was in a pliable mood.

These histrionics did not please everybody. A New Haven critic predicted that "his course as a lecturer will end when the curiosity of his thousands of readers shall have been satisfied by a good square look at him." Dismissing the Sandwich Islands as "a tissue of nonsense from beginning to end," this reporter called the delivery "as disgusting as the lecture is foolish." Yet "people clamor for a look and . . . one will be enough for the most ad-miring."[30] Some complained of the substitution of stunts for sub-stance, others of audiences who laughed too easily at vaudeville antics. Yet Mark Twain hit so near the center of popular taste that, if carped at by the esoteric, he had a safe majority. One editor accurately summed up platform purpose and appeal:

Twain's lecture was *not* intended as . . . moral reform . . . an histori-cal essay, an archeological research, a political stump speech, a de-scription of scenery. . . . It was *nothing* and intended as such. . . . He is to the comic world what Wendell Phillips is to the serious and philosophic. . . . Mark Twain is and pretends to be nothing *but* a joker.[31]

Exactly, but stern-minded critics would not permit him to be him-self; persistently they condemned his failure to be something other than what he was.

As advancing age made him aspire to be a sort of philosopher, the label of joker ruffled him, but it was a fair one. On the plat-form he was primarily, if not almost entirely, a joker. He admitted as much when he said to Andrew Lang twenty years later that he had "never tried in even one single instance to help cultivate the cultivated classes," but had

always hunted for bigger game—the masses. . . . To simply amuse them would have satisfied my dearest ambition at any time; for they could get instruction elsewhere, and I had two chances to help to the teacher's one: for amusement is a good preparation for study and a good healer of fatigue after it.[32]

Going out of his way to be funny, he continually sacrificed the serious to the facetious. At Washington, D. C., he invented a new flippant comment for the celebrated word painting of the Kilauae eruption: "Let someone beat that for harnessing adjectives together." The quip brought the satisfying laughter that meant more to him than any other response. Yet on December 9 the critic of the *Daily Morning Chronicle* refused to give him top marks as a humorist. Observing that "Mark fell . . . below the estimate which had been formed of him from his humorous writings," he said:

It would be doing an injustice to the memory of poor A. Ward to say that the droll Mark was his equal in . . . genuine wit and humor. . . . in that genial, modest, and sparkling flow of fun . . . Artemus . . . was by far his superior.

After Washington the trail wound in and out of Pennsylvania, New York, Connecticut, and Massachusetts: Germantown, Mt. Vernon, West Meriden, New Britain, Warren, Pawtucket, Waltham, Abington, Canton, and Hudson. On December 22 he was in Portland, Maine, where the *Transcript* printed a three-column synopsis, then dropped down to Rockport, Slatersville, New Haven, Trenton, Newark, Wilkes-Barre, and Williamsport. The last leg of the tour, in January, 1870, was all in New York: Amenia, Cohoes, Albany, West Troy, Rondout, Cambridge, Utica, Oswego, Baldwinsville, Buffalo, Fredonia, Hornellsville, and Jamestown. For six weeks he was a steady trouper, speaking four and five nights a week, using Boston as a base when he could, and resting on weekends, which he generally spent there or in the largest city convenient to his Friday or Saturday performance. Although railroad trips were not so hard as those of the previous year, he complained that his "nerves, & . . . whole physical economy" were "shattered with the wear & tear of travel."[33]

Usually he attracted larger audiences than his more serious circuit contemporaries. Papers, reporting with stereotypes relieved by occasional originality, were generally favorable, though not unanimously so. At Pawtucket he was "intensely interesting to those who are intensely interested . . . a fair lecturer but he writes much better than he talks."[34] The New Britain *Record* maintained that "when he walks lazily about the platform, drawling out the dryest jokes . . . he is a thousand times more the humorist than in his book."[35] A New Haven editor thought differently. "An hour with Mark," he said,

is like gentle dew upon a withering flower; when he . . . comes as Mr. Clemens, the lecturer, it is like the tickling of a sleepy boy with a feather—perfectly ravishing until the eyes are opened, but which he doesn't care to experience for a second time."[36]

At Oswego, after two heavy lectures in the series, "Twain's was thrown in just at the right . . . time to make the course rest a little easier on our stomachs . . . like the wine after dinner."[37] At Cohoes the puzzling manner was "so different . . . from what people usually hear from the platform, that the audience was . . . disappointed."[38]

The last engagement of the tour, at Jamestown, New York, on January 21, precipitated a lively outpouring of opinion. A week later the Jamestown *Journal* summed up the performance thus:

Take the whole of last evening's lecture and place it into an hydraulic press, bring it to its maximum density; result: 225 pounds of solid matter decomposed as follows: common sense, 1 ounce; wit 1½ ounce; nonsense, 224 pounds, 13½ ounces.

In the same issue "an Indignant Spectator" used the *Journal* to "pitch into Mark Twain's lecture." He complained that the title, "Our Fellow Cannibals," was "a slander on the people of this great and enlightened nation," that there was no sense in speaking of a man "dressed in an umbrella," that baked dogs were disgusting, particularly since the speaker had admitted that he did not care for the dish. Failure to find a moral in the story of a cannibal who devoured a tough old missionary was evidence of "Twain's excessive stupidity." The story of the man docked for time lost when he was blown up was "preposterously unlikely." Requesting an infant to illustrate cannibalism was silly because "He knew perfectly well that in such an advanced community as this, infants are not allowed in the lecture room." Ranting against irrelevance, senselessness, and trash, Indignant Spectator reproved the lyceum committee for engaging Mark Twain, who had

offended the good taste and religious scruples of the sober portion of this community by introducing his ill-timed levity and in this opinion I am sustained by nine-tenths of that portion of the community.

The concluding remark sounds like the genuine huffiness of an ingrown small town, but the letter as a whole has all the earmarks of a hoax. The *Journal* editor, professing to take it seriously, explained that the audience had been mistaken in expecting "valuable information about the Sandwich Islands," and that "if some . . . were 'mad at themselves for laughing at such nonsense,' the lecture was all the greater success. It takes a smart man to provoke an unwilling laugh." Calling Mark Twain "an honest jokist," the editor advised him "to settle down on the conviction that his *forte* is not that of a missionary, a preacher, a philosopher, a reformer, a teacher nor any of these solemn callings."

These words, intended to soothe local feelings, did not soothe Mark Twain. It is hard to believe that he took at face value the ravings of Indignant Spectator, yet, paradoxical as usual, he was incensed by the nonsense label he had deliberately sought, and irritated by the *Journal* editor, by Spectator, by Jamestown generally. Instructing Redpath never to schedule it again unless compelled by Providence, he called the town a place "all lecturers hate." Sixteen years later irritation still remained, for when the supposed Indignant Spectator asked Mark Twain's endorsement for a consulship, he replied with a warm—though unmailed—denunciation of the 1870 *Journal* letter, and referred to the editor as "that buzzard," "ostentatiously pious, half-human." Recommending a rope instead of a consulship, he said to the applicant: "I will send you one—the thing for you is a burial permit. You have only to speak, I will see that you get it."[39] If the whole thing was a joke, the long-standing distemper is one more proof that Mark Twain was not amused when the joke was on him.

Thus the tour ended in a flurry of controversy that was pleasurable, if annoying. Immediately he departed for Elmira, where he was caught up by the delirious bustle preceding marriage to Livy twelve days later. He interrupted his stay to give the Sandwich Islands lecture in Hartford on January 31 for the benefit of Father Hawley's orphans. A full house netted $1500, and there was no audible dissidence by captious critics. Soon after, the lecturer became husband, honeymooner, and Buffalo newspaperman, and for over a year there was no more trundling around the lyceum circuit. Out in the Washoe country the Virginia City *Enterprise* sardonically commented:

So Mark got hooked at last. Well, he had many narrow escapes in this land of sage, even some of the tar-head bells [*sic*] used to cast soft glances upon his manly form as he strode forth, notebook in hand, to view the wonders of some particularly rich streak of granite, a hole 15 feet deep and an old windlass.[40]

8

Interlude

AFTER his marriage on February 2, 1870, Mark Twain was sure that his speaking days were over. Picturing himself as no longer a rover, he seemed content to be a staid householder, his life complete within the walls of home, his spirit seeking no solace beyond the comfort of his own fireside. He had told Mother Fairbanks that, once settled in Buffalo, "I doubt if we *ever* move again, except to visit home & you."[1] Bemused by the joy of the honeymoon, he was for the moment blissfully domestic. Blithe days, swinging by with what he called "a whir & a flash," would not allow him to put his mind on serious work. The marriage was a happy one. Olivia Clemens was neither the forbidding disciplinarian of popular legend, nor the paragon her husband sometimes said she was. She was human enough to come to terms with his unconventional ways, to exercise the good sense that more than once prevented him from making a fool of himself, and eventually to drift further in the direction of his heterodoxy than he did toward her genteel tradition. His regard for her was not the calf love of Tom Sawyer for Becky Thatcher, as sometimes implied, but a strong and mature affection that she returned with like sincerity. There was more genuine understanding between that pair than critics have yet discovered.

He so often underlined his determination to give up speaking that conviction was, as usual, suspect. In January he had said, "I lecture no more after this season, unless dire necessity shall compel me."[2] In March he told Redpath, "I am not going to lecture any more forever."[3] In May he said, "I am making more money than necessary—by considerable, and therefore why crucify myself nightly on the platform."[4] He turned down Redpath's offer of $5000 a month, one-half in advance. But the proposal must have been tempting, for he modified the "forever" of his assertion to a resolution not to lecture for one year. Sometime in 1870, also, he dreamed again of a California tour and of using the "Curiosities" lecture there.

The news that he contemplated retirement from the platform brought protests. Josh Billings urged him to reconsider, saying that a humorist, like a doctor, was good for people. "Mark Twain, before an audience," he said,

iz as easy tew understand az strawberries and cream. . . . Mark Twain has grate wit, he has grate literary pretenshuns, but he iz a poor punster, and he ought tew be thankful for that, for there aint nothing (unless it iz three cent gin) that iz more demoralizing than punning.[5]

Apprehension was needless. After a year of a routine newspaper job in a city he disliked, he would be as eager as ever to sally forth again.

Meanwhile, duties on the Buffalo *Express* becoming a bore, he assumed in March the editorship of a department, "Memoranda," in the New York *Galaxy*. That job, together with doing sketches for the *Express*, gave him, he said, "fully six days' work a month." By July he was planning a long book about Nevada and California, and by late August *Roughing It* was under way. Into it went some of the material he had used in Sandwich Islands lectures and had sketched for the unused "Curiosities." If lecturing was not on his agenda, it was on his mind and that of the public, although some thought that the public mind needed renovating. The New

York *Times* thought that the lyceum circuit was withering away for lack of patronage, and a good thing, too, because it contributed only to intellectual shallowness.

For one man who is driven to the full investigation of a subject by hearing a lecture upon it . . . at least twenty . . . depart with the complacent consciousness of having mastered it, and are, in virtue of this conviction, more intensely ignorant than before.[6]

A disgusted midwestern editor muttered about the high prices charged by "itinerant retailers of stale platitudes." In San Francisco *The Golden Era* wearily remarked upon the annual shipment of speakers from the East:

Dilapidated showmen bereft of all their gifts. . . . Worn out story writers. . . . old hacks lecturing on moral reform—inebriates preaching temperance—thin-voiced clergymen . . . humbugs and charlatans . . . boring people by their tedious moralizing or . . . melancholy humor. . . . The invasion of these lecturing locusts has driven all recognized ability from the field.[7]

Josiah Holland, first editor of *Scribner's Monthly,* and as "Timothy Titcomb" hailed as great poet and thinker, published in March, 1871, a gloomy analysis, "Lecture-Brokers and Lecture-Breakers." Lamenting the passing of the platform's lofty purpose and high moral tone, he condemned lecture bureaus for ruining the profession by introducing "great numbers of men and women who have nothing to say," also "literary jesters and mountebanks" who debased the lecture system to "a string of entertainments that have no earnest purpose, and minister to no manly or womanly want." In February, 1872, he published another blast, "Triflers on the Platform," which scored nonsense-mongers and literary buffoons who exerted "a . . . degrading influence upon the public taste." These low fellows "disseminated slang and vitiated the taste of the impressible, and excited unworthy ambition" because they "never aimed at any result but a laugh, and . . . did not hesitate at any means . . . to secure the coveted result."

This criticism irked Mark Twain. It touched him in a tender spot, for he made capital of nonsense and used all the tricks he could think of to make people laugh. His bile rising, he said that he was "going for" Timothy Titcomb by giving him evidence to "chaw over" that " 'buffoons & triflers' are not scorned by everybody." In an unpublished manuscript, entitled "An Appeal From One that is Persecuted," he compared Holland to the sentimental Tupper, and defended nonsensical lecturers as a necessary relief from solid instruction and high-minded purpose. Popular buffoons, he said, filled auditoriums and made up deficits created by the solemn. In a letter to Redpath he remarked that one of Nasby's letters had "done the country more good, than the entirety of Mr. H's commonplace existence. *He* to talk about the buffoons!"[8]

Holland had a point in his recognition of changing tastes that permitted now a larger infusion of the gossipy, the frivolous, even the scandalous. In the seventies a lecture course was less likely to be heavy with discussions of public questions or fervent with moral exhortation than it was to be a variety show similar to a chautauqua. Large numbers of itinerants, both serious and foolish, continued to travel and to talk.

Those warhorses, Beecher, Gough, Phillips, and Nasby, were going strong, and would be for years to come. Anna Dickinson had an annual income of $20,000, and she was said to have had two hundred offers of marriage. The aging Emerson lectured in towns as far west as Illinois. Olive Logan, in plain silk dress, water color, her hair bound up with a gold clasp, spoke of looking on the bright side, cultivating cheerfulness, love, and laughter. Anybody can do it, she said. In New York she always dined at Delmonico's, and in Chicago she murmured, "I adore literature." Woman's rights stalwarts—Susan Anthony, Elizabeth Cady Stanton, Mary Livermore, Matilda Joslyn Gage, Julia Ward Howe—strove to make converts to political and social enlightenment, not always successfully. Mrs. Livermore's strictures on tight lacing that made the complexion pale and the eyes unnaturally bright merely increased sales of corsets.

Victoria Woodhull blazed into prominence in 1870, when she and her sister became the first female stock brokers in New York, making a small fortune under the sponsorship of Commodore Vanderbilt. The phenomenon of successful businesswomen enchanted the town: smartly-coiffed beauty set off by dark blue empress walking dresses, the strictly business air of gold pens behind dainty ears. Even more exciting was *Woodhull and Claflin's Weekly,* advocating suffrage, labor interests, birth control, a single standard of morality, free love, spiritualism, and Victoria Woodhull for President. Having divorced two husbands and remarried one, she lived with both in an atmosphere so charged with sultry implications that it was irresistible everywhere, except in Boston. Barnstorming at $250 a night from New York to Iowa, she entertained overflow audiences with a lecture on "The Principles of Social Freedom, Involving Free Love, Marriage, Divorce, etc." Taking up the cause of feminism, she became one of the most successful speakers on woman's rights, astounding everybody by an exquisite femininity far removed from the brusque mannishness that had come to be accepted as characteristic of the feminist. To the rigidly righteous she was "that bold, bad woman." Others admired her Grecian profile, her soft voice, more mellifluous than Anna Dickinson's, her graceful gestures, polished manners, modern ideas, and frequent good sense. Notwithstanding the lurid aura in which she moved, she was not a crackpot, as the twentieth century has discovered by accepting a number of her proposals for social regeneration.

Robert Ingersoll, assaulting all organized religions, jammed New York auditoriums while ticket scalpers reaped a harvest. George Francis Train was in the public eye. Fellow-traveler of Fenians and Communists, self-styled "Champion Crank," and called by others "the great incoherent," he had a lecture entitled "Concupiscence, or Mental Adultery"—"No eunuch admitted to the dress circle." Another was "Muscular Christianity," its text a paraphrase of Matthew xiv, 27: "Hit his I; be not afraid."

Such strong meat, hardier fare than the bland diet of traditionalists, was symptomatic of greater platform variety than heretofore. Yet among the ranks of speakers were many clergymen, eloquent and humdrum, many sobersides and old-fashioned uplifters. Lyceums could still get whatever kind of lectures they preferred, and societies were very much in the market. In 1870 so many invitations poured in upon Mark Twain that he sent a printed form letter answer, regretting that he would "not be able to lecture again during the present season." In popularity he stood among the leaders.

In the September *Galaxy* he published a sketch on "The Approaching Epidemic" of memorial lectures certain to follow the recent death of Charles Dickens. "All the vagabonds who can spell," he said, "will afflict the people with 'readings' from Pickwick and Copperfield, and all the insignificants who have been ennobled by the notice of the great novelist or transfigured by his smile will make a marketable commodity of it now." He invented titles:

"Remembrances of Charles Dickens." . . . By John Jones, who saw him once in a street car and twice in a barber shop. . . . "Readings from Dickens." By John White, who has the great delineator's style and manner perfectly. . . . Upon this occasion Mr. W. will exhibit the remains of a cigar which he saw Mr. Dickens smoke. . . . "Heart Treasures of Precious Moments with Literature's Departed Monarch." . . . By Miss Serena Amelia Tryphenia McSpadden, who still wears, and will always wear, a glove upon the hand made sacred by the clasp of Dickens. Only Death shall remove it.

Sure enough, William Winter, a New York dramatic critic, displayed as a treasured possession the identical glass from which Dickens drank his last jigger of brandy before boarding ship for England. And sure enough, a phalanx of Dickens readers and

lecturers marched to the platform. In the Middle West an elocutionist named Ogden Hoffman Feathers "made all cry with his
'Will the New Year Come To-night, Mama?' and . . . strained
whalebones fearfully with Sam Weller's 'Walentine.' "[9] In San
Francisco the Rev. Dr. Stebbins stepped forth with "Dickens and
His Religious Critics," and Mrs. Mattie Field lectured on "Dickens." Another Dickensian was Kate Field, known as "The Rose
of the Rostrum."

Mark Twain considered her one of the insignificants. He did
not think highly of women lecturers in general, except perhaps
of Anna Dickinson, although he admitted that they did well
enough with "Tenderness, pathos, tragedy—the earnest, the beautiful, the majestic." That a woman should attempt a humorous
talk he thought "the ghastliest conception to which the human
mind has yet given birth. . . . wholly out of the question."[10]
Puzzled by female presumption, he was especially perplexed by
the success of Miss Field. Twenty-eight years later he rated her
among the house-emptiers. Her platform manner, he said "was
poor and her delivery repellently artificial,"[11] yet she was good
enough to earn $10,000 a year. He must have forgotten that he
had once thought better of her, for she was leading woman, opposite Raymond, in the dramatization of *The Gilded Age*. Contemporary criticism praised her ease, vivacity, intense earnestness,
and reformer's zeal as journalist, author, actress, and lecturer. A
versatile woman of strong, if eccentric, intellectual gifts, Kate
Field was not the fleeting incompetent of his unreliable memory.

To hear her on Dickens in New York on December 6, 1870, a
capacity audience congested Association Hall, and the fair performer so dazzled the *Times* man that in his story next day he
almost forgot to mention the lecture. He gave her a full column
on page one, more space and more prominent space than Mark
Twain had ever got in a metropolitan paper. With her hair swept
back in a shower of ringlets and a red rose in it, she wore, said
this reporter, "a rose-colored silk, with train, trimmed with narrow

flounce and roses," relieved by "white point lace . . . at the throat
and sleeves." The waist was

cut in postillon jacket, with pointed ends in front, and caught at the
bust with rose-buds, open at the throat . . . revealing a velvet necklace
fastened with a diamond pendant, which, with gold bracelets and a
few handsome rings, completed . . . a very tasteful toilet.

The lecture, he added as an afterthought, was "crisp, but coherent
. . . vivid in description, crammed with anecdote and information," the delivery "piquant and graceful," the voice "exceedingly
sweet, clear and effective." This lady had admirable platform
equipment in herself alone, and she knew how to assist it with
good clothes.

Mark Twain's aversion for female lecturers may have been
flavored with sour grapes, for the best of them made more money
than he, and got more attention. Perhaps he did not understand
that women appealed because they were women. In isolated
towns, inhabitants who looked glumly upon the same frost-bitten
faces day after day, the same frumpiness of pre-mail order times,
may have been like forlorn soldiers in remote camps, hungry for
the sight of a new feminine countenance. So they turned out for
unfashionable representatives like the matronly Mrs. Stanton and
the austere Miss Anthony, and they welcomed the snarling Anna
Dickinson. Editors enjoyed poking mild fun at the ladies: "Miss
Lizzie Boynton, of Indiana, announces herself for Congress. She
has blue eyes, short hair, a prominent nose—and such cheek!"[12]

The appeal was greatly heightened when femininity was good-
looking and artfully adorned with dashing clothes, jewelry, and
smart coiffure. These aids made even a blasé city audience take
notice, and they bowled over impressionable males. Of the glamor-
ous Lillian Edgarton, one reporter said that she was "very popular
with all except long-haired men, short-haired women, grass widows
and scolding wives."[13] She had a voice described as "clear and
silvery." Nobody ever said that about Mark Twain.

He carried on through 1870, writing nothing of consequence, and becoming so bored with the *Express* that by the end of the year he was dropping in at the office for a brief call only about once a week. The routine job was tiresome, the Buffalo winter dreary; the newlyweds scarcely left the house, saw nobody but occasional out-of-town visitors. Old California friends who landed there reported astonishment at hearing Mark Twain say grace at table. He said he didn't know what it was for. "But they all do it around here and it won't hurt anybody, anyway."[14] They were puzzled, too, when no whiskey came forth to wet parched western throats. But about bedtime he sidled over to whisper that, if they hunted, they could find a jug stashed in the library.

Work on *Roughing It* was so desultory that he did not get a good grip on the book until the next spring. He skirmished over plagiarism alleged of himself and others, and fretted over the implications of some critics that he was only a publicity-seeker and an imitator of Bret Harte besides. In a letter to his brother, Orion, in early 1871, he expressed disgust at "seeing my hated nom de plume (for I do loathe the very sight of it) in print *again* every month."[15] Possibly he was becalmed in temporary doldrums; possibly he was bored with himself. Marriage was splendid and domesticity was delightful, but they did not stimulate the professional man.

9

Most Detestable
Lecture Campaign

By APRIL, 1871, Mark Twain had left the *Express* and wretched Buffalo. At Elmira and Quarry Farm morale improved as he made headway with *Roughing It*. His stock was "looking up," he said, for he was getting "the bulliest offers from publishers," and he was "flooded with lecture invitations." A return to the platform was inevitable. Redpath cogently argued for another tour, but Mark Twain probably needed no strong urging to entice him back to the circuit.

Still, he laid down seventeen conditions, among them these: a fee equal to Nasby's; all travel to be on main lines, no steamboat or stage trips; no engagements west of St. Louis; short hops, mainly in New England, and a fee of $125 for all places elsewhere; the best hotel in every town.[1] Perhaps Redpath did not take these injunctions very seriously, knowing from past experience the vagaries of his changeable client. Mark Twain bombarded his agent with instructions. He wanted to start the tour with eclat in the Boston Music Hall; he did not care to speak in a church because the pious hush made people afraid to laugh there; he refused to appear in Buffalo because he "mortally" hated that lyceum society; he was indignant because inaccessible Rondout had not been scared off by a high price; he debarred any engagement at Jamestown, New York. When Redpath had trouble keeping up with these weekly directives, Mark Twain explained:

I am different from other women; my mind changes oftener. People who have no mind can easily be steadfast and firm, but when a man is loaded down to the guards with it, as I am, every heavy sea of foreboding or inclination . . . shifts the cargo. See? Therefore . . . one week I am likely to give rigid instructions to confine me to New England; next week, send me to Arizona; the next week withdraw my name; and the week following modify it. You must try to keep the run of my mind, Redpath, it is your business being the agent, and it always was too many for me.[2]

That Redpath kept the run of Mark Twain's revolving mind and coped with the whimsies of his difficult charge is a tribute to his managerial skill.

Storm and stress evolved a long tour of sixteen weeks and seventy-six performances in fifteen states and the District of Columbia. Only about one-fifth of the stops were in New England. A number of small towns were not on main lines, and some auditoriums were churches. Hotels were evidently satisfactory, in the main, for only rarely did he growl about them. The fee probably did not equal Nasby's reputed $200. In the fall he estimated that the tour should gross $10,000; at the end of it he said that he had "lectured eleven or twelve thousand dollars' worth."[3] Which of those figures was correct, if any, is impossible to say. A surmise is that in towns of about twenty thousand—thirty of them, of which fifteen were villages of less than five thousand—he received $100 to $125, increased to $150 in larger cities, perhaps more in Boston, New York, and Philadelphia. On that basis, total income was between ten and eleven thousand dollars. No clear evidence shows that Mark Twain, at any time during his circuit career, ranked with the select group of the most-highly paid: Beecher, Gough, Nasby, Phillips, Anna Dickinson. His willingness to accept second-class fees is merely another indication that he talked because he liked to talk, because he could not help talking.

Ranging from Maine to Illinois, the schedule was longer than either previous one, more far-reaching yet more concentrated. Five performances a week was the usual stint, sometimes six. Besides the harassments of awkward timetables, nagging committeemen, and recalcitrant audiences, a further handicap was his several capricious changes of subject. Multiple vexations made him call this tour "the most detestable lecture campain [sic] that ever was. . . . a fatiguing, sleepy crusade."[4] Fatiguing it may have been, but hardly sleepy, for this campaign set off critical fire so hot and loud that it was no inducement to slumber.

By late June he had written two lectures. One, called "Boy," the Lyceum Bureau advertised as "An Appeal in behalf of extending the Suffrage to Boys." Nothing remains of it except the title, which suggests satirical treatment of a pseudo-serious subject. The other he cryptically referred to as "D. L. H.," but what those letters mean and what the substance was are a mystery, for this manuscript is also non-existent. Pleased with both, he said that in July he would choose the one he preferred, but by that time he had written a third, called "Reminiscences of Some Pleasant Characters Whom I Have Met," this title later revised to the more unwieldy "Reminiscences of Some Uncommonplace Characters I have Chanced to Meet." It was a medley, he said, about his acquaintance with "kings, lunatics, idiots and all": Artemus Ward, Dick Baker and his cat, Dr. Jackson disconcerting European guides, the Rajah of Borneo, the eccentric Emperor Norton of San Francisco, the King of the Sandwich Islands, the Emperor of Russia, and others. This one so took his fancy that he chose it for the coming season. It was "tip-top," he said, a first-rate job that "I just know will 'fetch' any audience I spout it before."[5]

Yet he did not get it well in hand, for at the first stop, Bethlehem, Pennsylvania, on October 16, he was still rehearsing up to the moment of going on stage, and finding the lecture twenty-five minutes too long. Curtain time was a late hour to discover that defect. Perhaps his twenty months' absence from the platform had made his technique rusty, or had begot overconfidence that made him think he need not prepare thoroughly. If so, complacence was abruptly jarred. At Allentown the next night the tiptop "Reminiscences" suddenly turned sour, pleasing neither audience nor speaker. After a painful evening with a stolid house, he dispatched a troubled note: "Livy darling, this lecture will *never* do. I *hate* it & won't keep it. I can't even handle these chuckleheaded Dutch with it."[6] At Wilkes-Barre on the third night, he called the evening miserable. In a panic he begged off from the next two engagements, at Easton and Reading, promising both societies free lectures later if they would release him now. When they consented, he put them on the schedule for late November, and gained a breathing spell of several days to pull himself together.

Thus the tour got off to a lame start, but it was normal in one way, for immediately he began to groan and swear over the unhappy lot of the lecturer, and the woes of the lorn traveler at the mercy of thoughtless intruders. Having brought along a chapter of *Roughing It* to revise, he complained that he had no opportunity to work on it because of travel, talking, and the pestering of various idiots. Besides, three poor performances in succession made him unfit for much except fretfulness.

In a tight spot because of the collapse of "Reminiscences," he hastily blocked out a new talk on Artemus Ward. On the theme of Ward as humorist, the lecture embodied biographical data of dubious accuracy about his boyhood in Waterford, printing apprenticeship at Skowhegan, experience on the Boston *Carpet Bag*, newspaper days in Cleveland, editorship of *Vanity Fair*, success as a lecturer with "The Babes in the Wood." These items served only as pegs on which to hang jokes by Ward and by Mark Twain, so well mixed that he once introduced himself as "Charles F. Clemens" (after Charles Farrar Browne, Ward's real name), and led one reporter to call the mixture "Mark Ward on Artemus Twain." The preacher who spilled the playing cards hidden in his gown; the showman who charged admission to see an eclipse from a tent without a top; the epitaph of the housewife burned up by her kitchen stove—"Well done, thou good and faithful servant"; "Did you ever hear of Adam?"—"What was his other name?"; "What'll you take for one hundred nights in California?" —"Brandy and water": these and other standbys went in. They were like old friends to audiences of the seventies. Yet using Ward's stories was risky, for it made Mark Twain seem barren of original humor, and allowed people who had heard Artemus in person to make damaging comparisons.

The tone of the lecture was partly good-natured, comradely with the jibes permissible to friendship, as in the description of Ward:

He looked like a glove-stretcher; his hair, red, and brushed well forward at the sides, reminded one of a divided flame. His nose rambled on aggressively before him with all the strength and determination of a cow-catcher, while his red mustache . . . seemed not unlike the unfortunate cow.

Yet there were overtones of condescension, if not malice: priggish allusion to Ward's coarseness, and pious regret for his failure to develop into a polished wit; the patronizing inference that, although the man was a good companion, he was rather a low fellow; invidious comparison of his humor with that of Harte and Holmes; and the implication that the illiterate showman of the badly-spelled sketches was only the alter ego of Ward himself.

It has been surmised that Mark Twain disparaged because he was envious of the fame of the other. Envy was probably there: of Ward's popularity, so great that plenty of people still believed he was the better humorist; of his extraordinary lecturing fees, much larger than Mark Twain had ever received. Yet derogation was a strange way of repaying friendship and a large debt besides. To Ward, Mark Twain owed his eastern start with "The Jumping Frog," his lecture technique, even accessory devices, and probably the ideas for more than a few tall tales. The unfriendly treatment of his generous friend may show, as other episodes show, that playing second fiddle was not a congenial role for Mark Twain.

He tried the new piece in Washington, D. C., on October 23 before an audience of two thousand crammed into a hall built for fourteen hundred, the stage crowded with a hundred and fifty. Always stimulated by a large gathering, he generally assumed that its mere presence guaranteed success. He was not entirely at ease, being so unfamiliar with the hurriedly devised talk that he had to read from his manuscript, a poor tactic as he well knew. Still, he said that this lecture suited him. It did not suit all others. One critic, scoffing at "this highly concentrated compound of old jokes," called him "a lamentable failure" who wearied everybody with threadbare witticisms. "He is 'played.' The water on this side of the mountains don't agree with him. His wit was genuine on the Pacific slope . . . but transplanting does not . . . improve the flavor."[7]

At Wilmington the next night results were not remarkable. On the day after, the *Delaware Gazette* condemned retailing another man's humor as "a confession of weakness that met the chilling reception . . . it deserved." Another insult was attributing "the paternity of his own stale jokes to the subject of his lecture"; there was no excuse for

an entertainment that could be more effectively enjoyed by a perusal of the *Galaxy Memoranda* for several years back . . . there are few more unsatisfactory efforts in the lecture field.

At Norristown on the 25th things got worse. In a harsh review, the *Independent* complained a week later that "the yarn . . . never rose to the dignity of a lecture." Reprimanding the speaker's "running up here at 7 o'clock and away at 10," the paper said:

his principal object seemed to be to pocket the fee, and palm off anything upon us. . . . MARK TWAIN you are a fraud as a lecturer, or . . . you concluded that anything would do for a country town. . . .

Sometimes he did treat small towns offhandedly, rushing in just before lecture time and departing immediately after. Such cavalier behavior displeased people. For fifty cents, considered a high price for a lecture ticket, and for an extravagant fee of $150, they wanted more consideration: a chance to meet the speaker, shake hands, and chat awhile. Railing against the social demands of touring, he appears not always to have recognized them as a necessary part of his job.

The equally critical Norristown *Herald and Free Press,* complaining of an unsympathetic manner and monotonous voice, said that "it was exceedingly bad taste . . . to twice mention the fact that Artemus Ward received five hundred dollars an hour for lecturing." The "grimaces and shoulder-shruggings" brought only "a murmur of applause," and the performance was a depressing rehash of ancient jokes:

We have passed through several new eras of humor since their day. . . . unless the "management" which manages him . . . be uncommonly skillful . . . like Othello, he will find his "occupation gone."

Many reverses in the first ten days made this season look like a disastrous rout. Matters did not improve on a short run into New England. Having been billed for "Reminiscences," he had to apologize for changing his subject. The shift did not ingratiate him with listeners, who felt defrauded when a speaker departed from his announced topic. To bridge the gap between the advertised lecture and the Ward one, he gave out the topheavy title: "Reminiscences of but *one* of the Uncommonplace Characters I Have Chanced to Meet." Then he went on to say that at the start of his "missionary tour" he had intended to talk about persons he had known, like Bunyan, Martin Luther, and Milton, but that he had not the time to discuss these boyhood companions, hence would confine himself to "one single great man."

Response was such a blend of the deceptively cheery, the half-hearted, and the negative that he became frantic as he practised on audiences, "feeling . . . pulses," he said, "& altering manner & matter to suit the symptoms."[8] They were favorable enough at Great Barrington to make him believe he had "convulsed" everybody, yet the *Berkshire Courier* maintained that of the crowd of four hundred, "at least three hundred and ninety . . . went away dissatisfied and disappointed. . . . we can only account for his plagiaristic lecture by the . . . same charge he lays upon Artemus Ward—laziness."[9] At Milford, people did no more than politely smile and faintly titter. At Brattleboro, the indignant *Vermont Phoenix* sympathized with the swindled lyceum committee and the "sold" audience. Any man, raged this paper, who peddled "stale anecdotes and secondhand jokes, and called it 'lecturing'" was "an insult to the public, and a disgrace to the 'bureau' that endorses it."[10]

Mark Twain was floundering badly. In two weeks he had been more savagely pounded than in both former tours together. The most disturbing complaint must have been of wornout material. Although he often remarked upon his boredom at hearing the same old jokes over and over, he seems to have forgotten that his own had been widely publicized, and that for years Ward's stories had made filler for newspapers everywhere. All of that was aged and tiresome. In distress, he looked to Boston to pull him out of the slough and restore his confidence. The city, he said plaintively, "must sit up & behave, & do right by me. As Boston goes, so goes New England."[11]

On November 1 Boston did well, giving him a Music Hall audience of two thousand, who were ready to laugh at anything. On November 2 the press was complimentary in a conventional way—"much merriment," "cordial reception," "quaint sayings . . . which have often . . . made us light-hearted and cheery"—but not ecstatic. The *Transcript* gave the performance eleven lines, as against fourteen on his previous Boston visit in 1869, the *Advertiser* less than a half-column instead of the full one before. Both papers nostalgically mentioned Ward's stories as if reporting a reunion of old settlers. Mark Twain may have entertained his audience, but he was not taking Boston critics by storm. The Hub was willing to put up with him as an amusing eccentric, but it did not smother him with affection.

Still, he made a respectable showing. Yet the belief that Boston opinion dominated New England must have been a lecturers' superstition, for it did not help him in half a dozen towns in New Hampshire, Massachusetts, and Connecticut. With serene independence, they damned more often than they praised. At Exeter, hopeful expectation of a jolly evening withered under the blight of those ancient jokes. The *News Letter* said that the speaker, who lacked "almost every element of humor," was

lamentably deficient in originality. . . . we . . . hope that the press everywhere may be so severe . . . as to force this plagiaristic lecture off the platform; for we believe that Mark Twain is capable of better things, and he owes it to himself and to the public to produce them.[12]

At Malden, said the *Mirror*, the "so-called lecture" was a "patchwork" of "anecdotal beads, threaded with a . . . filament of tattered biography. . . . Mr. Clemens's homely face, and . . . tipsy style speech, are somewhat against him, though we suppose they are natural." Still, this critic ironically concluded, the performance was "pleasing, and in our estimation, well worth $15, or even $20."[13]

Hartford administered a soothing poultice for bruises with a full and lively house in Allyn Hall on November 8. The *Courant* of the 9th, praising "happy hits," said:

The man who can give such an audience . . . an hour of innocent laughter is a public benefactor, and this we consider Mr. Clemens. No lecturer of the season has had such a hearty welcome.

Thus the shopworn witticisms that fatigued one audience delighted another. Heeding the howls of outraged critics, he may have twisted old jokes enough to make them seem new. He had the raconteur's skill at taking over a story and making it his own, putting the Mark Twain stamp upon it by embellishments that, assisted by tricks of delivery, could have brought it off. This lordly habit of lifting and adapting may have been in his mind when, a few years later, he accused Bret Harte of deliberate plagiarism and at the same time admitted that his own unconscious borrowings might have made him one of the world's foremost literary thieves.

After a brief upswing, the curve of success plunged again at Worcester. The lecture pleased some there, but others thought it was silly. Mark Twain believed that the grumblers were a majority, for he exploded about "1700 of the staidest, puritanical people you ever saw—one of the hardest gangs to move that ever was. . . . a man couldn't fetch them with a hundred thousand yoke of oxen." Besides, "the confounded chairman" sat behind him on the stage, "a thing I detest. He is the last one that can air his good clothes & his owlish mug on my platform."[14] He must have been in a frenzied state. In the way of men seeking a scapegoat, he attributed all his troubles to Artemus Ward. Continually "patching at" his lecture, he said that he was "trying to weed Artemus out of it & work myself in. What *I* say, *fetches* 'em—but what *he* says—don't."[15] That was an unfair thrust, also inaccurate, for Mark Twain had not been brilliant at fetching.

The long tour went on: Manchester, Haverhill, Portland, Lowell, Philadelphia, Brooklyn, Rondout, Easton, Reading. At Haverhill, delayed a half hour by a slow train, he tramped through the audience to the stage, put down his valise and, in full view of the house, divested himself of overcoat and overshoes. Then, in a short impromptu, he begged some indignant gentleman to rise up and deliver a strong fifteen-minute reproof for tardiness. That apology, he said, "broke the ice & we went through with colors flying & drums beating."[16] Drumbeats were not so loud as he thought, for the *Daily Bulletin* reported a divided opinion: "Some thought it good, others dubbed it 'Small potatoes.'" The papers did not always see eye to eye with Mark Twain. Like the device on a TV show, he measured effect by decibels of sound that, in retrospect, might seem to have been expended on "small potatoes." But since he did not pretend to purvey much of anything else, he was probably right in accepting transitory approval as a warrant of favor. As the *Bulletin* remarked, "Mark don't care whether he sells small or large potatoes so long as he sells them well, which he does."[17]

At Portland, on November 16, his audience was "highly entertained" by Artemus Ward, its motheaten stories "told in such a droll way that they never failed to excite laughter." At Philadelphia on the 20th he was "perfectly irresistible" with "Reminiscences." The next night at Brooklyn he so crowded Plymouth Church with "the usual Beecher people" that some unfortunate late-comers had to sit on folding chairs over hot air registers, which had been put there by Mr. Beecher, one reporter believed, as reminders of hell. A waggish Brooklyn journalist, calling Mark Twain "the Intellectual Treat," said that he appeared in full evening dress, his "swallow tails . . . of orthodox fashion, but well sat upon," his trousers showing "the gloss of respectable middle age." The same newsman recorded remarks by members of the audience:

"My, what a handsome young man to be a lecturer!" "He's married over three millions of money, and lectures for fun." "So he ought, if he's a funny lecturer." "He isn't a bit funny now he's married." "He's got a baby and that takes all the humor out of him."

Of the talk on Ward, this critic said that its biographical data were "remarkable rather for . . . inventive power than for strict historical truth, but he fibbed with such unction that the congregation . . . listened to the sermon with their sweetest Sabbath smile."[18]

To be more fetching, he interpolated a digression about Ward's Puritan ancestors. "I am a Puritan Father myself," he said, "at

least I am descended from one." Then he took off on foolery
about a forebear who

cut a conspicuous figure in the "Boston Massacre," fighting first on
one side and then on the other. He wasn't a man to stand foolin'
around while a massacre was goin' on. Why, to hear our family talk,
you'd think that not a man named anything but Twain was in that
massacre—and, when you came to hear all about it, you'd wish that
such was the case.

Another ancestor, at Bunker Hill, was "killed, wounded and
missing. He was a prompt, business-like fellow, and to make sure
of being the last of the three, he did it first of all—did it well,
too, before a shot was fired."[19] These absurdities, spoken with the
aid of verbal and other mannerisms, probably sounded funnier
than they look in cold type.

In a new ending, he led up to Ward's last days in England,
his longing for home, and untimely end in Southampton on April
13, 1867. Then he closed with a memorial poem written by
James Rhoades and published in the London *Spectator* a week
after Ward's death:

> Is he gone to a land of no laughter,
> This man that made mirth for us all?
> Proves death but a silence hereafter
> From the sounds that delight or appal?
>
> .   .   .   .
>
> For the pain in our heart lingered after,
> When the merriment died in our ears,
> And those that were loudest in laughter
> Are silent in tears.

This finale was universally approved. Read with feeling, as Mark
Twain knew how to read verse, the lines won respect, even of
critics who complained of everything else in the lecture.

Several good city performances were balm for wounds inflicted
in small towns. He was right in preferring the metropolitan

audience to that of the village. Eccentricities and puzzling humor had a better chance with a large, mixed crowd. It was sure to contain a number of people who asked no more than an hour's amusing palaver to chortle over, and whose gayety was likely to be infectious. On this tour cities were his best stops; most of the sneers came from lesser places. Immediately after the success of Brooklyn he made only an indifferent showing at Rondout, and at Easton he was called a "lamentable failure" with an "abortive lecture." Still existent in the provinces was a sturdy core of old-fashioned earnestness that resented as an immoral waste of time a full evening of frivolity.

Yet of one small town, Bennington, he made the strange complaint that the audience laughed too much. The man was hard to please. Between not enough laughter and too much, the proper quantity seemed dependent on his mood. At Bennington, as if determined to be not merely a clown, he said that any lecture of his should be "a running narrative plank, with square holes in it, six inches apart," these to be fitted, according to the temper of the audience, with pegs, "half marked 'serious' & the other marked 'humorous.' "[20] It was a good scheme, but the joker in him was too strong to allow it. Soon he would be sweating as hard as ever to make a poker-faced crowd laugh, and gloating over a noisy one, the noisier the better.

Getting control of the Ward lecture, he retrieved some ground lost in early failures by respectable performances in Albany and Newark, then in Oswego, Homer, Geneva, and Auburn. The pathos of the new ending, together with the poem, mollified objectors ready to protest against meager substance and ancient stories. Yet he was dissatisfied. "I am so sick of that lecture!" he said. "It makes me g-a-g to think of it."[21] Seeking an alternative, he hit upon the happy idea of composing a talk about Nevada and California in the manner of his new book, to be published within the next few months. Writing furiously on trains and in hotel rooms, he produced a draft that he tried out in

Warsaw, New York, on December 7. Announcing the title as "Roughing It: being Passages from my Forthcoming Book," he achieved, he said, "a tip-top success." Several things this season had been, in his estimation, tiptop. That some turned out otherwise is a comment on his unsure judgment.

This time the Warsaw *New Yorker* supported him by saying that "the hour and a half seemed robbed of half its clock-ticks," and commending eloquent description that held listeners in "the perfect stillness of rapt attention which marks the fine periods of Curtis or Anna Dickinson."[22] To be mentioned in the same breath with the hardy Dickinson must have been something like an accolade for Mark Twain. Perhaps one reason he captivated this audience was that he outdid himself in an extended self-introduction with vaudeville accompaniment. Striking an orator's pose, assuming the orator's resounding tone, he eulogized the lecturer's vast historical learning, his scholarly attainments in science, linguistics, and geography. He roared on about the patriotic ancestors of "the lecturer of the evening," who "fit into the war of the Revolution." As he worked up to a pitch of vehemence about the lecturer of the evening, with much shouting and arm-waving, apprehensive people wondered whether they were at the mercy of a lunatic. Then, pausing suddenly in a flight of rhetoric, he dropped his voice and casually identified himself. The crash of laughter was so relieved that it was all the more tumultuous.

The version of the new lecture at Warsaw contained remnants of the Ward one: the "Adam who?" story and others. He had not yet beaten it into workable shape, for at Fredonia the next night he confessed that, overcome by fatigue, he was "a dismal failure." The Fredonia *Censor* of the 13th agreed, deprecating an anecdotal hash that was "thin diet for an evening's entertainment. . . . In appearing this season with . . . such lack of preparation, making a tour 'on his reputation' . . . he does an injustice . . . to himself and the societies employing him." Undaunted, he was convinced that he had finally found a "tip-top" subject that was bound to "*fetch* 'um." On December 9 he returned to Artemus Ward for Erie, where the evening was one of those drawn battles of divided opinion: pros, cons, and the timid who did not dare say what they thought until instructed by the popular verdict. The Erie *Gazette* of the 11th remarked that to anybody who had heard the stories told by "the inimitable Artemus, their rehearsal was flat, but with the majority they took very well." After the performance there he spent the night ironing out the wrinkles in the new number, kept at it the next day, "though nearly dead with fatigue," and the day after that on the train to Toledo.

As it evolved, the lecture was similar to parts of *Roughing It*. Beginning by announcing the imminence of the book—a neat publicity gesture—he said that he was prepared to talk thirty or forty pages of it or the whole six hundred as the audience preferred. After brief mention of the stage journey across the plains, he described the vast Nevada country as a land of silver, little rain, and no thunder. Then followed a disquisition on sagebrush—no good as a vegetable, but useful as fuel—and a vivid description of the grand panorama visible from South Pass. The adventure with the Mexican plug, elaborated at length, Lake Tahoe, the healthfulness of the climate, difficulties of bagging an "American Shamwah"—"I believe that is the way the word is pronounced—I don't know"—silver mining and the Wide West lead, early experience on the *Enterprise,* Colonel Jack and Colonel Jim in New York: these items followed the trend of their counterparts in the book. The scapegrace Harris was in the lecture off and on, also brawls and murders of Virginia City and Carson. The ending varied. Sometimes he closed with the story of the abortive Nevada duel, accompanied by incongruous moral reflections. Occasionally he ended by reproving reporters for printing synopses of lectures, adding the story of Artemus Ward, who confounded one shorthand expert by substituting whistles for key words.

Not yet having a firm grasp of these materials, he talked on Ward at Toledo and Ann Arbor. At the latter, under the auspices of the Students' Lecture Association, he had his first experience with a crowd of college students. They made a good audience for him, so gay that the campus weekly, *The Chronicle,* reprimanded "the manifest boorishness of certain members of the professional departments and others." The paper called Mark Twain " 'one of the few immortal' ones," and ambiguously approved of the performance: "All appeared satisfied when the lecture closed."[23]

By laborious study he got "Roughing It" in hand for Jackson, Michigan, then used it, with some interruptions, for the rest of the tour. At long last, after two months of uneven showings, of false starts and harried experiments, he had a lecture that he believed in and that he could deliver with confidence. Thereafter successes became more frequent. Lansing gave him a crowded house of about five hundred, a good showing if not large by urban standards. Small wonder that Mark Twain would rather stand in a city auditorium before a heterogeneous audience of two or three thousand uninhibited by small town social pressures or by the hushed air of a village church. Yet he enjoyed himself in the Middle West, and his audiences generally enjoyed him. The Lansing *State Republican,* thinking that he might be hurt if not given "a pretty extended notice," published a long synopsis of the brand new talk. Little did the editor know that his misguided courtesy was a sure way not merely to hurt, but to infuriate, Mark Twain. But somehow this synopsis escaped his usually vigilant eye, and the Lansing man escaped the lightning.

On December 15 Grand Rapids did nobly with a crowd of 1300 in Luce's Hall, all seats filled, every foot of standing room taken. Everybody laughed, but on the day after the *Daily Morning Democrat* said that the evening was a failure, the *Daily Eagle* that the talk was thin. On reflection, citizens evidently agreed, for the *Eagle* also remarked that in the packed house "we thought we recognized . . . familiar faces, but it seems we were mistaken, the audience was composed of strangers, as today we can hear of no one who was there." Still, as the paper observed,

Americans . . . want something ludicrous, something odd, something to laugh at, at times, and in this respect they perhaps get their money's worth in attending Mark Twain's lectures.

That was an apt comment. He was a dead loss to anybody who expected a message or a moral lesson. On the platform he was not at home in the realm of ideas. In the formal sense he was not a lecturer at all. He was a story-teller, a yarn-spinner. What he called a lecture was a series of anecdotes interspersed with descriptive passages, the whole loosely held together, and sometimes revolving vaguely about a central theme, sometimes not. Hence, serious-minded listeners, though they might laugh freely, often felt uneasy, like a respectable burgher suffering twinges of conscience over the memory of having enjoyed a raffish escapade. Yet as more than one critic had pointed out, Mark Twain's forte was humor and fantastic exaggeration, and audiences had no right to expect more.

At Kalamazoo he congested Union Hall with the largest crowd since John B. Gough had filled the place the year before. People from outlying towns for miles around began sifting in at seven o'clock. The *Gazette* said that "No man, without it be Gough . . . had more perfect control of his subject, himself and his listeners," holding them spellbound with lyrical description, then dropping a droll remark that was "like the spark in a powder magazine."[24] The *Daily Telegraph* scolded:

Mr. Clemens had no right to impose . . . such desultory trash. . . . He should have . . . not put us off with a . . . disconnected talk about a hackneyed subject, *sans* wit, *sans* information, *sans* sense.[25]

Contradictory opinions leave the truth in doubt, but a certainty is that no cankered criticism diminished crowds in the Middle West. As large as halls permitted, often record-breaking, they proved that, regardless of critics, Mark Twain was a great popular favorite. The success of *The Innocents Abroad* had made him something like a national monument that people swarmed in to see.

The aftermath of Kalamazoo was another variety of travel contretemps that dogged the lecturer's trail. Staying up until well after midnight, he turned out at 4 A. M., missing breakfast, to catch a train for Chicago. On a scheduled two-hour run it "fooled along," he said, for eleven hours. Without food all that time he arrived famished, but after lugging his bags, "a couple of tons apiece," half a mile to his quarters, he broke his fast with

a perfectly enormous dinner (a roast turkey & 8 gallons of Oolong tea—well it was "long" something—it was the longest tea that ever went down my throat—it was hours in passing a given point).[26]

Then he and his host, Robert Law, spent some time viewing the devastation wrought by the great fire of two months before, destruction so widespread that he could not recognize the city. After that he talked for hours, then sat up until midnight revising his lecture. He was a good night owl. Given enough sleep —he generally spent the morning in bed unless he had to catch a train—he had the stamina to keep going most of the night. Despite roars over the hardships of travel, he measured up to them with agility and vigor, boasted of good health, ate prodigious dinners, and with combative joy coped with the perversities of dawdling trains and outrageous time schedules.

Two Chicago performances were triumphs. At the first, in the Michigan Avenue Baptist Church, he had a fine crowd of two thousand that filled the main auditorium, lecture room and Sunday School room, filled aisles and packed standees all around. The *Tribune* of December 19 described the speaker as

not handsome, but having a bright, intelligent look, and an eye with a humorous twinkle. . . . There is nothing finical about his style of dress. . . . and his manner of wearing his hair, which is abundant, shows that he is his own tonsorial artist.

Throughout the lecture he looked "as grave and solemn as the visage of an undertaker when screwing down a coffin lid." The *Evening Post* good-humoredly commented upon "the lank, lantern-jawed and impudent Californian," who spoke "in a fascinating nasal snarl, looking and speaking like an embarrassed deacon," and who craned his long neck around "like a bereaved Vermonter who has just come from the death-bed of his mother-in-law, and is looking for a sexton." Remarking upon awkward gestures— churning the air "as if fighting mosquitoes," rubbing his hands, putting arms akimbo "like a disgusted auctioneer"—the *Post* said that once

he got his arms tangled so badly, that three surgeons were seen to edge . . . quietly toward the stage, expecting to be summoned; but he unwound himself during the next anecdote.

That raillery was like the hoots and jeers of Virginia City and San Francisco. In a raw and robust city closer to the West than Boston, both geographically and temperamentally, Chicagoans felt at home with Mark Twain, and he was at home with them. His second appearance, in the Park Congregational Church, was as hilarious as the first. However much a churchly atmosphere might subdue a small town audience, it did not repress anybody here.

The only flaw in these pleasurable proceedings was that the *Tribune* published a detailed synopsis of "Roughing It." Mark Twain wrathfully invited damnation to descend upon the "cursed" sheet. Believing that the paper had destroyed the freshness of the new lecture for nearby towns, he returned to Artemus Ward for Aurora, Sandwich, Princeton, and Champaign. "If these devils incarnate," he raged, "only appreciated what suffering they inflict with their infernal synopses, maybe they would try to have humanity enough to refrain."[27] When he thought he was out of range of the *Tribune,* he went back to "Roughing It" for Tuscola, Danville, Mattoon, and Paris.

In prairie hamlets he was not always the conquering hero of

the city. Champaign and Tuscola papers failed to comment. At Princeton, the *Bureau County Republican* said that of the Artemus Ward kind of lecture, "One is enough to satisfy almost anybody; two . . . would be too many, even for the strong stomachs of a country audience." Ward's stories were only "passably told . . . not in any way up to the standard of the original storyteller."[28] At Danville, the editor of the *Commercial* snarled that since the visitor took all his meals in his hotel room, he might have made money if he had "charged 25 cents admission, for all suckers who wished to see him." Then he damned the whole tribe of humorous lecturers:

Take Doesticks, Billings, Twain, Fat Contributor . . . most of what they say is chaff . . . a thousand bushels of chaff to one hundred of sound grain—must be lots of fanning to separate the no account from that which is of *some* value.[29]

Besides uncertainties of reception was the labor of shuttling between towns. Getting from Chicago to Champaign, 128 miles, took almost six hours. The Champaign hotel was so shabby that after the performance he took off in a huff for Tuscola. Arriving there at two-thirty A.M. on the coldest night of the year, he found every hotel room taken. So he sat up the rest of the night in an unheated office, draping himself in an overcoat and trying to keep his legs warm by wrapping around them all the shirts in his valise.

Enjoying the stop at Paris, he sent from there a lively story of a church service that took him back in memory to the Hannibal of twenty-five years before: "the high pulpit, with the red plush pillow for the Bible. . . . stiff pews. . . . the wheezy melodeon . . . the old maid behind it in severe simplicity of dress." The choir poured forth "a grand discordant confusion" that ended with "a triumphant 'Oh, praise the L-o-r-d!' in a unison of unutterable anguish." The minister woodenly read a hymn: "Come, thou FOUNT. Of every Blessing./Tune my HEART. To sing thy PRAISE." The "ineffable" tenor rendered "Oh, for a sweet, inspiring ray" in a manner that sounded like "Ow fra sub-weet insphiring rye." After the missionary appeal,

the sexton and the deacon went around, while the choir wailed, and collected seventy cents for the carrying of the glad tidings of great joy to the lost souls of Further India.[30]

Turning eastward, he was in good form with "Roughing It" at Indianapolis on January 1, 1872. Next day's *Journal* spoke of an appreciative house, "with the . . . exception of one young lady, who looked on mournfully while her neighbors were convulsed with laughter." Mark Twain was delighted with everything. "Had a splendid time," he said, "with a splendid audience in Indianapolis . . . a perfectly jammed house, just as I have had all the time out here."[31] At Logansport on the 2d he filled the Opera House, but failed to satisfy the critic of the local *Sun*. This acrimonious fellow said two days later that "No man not . . . a fit candidate for a lunatic as(s)ylum . . . would dignify the performance by calling it a lecture." The manner was clownish and the humor inferior to that of J. Proctor Knott, "who excels him in extravagant . . . descriptive powers as far as an ocean steamer does a tea-pot." The Nevada story was neither moral nor elevating:

Does . . . Jack Harris, with his coarse allusions . . . benefit the people? If not, then in the name of society, let us have no more of such performances under the auspices of the Christian Association.

The accusation of coarseness had not reared its scaly head for five years or more, though the offensive "allusions" were not identified. The *Sun* man was evidently an old-line champion of righteousness. Yet the most unkind cut must have been the superior rating of J. Proctor Knott. Mark Twain considered him so feeble that a few years later, when the *Library of Humor* was under way, he refused to put into it anything by Knott.

After Richmond, Indiana, he went on to Ohio towns: Dayton,

Columbus, Wooster, Salem, Steubenville. At Dayton, a clergyman who met his train asked whether he had any objection to opening the evening's entertainment with prayer. "Why, my dear sir," was the cordial reply, "on the contrary, it will give me great pleasure— I should be very glad to know that the lecture was going to be started right, anyhow."[32] The minister led off with a long prayer of twenty minutes or more, concluding with the fervent plea:

O Lord, we have with us to-night a man . . . known throughout all the world as the great American humorist. Help us, O Lord—help us to understand what he is about to say, and to be amused by it . . . if possible, grant that we may derive some real benefit from this lecture.[33]

What Mark Twain had to say after that about invoking the aid of the Lord to find amusement and "real benefit" is not on record. Possibly the two discussed the point, for he could not escape putting up at the parsonage. Although he did not complain as loudly as usual about the handicaps of a strict household, there was latent irritation in his remark to Livy that a lecturer "*dreads* a private house—Oh, more than he dreads 200 miles of railway travel."[34]

At Columbus, to avoid getting up for a train at two in the morning, he chartered a locomotive for $75 to take him to Wooster. Then he gave fifty dollars to a poor devil of a hardup poet. Spending freely, besides paying off debts, he was generally low on cash; on this tour he said that he "squandered no end of money." Slim returns for hard work made him reflect on the miseries of touring. "I *do* hate lecturing," he said at Wooster, "& I shall try hard to have as little as possible of it to do hereafter."[35] Yet three days later at Steubenville, quartered in the Female Seminary, he found lecturing not at all hateful in the midst of seventy girls, described as "a mighty handsome lot," who all attended the performance and showered him with attention.

Moving on, he paused at Wheeling, then at Pittsburgh, where

he attracted to Liberty Hall the largest audience that had ever attended a lecture there. Everybody was gay, and he did not complain of too much laughter. By contrast, Kittanning struck him as "a filthy, stupid, hateful Dutch village, like *all* Pennsylvania." After speaking to the "leatherheads" there, he hurried back to Pittsburgh for a weekend of "dinners & things" in "that black but delightful town."[36] Apparently it was not a part of Pennsylvania.

After Lock Haven and Milton, he moved on to Harrisburg. Such a crowd surged into the Court House there that wives became separated from husbands, children from mothers, and there was more feverish jostling and squeezing than even the popular Methodist pastor had ever induced. "Such a minister as Twain is," said the *Patriot,* "for drawing people would be a valuable auxiliary for revival purposes. Some denomination ought to 'call' him in." Seats full, aisles full, windowsills occupied,

the gas brackets could have been useful for hanging the children to. . . . The only vacant place left when the lecturer commenced was his mouth, and that nobody crowded down his throat was astonishing.[37]

No doubt such a reception made him forget the stupidity of hateful Dutch villages. When he boldly invaded the real Dutch country at the staid old town of Lancaster, he made no slighting remarks about chuckleheads or leatherheads. At Carlisle a packed house of six hundred gave him a hearty welcome. The *American Volunteer* paid a high compliment by saying that of all humorous lecturers only two were worth listening to: the late Artemus Ward and Mark Twain.

He went on to Baltimore. Then, on January 24 in Steinway Hall, he spoke to a New York audience for the first time in almost five years. Still bearing a grudge against Governor Nye for defaulting on the Cooper Union assignment in 1867, he inserted in his introductory remarks satirical praise of the governor. He was, said Mark Twain, a real father to those poor Nevada Indians. He gave them . . . blankets and hoopskirts. You could see an Indian chief with a string of blacking boxes round his neck, and over his red blanket four or five . . . hoopskirts, walking the streets as happy as a clam, with his hands sticking out of the slats. And yet . . . notwithstanding all the efforts and civilizing kindness of the good Governor, those Indians didn't step out of their savage condition—they were just as degraded as if they had never seen a hoopskirt.[38]

The press next day unanimously approved. The speaker, said the *Herald*, was "exceptionally funny," the audience shaken with "uproarious mirth." The lecture, said the *Times*, was "meteorological, historical, topographical, geological, zoological, and comical." The *Tribune* sounded a new note by saying that "He is the finest delineator of the true Pike accent." New York, like Chicago, was hospitable to Mark Twain. He was better acclimated to the breezy spirit of such places than he ever was to the more rarefied air of Boston.

Backtracking to Scranton, he then returned to Jersey City and Paterson, and ended the long tour at Troy on February 1. "Roughing It" going well at these places, he salvaged some satisfaction from the fag end of this "detestable" season. It was, he said, "one eternal worry." Still, if the first half had been rugged with failure and critical disapproval, the latter part had produced a number of triumphant successes. Yet liberal spending and paying off debts left him, he said, with "less than $1500" as a reward for "all that work & misery."[39]

10

Erstwhile Innocent Abroad

WITH AN AIR of disgust he once more renounced the platform. "I ain't going to ever lecture any more," he told Mother Fairbanks, "—unless I get in debt again. Would you?"[1] But he was immensely pleased by the steady flow of invitations. Sharp criticisms on the recent tour diminished neither the number of requests nor the size of proposed fees. One munificent offer promised $10,000 for one month in several large cities, or $5000 for twelve nights. In midsummer Redpath inquired: "Will you? Won't you? We have seven thousand to eight thousand dollars in engagements for you"[2]—in principal cities from Boston to St. Paul. These temptations he resisted. Another season was out of the question, he said, because he expected to spend the next winter either in England, Florida, or Cuba.

England was the choice. To keep *Roughing It* out of the clutches of British pirates like John Camden Hotten—lampooned as John Camden Hottentot—and to take notes for a book on Britain that he never wrote, Mark Twain sailed in August, 1872. The time was propitious, for Britishers were friendly to American writers. They had taken Artemus Ward to their hearts, and they welcomed his countrymen who followed. England in the seventies, particularly London, attracted American authors much as Paris

173

enticed them fifty years later. Visiting Britain was like a pilgrimage for Californians. Bret Harte was to become an English expatriate. Joaquin Miller delighted Londoners with his drawing-room war-whoops and his wild west outfit of high boots and jingling spurs; the mild Charles Warren Stoddard was at home abroad; crusty Ambrose Bierce was boon companion of hard-living journalists of Fleet Street; even so self-effacing a San Franciscan as Prentice Mulford clung to the hand-to-mouth bohemianism of Bloomsbury.

Mark Twain received a profuse outpouring of good-will. Remaining in England over three months, he was both busy tourist and social lion. He roamed London—Westminster Abbey, Crystal Palace, the Tower, St. Paul's—visited Kenilworth and Warwick Castle, and reveled in the beauty of Oxford. The tower of Magdalen College, decked with Virginia creeper pouring down a cataract of green, gold, and crimson in what he called "a wasteful, graceful, gorgeous little Niagara," struck him as "the darlingest, loveliest picture I ever saw."[3] When not sightseeing, he was the center of flattering attention: guest of honor at dinners of the Whitefriars Club and Savage Club, at both of which he responded with humorous after-dinner speeches; wildly applauded at the Guildhall, and escorted by the Lord Chancellor through the assemblage at the Lord Mayor's dinner; watching a stag hunt, complete with whoop and halloo and red-coated riders, at War-grave-near-Henley. The socially prominent and the distinguished wanted to meet Mark Twain: Tom Hood, Henry M. Stanley, Charles Reade, Henry Irving. It was a heady experience. Yet, after initial surprise at such effusiveness, he was seldom at a loss. Dubbed "the Belle of London," he relished the applause, basked in the warmth of compliment, rapturously reported on gatherings at which he was the main attraction, and mentioned, with pleasure and awe, grandees who cultivated his acquaintance. He was received, he said, "Just the same as if I were a Prodigal Son getting back home again."[4]

British societies begged him to lecture, and British friends urged him. George Dolby, the manager of Charles Dickens, exerted all his jovial charm to induce Mark Twain to take to the platform. Everybody, he remarked, kept telling him to lecture, "but I have not the least idea of doing so—certainly not at present."[5] In November he wrote Redpath: "When I yell again for less than $500 I'll be pretty hungry, but I haven't any intention of yelling at any price." That apparent certainty was merely another hint of insecure conviction, for in the same letter he said that he was "re-vamping, polishing . . . fixing up" the "Roughing It" lecture to deliver "in London a couple of times, about a month from now, just for fun."[6] He could no more stay off the rostrum than he could become a hermit. In late November he informed the press that he had "partly promised" to speak for British societies, but that he could not do so because a cablegram had called him home. Announcing a return to England with his family for most of the following year, he assured admirers that he might then be able to lecture a month "upon such scientific topics as I know least about and may consequently feel less trammeled in dilating upon."[7]

In the United States Redpath was after him immediately with lucrative offers, like $400 for one night in Philadelphia. Mark Twain turned them down, yet by January, 1873, the old urge made him feel that he must lecture a few times, compelled by no other force, apparently, than the magnetism of the platform. As a prelude, he published in the New York *Tribune* on January 6 and 9 two long articles on the Sandwich Islands. Concluding with an ironical plea for annexation of Hawaii, he said:

> We can make that little bunch of sleepy islands the hottest corner on earth, and array it in the moral splendor of our high and holy civilization. . . . "Shall we to man benighted, the lamp of life deny." . . . we can furnish them some Jay Goulds who will do away with their old-time notion that stealing is not respectable. We can confer Woodhull and Claflin upon them. And George Francis Train. We can give them lecturers! I will go myself.

On January 31 he gave "Our Fellow Savages" at Hartford for the benefit of Father Hawley's City Mission, netting the good sum of $1500 from a crowded house. Next day's *Courant* praised the lecture as "the same Mr. Clemens once delivered here . . . yet not the same. It was greatly improved . . . in fact, by far the best of the lecturer's efforts here." Variations were minor. Omitting the skinned man-stabbed man preamble improved the beginning; leaving out the offer to illustrate cannibalism was no loss. He introduced new material, such as the Islanders' fondness for the American game of seven-up, in which their abysmal ignorance rated a tenspot higher than an ace; and their capabilities as future voters. Since they did everything wrong-end-to, they would probably "elect the most incorruptible men to Congress." A revised ending dwelt lyrically upon

a dreamy, beautiful, charming land. . . . ever so vague and fairy-like. . . . Sunday land, the land of indolence and dreams, where the air is drowsy and lulls the spirit to repose and peace, and to forgetfulness of the labored turmoil and weariness and anxiety of life.[8]

Otherwise the substance was little different from that of the previous version. Some of the phrasing was almost identical, as in the joke about native dress: "In the rural districts the women wear a single, long, loose gown. But the men don't." Yet the manner may have seemed different in 1873. By that time, when the Sandwich Islands had slipped further into the romantic haze of the past, nostalgia probably bathed the text in a mellower warmth.

On February 5 and 10 he appeared in Steinway Hall, New York, for the Mercantile Library Association on a basis of half profits, earning $1300 as his share. Packed and roaring houses greeted him, hundreds of disappointed people having been turned away. On the 5th various celebrities sat on the stage. One of them, called "the Rev. Petroleum V. Nasby," later escorted the speaker to the Lotos Club where, with convivial friends, they talked most of the night away. For that sort of sociability the metropolis was vastly preferable to small towns. They could not pay Mark Twain's rising fees, and they were short on clubs and celebrities. Between the New York engagements he filled the Brooklyn Academy of Music. The *Eagle's* two-column review with frequent interpolation of "[Laughter]," "[Prolonged laughter]," and "[Prolonged laughter and applause]" testified to a rousing audience and a contented speaker. The *Daily Union* praised handsomely by likening the comic spirit of Mark Twain to that of Rabelais' and Charles Lamb.

Meanwhile lecture invitations continued to arrive, twenty or more from New York City alone. One generous proposal from an unidentified source offered $500 to $800 a night for twenty to thirty nights.[9] Mark Twain replied that he could not accept because Livy disapproved. Evidently she had had enough of being a lecturing widow. He said he was not sorry, yet rejecting so opulent a prize as $800 a night must have been painful. He had need of money now, for the new house being built in Hartford was an expensive undertaking. An imposing affair, it was to be three stories high, 87 x 111 feet overall, set in spacious grounds equipped with commodious stables: an elaborate place that was eventually to cost, exclusive of furnishings, about $135,000. That was a tremendous figure for the seventies, and it is no small one even in the inflationary twentieth century. Mark Twain's preferred style was that of the tycoon. If his lecture fees were going up, so was the cost of living.

Back to England went the whole family in May, 1873, to be caught up in a furore of making and receiving calls, hobnobbing with lords and ladies, lunching and dining and talking with Herbert Spencer, Robert Browning, Wilkie Collins, Anthony Trollope, Sir John Millais, Charles Kingsley, and all sorts of others. Mark Twain said that this frenzy was like being "ground up" in a mill, "a kind of foretaste of hell." But since he was a social being, like Dr. Johnson, the mill was probably less hellish than exhilarating. He loved the swirl of action. In early summer he rushed off to Ostend to cover the visit of the Shah of Persia for the New York *Herald*. The paper reported his adventures in several long stories under impudent headlines: "The Man of Mark Ready to Bring Over the O'Shah"; "Mark Twain Gets O'Shah on Board and Proceeds With Him to Hold Hingland"; "The Pilgarlic Pilgrim's Progress to Portsmouth." He made a rambling yarn of his troubles, real and imaginary, in trying to catch up with the royal visitor, whom he contemptuously dismissed as

a man who has never done anything to win our gratitude or excite our admiration, except that he managed to starve a million of his subjects to death in twelve months. If he had starved the rest I suppose we would set up a monument to him now.[10]

He made a few dinner speeches. Responding to the toast, "The Ladies," for the Scottish Corporation of London, he pretended to get stuck on the poem written by "the most noble, the most gracious, the purest, and sweetest of poets": "Woman! O woman! —er—Wom—" then went on to cite famous women like Sairey Gamp and Josephine, also great men of Scotland, "Scott, Bruce, the warrior Wallace, Ben Nevis—the gifted Ben Lomond, and the great new Scotchman, Ben Disraeli."[11] At a dinner of the St. Andrews Society, responding to the toast, "The Guests," he said that he felt at home in Scotland, where he had been taken for a native.

I had my clothes . . . colored tartan. . . . I stuck a big feather in my cap too, and the people would follow me for miles. . . . some of the best judges in Scotland said they had never seen a Highland costume like mine. What's more, one of those judges fined me for wearing it— out of mere envy, I suppose.[12]

Since he found people more interesting than historical land-marks, his intention of writing a book about England fell by the wayside of comings and goings with fascinating new acquaint-ances. "I find," he said, "that the *really* great ones are very easy to get along with, even when hampered by titles." But "mediocrity with a title . . . is a formidable thing to encounter—*it* don't talk, & I'm afraid to."[13] That remark was surely blarney, for it is impossible to imagine that he was ever afraid to talk.

This time there was no coy diffidence about lecturing, and he soon came to terms with Dolby. Choosing the Sandwich Islands for his British debut, he published in London papers in early October an announcement of his intention to speak because of "the inflamed desire of the public to acquire information concerning" the Islands. No one, he said,

can allay this unwholesome excitement as effectually as I can. . . . I feel and know that I am equal to this task, for I can allay any kind of an excitement by lecturing upon it. . . . I have always been able to paralyse the public interest in any topic that I chose to take hold of and elucidate with all my strength.

Dolby advertised a week of performances, from October 13 to 18, at the Queen's Concert Rooms in Hanover Square. The place was too small for Mark Twain, who said he felt cramped there, but it was fashionable. For five nights and a Saturday matinee notables of London crowded the auditorium: men and women of rank, people famous in the arts and sciences, and a sprinkling of Americans, including P. T. Barnum. These assemblies were the starchiest Mark Twain had ever faced. If he was not entirely at ease with them, the stiff British front only intensified his insouciance. With a casualness that barely escaped swagger, he shuffled upon the stage, said one reporter, as if "assured of the success . . . so speedily won." As Huck Finn remarked of another occasion: "Tom had his store clothes on, and an audience—and that was always nuts for Tom Sawyer."

In his introduction he endeared himself by saying that he was speaking out of gratitude to England for her generosity in sending many lecturers across the Atlantic. The mother country, he said, "should not give all and the child nothing." The nasal twang and western dialect offended some cultivated ears. Defending the speaker, the *Standard* asked:

Is the . . . Irish bull . . . less palatable because it is served up with brogue sauce; or the high dried Scotch jest . . . less pungent because . . . of . . . an accent only procurable north of the Trent? Wherefore then should not the delicious dialect of California . . . enrich the quality of American humour? With Mark Twain it does so.[14]

The *Post* could say only that "the full-flavoured American dialect" was not "unpleasant to listen to when spoken by Mr. Twain in its integrity."[15] The *Cosmopolitan* considered the voice "not particularly . . . musical." Another paper disparaged the nasal tone as typical "of some portion of the Americans." He was a long time overcoming British distaste for American speech habits, if he ever did overcome it. Some years later, after a reading at the British Embassy in Paris, he was distressed when the only comment he overheard was: "What a beastly American accent that man has!"[16]

Still, Hanover Square crowds enjoyed his jokes, the quips about mountaintops "where it's so cold you can't speak the truth. I know, for I've been there!" and about Kanaka men who wore nothing but "a smile, or a pair of spectacles, or any little thing like that." Springing the nub of a joke as an insignificant afterthought made the British miss the point occasionally, as of "the long green swell of the Pacific." They applauded brilliant word pictures of "gem-like isles, set in their verdant beauty in the midst of a silvery fringe of spray," admired the ostensible unconcern, laughed at exaggerated awkwardness and grotesquerie—as in the story of the cannibal who wanted to see "how Europeans would go with onions." He was praised as "an actor of no mean powers," commended for "artlessness and apparent ingenuousness," for "good mimicry and anecdote, and not a little commonplace fun."

The dissenting *Daily News,* lumping Mark Twain with Nasby

and Artemus Ward, remarked that their humor, though fresh and original, was "certainly not that which any educated American would acknowledge as typical of the best wit and satire and mirth of his country's literature." According to the *News*, the most acceptable American humorist was James Russell Lowell. Hence the paper doubted whether Mark Twain's drollery was "destined to amuse the world for long; or whether anything more than ashes will be left when its fire goes out."[17] Probably a number of educated Americans shared that belief. Long bemused by the literary dominance of New England, traditionalists among Mark Twain's countrymen would not for decades recognize his earthy native genius.

London critics made the expected comparison with Artemus Ward. In a scholarly analysis the *Spectator* of October 18 said that "perfect calm and assumed earnestness of manner" were common to both, but that Ward was "much more comically child-like," and that in his humor was "much more of serious inward embarrassment and bewilderment." Mark Twain was "the easy man of the world." His humor

consists in the unconscious, matter-of-fact way in which he habitually strikes false intellectual notes, the steady simplicity with which he puts the emphasis of feeling in the wrong place, with which he classifies in the most unassuming way, as families of the same tribe of things, the most irreconcilable of common nouns, and so glides into sarcasm or caricature, while seeming to pursue . . . the even tenor of his way.

That was as perceptive a comment on Mark Twain's lecturing technique as any critic ever wrote. The *Spectator* concluded that, although "happy extravagance was no insignificant part of the fun," the excess showed "its inferiority to Artemus Ward's, whose humour was everywhere penetrated with a moral coherence which very much set off its intellectual incoherence." Perhaps that preference for Ward was not universal, yet it was a reminder that he had been a tremendous favorite. His London lecture series, beginning in late 1866, had continued over two months and in a larger hall than Mark Twain's; only fatal illness had cut short what promised to be an indefinite run. Remembering this greatly-loved American, his admirers were loath to give his place in their affections to a newcomer.

Niceties of judgment did not influence the popular verdict that Mark Twain was a success. He was so much affected by six days of hearty receptions that when he was recalled to the stage at the close of the final performance, his customary aplomb was shaken by emotion. "I only wish to say that I am very grateful," he said. ". . . it is something magnificent for a stranger to come to the metropolis of the world and be received as handsomely as I have been. I simply thank you."[18]

On October 20 and 25 he spoke at Liverpool, where he excited such a fever of curiosity that traffic jammed avenues leading to the hall of the Institute. The Liverpool *Journal* remarked upon his "air of improvisation," lack of elocution, "strong American accent," and

low, rather droning monotone. He never, even in burlesque, raises his voice or gives himself any trouble to do more than talk, and does nothing for effect except to pause and deliver the real point of his jokes after the audience has stopped laughing at them.

A surprise was "the sudden introduction . . . without any notice or change of manner of two of the most eloquent pieces of descriptive composition that ever fell from the lips of man."[19] Since nothing was said about flippant remarks after the eloquence, he had evidently discarded that cheap device for getting laughs.

In a brief tour of duty he won two cities of Britain. He might have continued to conquer had he not been obliged to escort his family back to the United States, Livy having become home-sick and fatigued by the relentless social pressure. London *Figaro* of November 16, in its "Town Crier" column, probably written by the acidulous Ambrose Bierce, regretted the departure of "one of the Great American Humourists." But Mr. Hotten, said this ironic columnist, would no doubt import

at least six other G. A. H.'s to take his place. The importation of American humourists . . . has, for some time past, averaged exactly three humourists and a quarter per week; and I really think that, in our present state of civilization, we cannot, honestly, do with more.

Bierce was not an admirer of humorists, yet he was probably envious, or at least respectful, of the popularity of Mark Twain. The two men met once in London, but no friendship ever developed.

Mark Twain had no intention of allowing any number of importations to displace himself. Having shepherded his family back to Hartford, he immediately re-embarked for England, and by the latter part of November he was again in London. Notwithstanding his affection for Livy, his loneliness when they were apart, home ties were not unbreakable bonds to this unquiet man. He was too fond of movement to be a sedentary citizen. As he had written to the New York *Graphic* in April: "I love stir & excitement." With the coming of spring, he had said, "I grow restless, I get the fidgets; I want to pack off somewhere where there's something going on."[20] The only error in that statement is the inference that the fidgets were uniquely vernal. He had them the year around. He was like Huck Finn who shocked Miss Watson when he said he wished he was in the bad place: "All I wanted was to go somewheres; all I wanted was a change, I warn't particular."

In London he was soon back on the platform, beginning on December 1 with the Sandwich Islands, again at the Hanover Square Rooms. Once more the shining carriages, some with liveried footmen, rolled up to the entrance, once more the smartly-dressed audiences swept in. He might have carried on for some time, but after a week he grew tired of this lecture. Little wonder perhaps, for in its various forms he had given it about a hundred times. That was a small number compared to some records— Wendell Phillips' two thousand repetitions of "The Lost Arts," for instance—but it was large for a variable man like Mark Twain. On December 8 he changed to "Roughing It on the Silver Frontier," which he gave for two weeks, five nights each and Saturday matinees.

For this London campaign he had an entourage, having hired Charles Warren Stoddard at $15 a week to serve as so-called secretary, companion, and amateur stage manager. The wages were theoretical, for Stoddard refused to accept pay for congenial duties. Different from some of his rowdy California contemporaries, he was a gentle, unworldly man, good-hearted, sensitive, somewhat effeminate, yet hearty enough to have been the "Prince Charlie" of boisterous San Francisco adventures in the sixties. Mark Twain once called him "such a nice girl," but he was taken with Stoddard's charm, his generosity and honesty, and found him so affable a companion—"when he was awake"—that these two men of opposite temperaments got on well together.

They moved into a large corner suite of the Langham Hotel, overlooking spires and hundreds of smoking chimney-pots, and fell into a pleasant routine. The day began with breakfast of chops and coffee, occasionally with friends, at twelve-thirty. Then they read the papers and the mail, which usually came up with the first round of toasted muffins. After that they took a walk through a park or Hollywell Street or into Portland Place to see the Horse Guards. Returning to the Langham they mixed afternoon talk with music, Mark Twain singing jubilee songs or "Ben Bowline" to his own piano accompaniment. Sometime during the day Stoddard brought the scrapbook up to date, scanning a dozen papers for notices that he carefully clipped and pasted in with such loving care that his neat work is a striking contrast to slap-dash scrapbooks kept by Mark Twain.

After dinner they donned evening dress, and at 7:30 arrived

at the anteroom in Hanover Square. For the next half hour Stoddard stood at the window counting carriages, while Mark Twain strode about the room with such restless impatience that Dolby sometimes had to calm him down. At eight precisely Stoddard escorted the speaker to the foot of the steps leading to the stage, then retired to the royal box. Mark Twain's first action was to walk to the footlights, look over the house, and rub his hands like Lady Macbeth. Stoddard noted the extreme deliberation of speech and the varying effect of jokes: a pleasantry that brought down the house one night caused only a mild ripple another. Laughter was sometimes hearty and spontaneous, sometimes sporadic, sometimes an isolated outburst that gradually spread over the whole audience. Once fog, laden with soot, seeped in to becloud the auditorium in such hazy gloom that Mark Twain, a shadowy figure haloed by misty light, reassured his listeners: "Perhaps you can't see me, but I'm here."[21]

He described the silver frontier as a land of no dew, no thunder and lightning, no twilight; as a country inhabited by editors and thieves, blacklegs, lawyers, miners and gamblers. He brought in Lake Tahoe, Sierra Nevada scenery, sagebrush and jackrabbits, the Washoe zephyr. He told anecdotes of Nevada journalism, drawing an exaggerated picture of himself as a reporter with a pencil in one hand, a revolver in the other. He talked about Indians, hunters who could hunt for a year without finding game, and the desperado, Jack Harris, who, under the benign influence of a clergyman, gave up bowie knife and pistol in favor of a double-barrelled shotgun. Concluding with the story of the farcical duel, he anxiously expressed the hope that nothing he had said might lead to the depopulation of England by a wave of emigration to this western country. The London *Times* called that the height of the Artemus Ward kind of irony because Nevada

Save for its abundant silver . . . seems to be, whether considered from a moral or a material point of view, the most objectionable place on the face of the earth.[22]

In Britain, as in America, some people expected more than they got. One listener said that "We had not time to get accustomed to his peculiar way, and there was nothing to take us by storm." The audience was "very well interested and gently simmering with amusement," though laughter was not uproarious or long-continued. As for himself, he said that he "got no information out of the lecture, and hardly a joke that would wear, or a story that would bear repeating. . . . in the art of saying nothing in an hour, he surpasses our most accomplished parliamentary speakers."[23] Possibly that was intended as a compliment.

After every performance a crowd surged into the green room for an informal reception. Then Mark Twain, Stoddard, and Dolby returned to the Langham, to easy chairs before a fire, drinks, and an animated swapping of yarns that went on for several hours. Dolby was a ruddy, hearty man, as elemental as Nasby, an interminable talker with an endless stock of anecdote and reminiscence. He was a spirited match for Mark Twain, though somewhat of a trial to the sensitive Stoddard, who was always distressed by the bawdy stories the burly manager made a point of telling him. "It was a choice and satisfactory menagerie," Mark Twain recalled many years later, "this pensive poet and this gladsome gorilla."[24] After Dolby had departed about midnight or after, Mark Twain kept on talking, walking the floor as he did so, while Stoddard calmly went to sleep on the sofa.

The daily and nightly doings should have been agreeable. But midway of this short "season" Mark Twain told Livy that he was very tired of lecturing. Saying that he enjoyed himself while he was on the platform, he admitted his pleasure in the gleaming shirt-fronts and jewels, and in the delicious hubbub of fashionable people arriving in polished carriages. But leading up to those satisfactory moments were long daylight hours he found boring.[25] The confession epitomizes his whole speaking career: an hour upon the stage was worth many aimless hours preliminary to it.

Ensconced at the Langham with friends, or rambling around

London, he may not have been so bored as he said. Apparently he found the city stimulating, for it inspired him to make a publicity gesture like those western inventions of 1866. Following the lead of Artemus Ward's letters to *Punch*, Mark Twain published in the *Morning Post* of December 10 an apology for his failure to provide "the attendance of some great member of the Government to give distinction to my entertainment." A waxworks owner had agreed to supply "a couple of Kings and some nobility, and he said they would sit out my lecture, and not only sit it out, but that they wouldn't even leave the place when it was done." Hence he had been prepared to advertise that on one evening "his Majesty King Henry VIII. would honour my entertainment," that on another "his Majesty William the Conqueror would be present," and that on the next night "Moses and Aaron would be there." Unfortunately a porter, falling downstairs with Henry VIII, smashed him; something "let go" in William the Conqueror, and he lost all his sawdust. In lieu of this damaged royalty he had considered several dukes, but "they were so seedy and decayed that nobody would have believed in their rank; and so I gave up, with almost a broken heart." As for Moses and Aaron, the wax-works man had been fraudulently exhibiting "what any educated person could see at a glance . . . were only the Siamese twins." I wish, he concluded wistfully, "I could get a king somewhere, just for only a little while, and I would take good care of him, and send him home and pay the cab myself."

That nonsense was audacious. He must have been in fine fettle to joke the British in such an airy fashion. He had taken no such liberties with the traditions of Boston (though a few years later he would do so at the much-discussed Whittier birthday dinner). Possibly he sensed that in London he was more of a hero than he was at home, and that indulgent Englishmen would accept any japery of this eccentric American. Yet if the seedy dukes and saw-dust king forecast the scorn that would find expression in *A Connecticut Yankee*, perhaps he nursed a real hope that his plea might attract some member of the royal family. He could poke fun at titles, but, like all good Americans, he relished association with crowns and coronets. But royalty remained aloof from Hanover Square, and Stoddard, unchallenged, continued to occupy the royal box.

On December 22 Mark Twain had intended to begin a tour of Great Britain: two or three performances each in Glasgow, Edinburgh, Belfast, Dublin, Cork, Manchester, and Liverpool. This plan fell through when he was unable to engage halls large enough to suit him, all the best ones having been taken for holiday entertainments. He did appear in Leicester on January 8, 1874, and the following two nights in Liverpool, giving "Roughing It" on the 9th and "Our Fellow Savages" on the 10th.

The short British lecture campaign was his most successful, so exciting that at the end of it his usual complaints of weariness and drudgery were overborne by regret that it was ended. Stoddard says that on their last night in Liverpool Mark Twain was in a mood of gloomy foreboding, his voice a melancholy minor as he solemnly said: "Remember now thy Creator in the days of thy youth." Ringing for a Bible, he read the Book of Ruth, then verses from Isaiah, "in a style," says Stoddard, "that would have melted the hardest heart; and his last words were, that if ever he got down in the world—which Heaven forbid—he would probably have to teach elocution; but this was at five o'clock in the morning."[26]

On January 13, he sailed for home. To Redpath and others he made one point crystal clear: that after a few appearances in New York and Boston in February, he was permanently retiring from the platform.

11

Under Shelter at Home

A STEADY succession of seductive invitations tested the strength of his resolve never to speak again. By late March, 1874, he was booked for three charity lectures in New York. Apparently he did not give them, but his willingness to speak indicates a wavering resolution. In early 1875 he spoke in Hartford for the benefit of Father Hawley's "clients," this performance, he said, being "the last and final time." But some months later, yielding to Redpath's plaintive appeal, he agreed to deliver "Roughing It" in Boston; while he was about it, he thought he might as well repeat several times in New York. Then, as if suddenly remembering his retirement resolution, he withdrew his consent. Yet during the following winter he considered going all the way out to Hannibal to speak there, but the plan miscarried.

Sometime during the winter of 1875-76 he gave a fifteen-minute reading at a concert in Philadelphia. That performance marked a change in his platform technique. From this time forth he relied entirely upon anecdotes, most of them from his own books, some having been used in his several lectures. The stories of the Mexican plug (which he worked into a curtain speech at the 100th performance of *The Gilded Age* in 1874); of Dick Baker, the miner, and his sagacious cat, Tom Quartz, who got "blowed up" and never thereafter approved of quartz mining; of grandfather's old ram, as told by a maundering narrator who floundered around in so many irrelevant details that he always fell asleep before he got to the remarkable ram; of the misguided blue jay that tried to fill an empty cabin with acorns and thereby became the laughingstock of a swarm of guffawing jays; of the incorporated company of mean men, the Nevada duel, the champion liar, the golden arm, the jumping frog: these and other familiars made a continually enlarging collection. Eventually he had a repertoire of fifty stories or more he could draw upon at short notice. Learning to speak them as if extemporaneously by much working over in notebook drafts, he rehearsed aloud to wring the best effect from repetitions of words and nicely-timed pauses. As he observes in "How to Tell a Story," the humorous narrative allowed him to "string incongruities and absurdities together in a wandering and sometimes purposeless way, and seem innocently unaware that they are absurdities," to slur the point, and to drop "a studied remark apparently without knowing it, as if one were thinking aloud." He was so taken with the story-telling method that he recommended it to Josh Billings. Advising against lecturing on "Nitro-Glycerine, with Experiments" because "The cost of keeping a coroner under salary would eat up all the profits," Mark Twain suggested: "Try 'Readings.' They are all the rage now. Yet how can you read acceptably when you cannot even spell correctly?"[1]

For the Philadelphia reading he received $300, which he regarded as so picayunish that he berated the manager as a skinflint, and remarked of the concert that he could get up a better one "with a barrel of cats." Concerts were not his dish. Yet he got involved with another musical affair when Redpath billed him as part of a "Grand Double Entertainment" in the Boston Music Hall on November 21, 1876, the other part being a soprano and the Mendelssohn Quintette Club. How Mark Twain fared he did not say.

In 1877 he tried hard to arrange a joint tour of about twenty-five large cities with the famous cartoonist, Thomas Nast. Dislike of lecturing vanished as he figured paper profits of $60,000 to $75,000 from seventy-five to one hundred performances—an estimate that within three months went up to $100,000. Abhorrence of touring went out the window as he excitedly faced the prospect of four months of "fun" on the road, "meandering around," he said, "(to big towns—don't want to go to the little ones)," Nast to draw pictures, he (Mark Twain) to talk about the drawings "and blackguard the audience."[2] But Nast, nursing his own distaste for public appearances, and perhaps irked by Mark Twain's having rejected a similar proposal in 1867, resisted the lure of this scheme, and it came to nothing.

Thus Mark Twain was his normal self, a compound of inconsistencies. Still, for ten years after his return from England he came closer than heretofore to his retirement resolution, for he lectured only occasionally. As he looked back over thirty years later, he remembered this period as a time of great calm and placid domesticity. Drawing a characteristically inaccurate picture, he recalled himself as a man who "after a weary life of wandering . . . remained under shelter of home for fourteen or fifteen years."[3] The impression is of a contented householder too happy under his own rooftree to bother with the bustling world outside. He must have forgotten a number of variations upon this imaginary theme of idyllic vegetation.

For one thing, the new house was unfinished when the family moved in, and for some time it was upset by the clatter and clutter of construction. In one harried letter to his mother Mark Twain spoke of being "bullyragged all day" by builder, foreman, and architect,

by the tapestry devil who is to upholster the furniture, by the idiot who is putting down the carpets, by the scoundrel who is setting up the billiard-table (and has left the balls in New York), by the wild-cat who is sodding the ground and finishing the driveway . . . by a book *agent,* whose body is in the back yard and the coroner notified. Just think of this thing going on the whole day long, and I a man who loathes details with all my heart![4]

Some years later, several months of remodeling again distracted him by turning the place upside down with the tramping and banging and littering of plumbers, carpenters, and decorators.

These years were also nervous with expectations of great profits from sundry inventions and businesses he bought into. He was the ever-hopeful Comstock prospector over again as he conjured illusory thousands out of Kaolatype, a patent steam generator, the self-pasting scrapbook, a steam pulley, the history game, the publishing company, and, most mistakenly of all, the Paige typesetter. Besides being a business man, he was a productive author who fancied himself a playwright, an after-dinner speaker, a working member of the Saturday Morning Club, a letter-writer carrying on a voluminous correspondence, and host to a continual parade of guests who turned the Hartford house into a hotel.

There were excursions beyond the shelter: six weeks in Bermuda with Twichell in 1877; seventeen months in Europe, chiefly Germany, in 1878-79, and another jaunt with Twichell; the journey down and up the Mississippi River in 1882; business trips, play directing, copyright affairs, after-dinner speaking, and social visits that took him to Boston, New York, Washington, Baltimore, Chicago, Montreal, and other cities. He had so many things on his hands that he told his mother in 1878: "I have a badgered, harassed feeling, a good part of my time."[5] That comment is more genuine than the reminiscent serenity alien to the turbulent spirit of Mark Twain. Rarely peaceful and seldom content, he did not and could not stay home so faithfully as he thought. Yet his reminiscence has in it some truth to spirit if not to fact, for he was in Hartford or at Quarry Farm much of the time, and there were no speaking tours until he set out with George W. Cable in 1884. He might have lectured profitably, for the times were favorable to the star performer, who could name his own price. In the seventies the lyceum course became a mixed show, that included concerts and opera, dramatic readers, and other novelties. The first chautauqua, in 1874, engaged its actors, musicians, and speakers through lyceum bureaus, which thus bridged the gap between the old and the new. Mark Twain's readings would admirably have fitted into the new system.

The Redpath Bureau was still prominent, but it had competition. James B. Pond got his start by taking a desk in the Redpath office. One of his first successful ventures was to manage the New England tour of Ann Eliza Young, nineteenth wife of Brigham Young. Known as "the rebel of the harem," she revealed the horrors of Mormonism so vividly in "My Life in Bondage" that she made $20,000 her first season. In 1875 Pond and George H. Hathaway bought out Redpath. Four years later they dissolved partnership, Hathaway retaining the bureau in Boston, Pond setting up an agency of his own in New York, and eventually managing all the famous speakers in the country.

Well-known talkers commanded such high prices that they were out of reach of the village. The difficulty was to find enough good ones, for some of the stalwarts were unavailable. Emerson had given up lecturing, Frederick Douglass was out of the country, Mark Twain said no. Anna Dickinson's scolding had become so tiresome that her audiences dwindled. In 1876 she quit the platform for the stage, appearing in her own play, "A Crown of Thorns." An untrained actress, she attempted to make the moral fervor of her lecturing serve in place of acting skill. New York critics did not accept the substitute. They condemned both her play and her acting so severely that at one performance, before a house one-third full, she stalked to the footlights to deliver an hour-long tirade against critics. Mark Twain, who admired the lady, planned a theater party with the Howells and Aldrich families for her Boston debut. There is no commenet about this performance, but later he made the general remark that "Talent is useless without training, thank God—as Anna Dickinson may yet discover before she gets done trying to skip to the top-round of tragedy at a bound."[6] Attempting Shakespearian roles and others beyond her ability, she did not rise above mediocrity. After a few years as an indifferent actress, she tried lecturing again, but her heyday was over.

Olive Logan's fortunes were on the wane. Newspapers still occasionally praised her "brilliant wit," "lofty and poetic fevor," and "perfect mastery of that shapely hand and well-moulded arm," but some critics were emerging from befuddlement induced by glamor. One reporter disparaged "a forced, stilted, Grecian bend-i-bus and agonizing style," and some impolite fellow, commenting on her second marriage, said: "Wirt Sikes is the victim, but, fortunately for him, he is hard of hearing."[7]

Beecher's prestige suffered when the Tilton scandal burst into the open in 1872, and continued to be wrangled over by press and public for several years. The trial for adultery brought on by Theodore Tilton in 1875 was an opera bouffe. Loyal Plymouth parishioners spread the odor of sanctity by filling the courtroom with flowers. " 'Floral Tributes,' " snorted the New York *Nation*, "seemed, in such a place, on such an occasion, like wreaths round the man-hole of a sewer."[8] The two principals behaved as if playing a parlor charade, the scurry of lawyers and witnesses was like a grotesque ballet. Redpath frantically attempted to salvage his high-priced lecturer by sending him telegrams composed in Latin to prevent telegraph operators from learning what was afoot. Sob sisters, or their Victorian equivalents, turned in columns of copy that was spread over front pages everywhere. Away out in Nevada County, California, the Grass Valley *Union* remarked that the testimony

makes nice Sunday reading for pious families . . . who are too good for this world, and who wouldn't study physiology . . . for fear that they might find out that it is normal for mankind to have legs, and that there is a procreative principle in this world.[9]

More absorbing than wars and rumors of wars, the discovery of gold in the Black Hills, treaties and politics was the story, as one

headline writer put it, of "Licentiousness in Sacerdotal Robes."
A New York merchant advertised the "Tilton Favorite" collar
and "Elizabeth Ruffles"; an Ann Street restaurant offered "Tilton
Stews" and "Beecher Pot-Pies"; a truss manufacturer sharpened
his advertising with Beecher's picture and letter of endorsement.

A hung jury left the legal truth in doubt, but Mark Twain's
verdict was guilty. To Howells in 1878, apropos of Elizabeth Tilton's confession and Beecher's denial, he said: "let the worn stub
of the Plymouth white-wash brush be brought out once more, and
let the faithful spit on their hands and get to work again regardless of me."[10] Beecher survived damaging courtroom publicity
and overrode scandalous imputations. To get back $118,000 the
trial had cost him, he took to the platform, under the management
of Pond, at $500 to $1000 a night. For awhile he had a rough
time with the hostility of jeering crowds in railroad stations, and
feeling the sting of being avoided like a plague spot. But people
attended his lectures, and he won them over. Complementing his
speaking skill was the enticing aura of brimstone and sin, which
made him a satisfactory attraction until his death in 1887.

Victoria Woodhull enhanced her notoriety by publishing in
Woodhull and Claflin's Weekly in November, 1872, a spicy account of Beecher's relations with Elizabeth Tilton. Whereupon
young Anthony Comstock, flexing his moral muscles as the self-
appointed guardian of public rectitude, had her jailed on a charge
of obscenity. "Free Love Filthily Feculent," screamed one headline: "Concubinage of Priest and Layman. . . . Free Love, Spiritual Incest and Debauchery." George Francis Train leaped to the
defense. To show the difficulty of interpreting the obscene, he
published in his own paper, *The Train Ligne,* full-flavored quotations from the Bible. He, too, was arrested for obscenity. Miss
Woodhull was acquitted, and Train never stood trial, the judge
dismissing him as a lunatic. Both kept on lecturing, their misad-
ventures, like Beecher's, being an added attraction.

Wendell Phillips steadily pursued his usual course of denunciation. In the seventies his subject was labor reform, and

the chief target of his wrath was the oppressive wage systems of soulless corporations. Conservative editors continually reproved him, yet they listened with a sort of wry respect for this perennial iconoclast; the New York *Times* faithfully printed his lectures in full. Robert Ingersoll, "the great agnostic," pleased skeptics and horrified believers by calling the God of the Bible a demon and condemning the Scriptures in toto. Crowds fought to hear him in large cities, but he was much too scarifying for hidebound small towns.

The old lecture course of enlightenment and uplift was never like this confusing babble. Mark Twain, looking back upon the late seventies and early eighties, remembered them as a time of "happy and holy silence." Not quite. The unholy din of many voices was not a silence, and it was more vexatious than happy. Perhaps he was thinking of his own comparative silence. Yet if not a traveling lecturer, he was in demand for after-dinner speeches and supposedly impromptu talks. Studying the technique of the dinner speech, he jotted down various ideas in his notebook. One was to bring up ridiculous accusations against people present, then refute them by dwelling upon the malice of the accusers.[11] Another, as a response to a toast to literature, was to ramble aimlessly on all sorts of topics except literature, bringing in incongruous quotations from the great poets, yet never saying anything about the subject.[12]

He was engaging in remarks that seemed extempore, though they had been studied beforehand. As a prominent person who could count on being asked to say a few words, he was generally ready with an "impromptu." Opening the Spelling Match of the Hartford Asylum Hill Congregational Church in 1877, he said that he saw no sense in "a uniform and arbitrary way of spelling words," and cited the refreshing letters of a correspondent who had "such a breezy unfettered originality about his orthography. He always spells Kow with a large K. Now that is just as good as

to spell it with a small one." He mentioned a lady who, out of
114,000 words in an unabridged dictionary, could spell only 180
correctly.

She steers clear of all the rest. . . . when she finds herself obliged to
write upon a subject which necessitates the use of some other words,
she—well, she don't write on that subject.[13]

Possibly he was thinking of Livy, whose uncertain spelling always
amused him. He did not win the spelling match, but he stayed
in over an hour, then went down on "chaldron," which he spelled
"cauldron."

At a dinner in Hartford in October, 1877, for the Boston Ancient and Honorable Artillery Company, he told the story of
his Civil War experience. It was a preliminary version of "The
Private History of a Campaign that Failed," first published in the
Century in December, 1885. "I have been through a stirring campaign," he said, "and there is not even a mention of it in any
history of the United States or of the Southern Confederacy. To
such lengths can the envy and malignity of the historian go."
Colonel Ralls, he went on,

made us swear to uphold the flag and Constitution of the United
States, and to destroy every other military organization, that we caught
doing the same thing. . . . Well, you see this mixed us. We couldn't
really tell which side we were on.

The narrative of the recalcitrant Orderly Sergeant, "19 years old,
6 feet high, 3 feet wide, and some distance through, and just out
of the infant school," the agile retreats, insubordinate backchat,
and casual disbanding, brought for the first time "the deeds of
these warriors . . . officially to the notice of humanity." He proposed a toast to

those . . . neglected and forgotten heroes, my footsore and travel-
stained paladins, who were first in war, first in peace, and were not
idle during the interval that lay between.[14]

At times he reverted to the Rabelaisian humor Mother Fair-banks naively supposed she had suppressed. De Voto and Wecter note his speech to the Stomach Club of Paris, "Some Thoughts on the Science of Onanism." It is well that Livy and Mrs. Fairbanks did not hear of that one. It is well, also, that neither they nor others ever completely inhibited his earthiness. However sniggeringly it may have been expressed at times, it was a gusty spirit. If his humor were occasionally of a behind-the-barn variety, he was probably incapable of a more open display. To Howells he complained that artificial refinement robbed literature of ribaldry, one of its choicest attributes, and in the concluding chapter of *A Tramp Abroad* he objects to the penalty of "nice and guarded forms of speech" imposed on writers. Yet in the same chapter, though he scoffs at fig-leaved statues, he is outraged by Titian's Venus, "the foulest, the vilest, the obscenest picture the world possesses." He commended the frankness of Fielding, but he was also a Victorian alert to public opinion that was quick to scent indecency. Intellectually he was a rebel, but practically he was a conformist unwilling, or afraid, to offend. Besides, it was more exhilarating to be bawdy and sinful in a furtive off-the-record way. As a censor of his own books he was as vigilant as Livy.

The scatological and macabre were funny to him, as they have been to other humorists and to people who enjoy backhouse jokes. To the Stanley Club of Paris he told a yarn, ostensibly about Roger McPherson, that later appeared in print as "The Invalid's Story." He and the audience found it laughable, but neither speech nor story seems amusing or even interesting. The corpse in the baggage car, the limburger cheese suggesting odorous decomposition, and the ghoulish remarks of the baggage master are more repellent than funny. It is a good example of Mark Twain's notion that death and decay are humorous. Still, that belief is in the same category as the fondness for bad smells of Smollet and Swift, who were both humorists of a sort, Rabelais' delight in physiological details, and perhaps even Shakespeare's occasional concern with superlative stinks.

Mark Twain was in good form for the Anglo-American Club of Students at Heidelberg, mixing English and German in a Fourth of July speech in 1879. He tossed in "meinem Freunde— no, meinen Freunden—meines Freundes—well, take your choice, they're all the same price," an "ich habe gehabt worden gewesen sein," an "Also!" now and then, and produced a stupendous omnibus word: "Freundschaftsbezeigungenstadtverordnetenversammlungenfamilieneigenthümlichkeiten." A corollary of this occasion was his meeting with Frank Harris, who delivered the invitation to speak. In the course of this meeting Mark Twain somehow got off on a violent criticism of Bret Harte, scoring him heavily as plagiarist and dead beat. Harris, having come prepared to be worshipful, was so disgusted by this outburst that he said: "I never want to see that man again; never again do I want to talk to him." Years later, the unpleasant memory still strong, he said that Mark Twain was "a friend of millionaires, and went about at the end like a glorified Hall Caine," called his humor "forced and unnatural," and dismissed *Joan of Arc* as "a dreadful book."[15]

Of all his after-dinner speeches the one that most disturbed him —and Howells—was the story he told at Whittier's seventieth birthday dinner on December 17, 1877, about Longfellow, Emerson, and Holmes as tipsy, euchre-playing miners in Nevada. It was the product of an irreverence fond of attacking all idols, and perhaps assisted by John Phoenix and Artemus Ward. Ward's "Among the Spirits" had John Bunyan, "old Bun," grinding the organ, taking tickets, and singing comic songs at a circus, other performers being Shakespeare and Ben Jonson. In "Fourth of July Oration" Ward said that trying to imagine George Washington and Patrick Henry as secessionists was as difficult as to think of "John Bunyan and Dr. Watts in spangled tites, doin the trapeze in a one-horse circus." As a close student of Ward, Mark

Twain may have found his inspiration there, yet his own imagination probably needed little more than a suggestion.

Over the Whittier dinner performance his soul-searching, self-laceration, and shifts of opinion as he read the speech from time to time went on almost to the end of his life. Suffice to say here that, as Henry Nash Smith demonstrates, the sense of insult to the proprieties and the sacred Brahmins was largely in the minds of Howells and Mark Twain, the tempest of protest having been stirred up not by Boston papers but by indignant editors in other New England towns.[16] On December 21 the New York *Times* dryly remarked that the fuss being raised in those parts was "Funnier than Mark Twain's speech at the Whittier dinner." That observation implies that New York, at any rate, was not insulted by ridicule of the supposedly sacrosanct.

At the opposite end of the scale was the great reunion of the Army of the Tennessee in Chicago in November, 1879. Eighty thousand men in line, two hundred bands, gold-braided commanders everywhere. General Grant was there, advertised by one flamboyant poster as

The . . . undisputed Military Genius of the whole world, the man . . . created by Providence to . . . crush to the earth those uncompromising TRAFFICKERS in human flesh, in their . . . unholy and unpardonable crime of attempting to destroy the most indulgent Government the sun ever shone upon.

Even former Confederates wired congratulations, except unreconstructed Robert Toombs. "Death to the Union," said he.[17] But that was only a minor irritant in a boisterous celebration. Never before had Chicago withstood such an hysteria of noisy patriotism and fervid oratory.

Mark Twain was in his element, sitting on the reviewing stand with a dozen generals, sitting with more generals on the stage of Haverly's Theater, and attending the huge banquet at the Palmer House. It was an elaborate affair, the room festooned with flags and flowers, General Grant's table decorated with a miniature man-of-war to symbolize the ship of state under full sail, programs printed on cream-colored silk fringed all around, a band playing patriotic airs. The dinner, followed by speeches, took almost all night. A hearty menu worked from blue points through turtle soup, fish, sweetbreads, potatoes and roast beef, venison, prairie chicken, fillet of wild turkey and duck to ice cream, ices, cakes and cheese, all washed down with four kinds of wines besides Roman Punch. At 10:45 the speaking began: toasts to "Our Country—Her Place Among the Nations," "The Army of the Tennessee," "The Army of the Cumberland," and so on. Emory Storrs, General Logan, and General Vilas spoke stirring words. Robert Ingersoll, standing on a table, loosed rhythmic oratory on "The Volunteer Soldiers of the Union." "Let us drink to those who died," he said,

where lipless famine mocked at want—to all the maimed whose scars give modesty a tongue—to all who dared, and gave to chance the care and keeping of their lives—to all the living and to all the dead.[18]

About three A. M. Mark Twain, placed last on the list to hold the crowd, responded to toast number fifteen: "The Babies—as they comfort us in our sorrows, let us not forget them in our festivities." Apparently the full assembly of six hundred diners was still there at that late hour, still drinking toasts and roaring for more. If some, perchance, did not roar because they were under the table, they were only expendable casualties of the Army of the Tennessee. Those fit for duty were an eloquent tribute to the banqueting stamina of our predecessors, and to the alcoholic capacity of the military man.

"The Babies" won the audience almost at once. Pausing at the end of every sentence to let the laughter subside, he carried on through a gale of hilarity, and concluded in a tumultuous explosion of merriment and applause. The speech even fetched General Grant, who had listened to toast after toast unmoved and stony-faced. "I broke him up, utterly!" said Mark Twain.[19] That feat must have been as satisfying as bringing down the house in the Boston Music Hall.

Finally reaching his hotel room about five o'clock after an hour and a half of handshaking and backslapping, he wrote Livy all about "the memorable night of my life." General Sherman had paid high compliments and shaken hands twice, Ingersoll was "that splendid old soul," whose speech was "just the supremest combination of English words that was ever put together since the world began. . . . Lord, what an organ is human speech when it is played by a master!"[20] So he babbled on, keyed up for days by exciting events. No doubt they were memorable. Aware of the insipid aspects of the great reunion, he was impressed by its ranking generals and politicians, its spread-eagle sentiments, its martial hurrah. Furthermore, during parades and speeches and cheers he had been a conspicuous and favored figure. It was nuts for Tom Sawyer, more gaudy than slouching into church under a black flag.

After a week of what he called "dissipation" in Chicago, the normal, if not quiet, run of affairs at Hartford was an anti-climax. Speaking at the dinner for Oliver Wendell Holmes in December, and remembering what he considered the painful Whittier debacle two years before, he took good care this time to offend nobody. On June 6, 1881, he entertained a reunion of the Army of the Potomac at Hartford, the audience distinguished by the presence of Robert Lincoln and Generals Sherman, Burnside, Sickles, Devens, and Porter. Responding to the toast, "The Benefit of Judicious Training," he quoted Martin Farquhar Tupper on the art of war: "Let the thoughtful civilian instruct the soldier in his duties, and the victory is sure." Then he took off on pseudo military lingo:

General Grant always sent an active young redoubt to . . . get the enemy's bearings. . . . General Sheridan always said: "If the siege-train isn't ready, don't wait—go by any train that's handy—to get there is the main thing." . . . See that every hod-carrier connected with a mortar-battery is at his post. . . . terrible as an army with bummers.[21]

By the early eighties he was in demand as an after-dinner speaker, an able rival of the popular Chauncey Depew. He could have made a career of dinner speaking, as he wellnigh did in later years, when no important banquet was complete without Mark Twain.

12

Genius and Versatility

By LATE 1881 Mark Twain was ready for another return to the platform. Planning a sentimental journey on the Mississippi River the following spring, he considered giving the "Roughing It" lecture on the way: three times in New York, twice in Chicago, St. Louis, and New Orleans; once in Cleveland, Louisville, and Memphis. Redpath, he hoped, would go along to manage the short tour. When nothing came of that plan, he broached to Joel Chandler Harris the scheme of a joint reading program. After meeting Uncle Remus and George W. Cable in New Orleans, he conceived a more elaborate traveling authors' troupe: himself, Harris, Cable, Howells, and Aldrich. But the shy Harris was too diffident even to try his voice in an empty hall; Howells and Aldrich did not fall in with the idea. It was just as well that the scheme fell through, for the "menagerie," as Mark Twain called it, might have been an unwieldy collection of clashing temperaments.

Still, he did not give up the hope of taking to the road with somebody. When Cable came north in 1883 for readings in Hartford, then read with some success in Boston and New York, Mark Twain again proposed a joint tour. In the summer of 1884 Cable consented, and Pond was engaged to manage a four months' sea-

son beginning in November. The contract specified that all
traveling expenses, cost of advertising, circulars, telegrams, and
hall rents be paid out of receipts; that Cable receive $450 a week,
hotel bills and railroad fares, no pay if sick, $60 for each extra
matinee; that Pond or his brother, Ozias, accompany the readers
and receive ten percent of net profits; that Mark Twain receive
the remainder of the net. In a "Special Announcement!" Pond
broadcast the news of the cooperating authors. The manager,
he said,

believes that in presenting them jointly he is appealing to the popular
heart, which . . . responds promptly to what is original and has in it
the broad elements of human sympathy and a humor . . . irresistible
and magnetic.

Cable, as a hired performer on a modest salary, considered
himself the lesser man of the two. That he felt complimented to
be the teammate of the spectacular Mark Twain appears in a
remark to his wife: "I think it's a great thing to be able to hold
my own with so wonderful a platform figure."[1] Twenty years
later, at Mark Twain's seventieth birthday dinner, he called the
tour one of the notable experiences of his life. Probably he felt
something like an apprentice in the company of a famous lecture
veteran and writer. Yet if less well known as a speaker, Cable had
a place in the "popular heart," which responded warmly to the
romantic charm of his genial humor and Creole dialect. One reporter said he "effectually dissipated the impression, if such pre-
vails, that his work was intended as a mere makeweight to that of
Mr. Clemens."[2]

Cable's literary reputation was almost the equal of the other's
—better, some thought. As one of the first local colorists, he had
published a collection of stories, *Old Creole Days,* a novel, *The
Grandissimes,* and a novelette, *Madame Delphine.* Another novel,
Dr. Sevier, was on the way. If less prolific than his overpowering
companion, he was, to defenders of the genteel tradition, more

literary. Of dignified demeanor proper to the usual notion of a
man of letters, he did not offend with outrageous yarns, offhand
manners, picturesque profanity, and vile cigars. One observer
analyzed the difference thus: Cable, "the dapper sort . . . polite
as a dancing master . . . precise, alert, brisk . . . his voice full of
quavers and graceful turns of enunciation"; Mark Twain, "the
man from way back, who has sat down by the stove at the corner
grocery . . . and is telling a story as only he can tell it."[3] Another
spoke of

a roughness in Twain's humor . . . perceptible in the contrast with
Cable's more refined thought . . . yet . . . each excels on his own
ground.[4]

The New York *Herald* reflected a segment of public opinion by
remarking upon the "mitigating circumstance" of Mark Twain's
being

made professionally one with Mr. George W. Cable, concerning . . .
whose pathos and dramatic force higher praise can scarcely be given
than that he acts as . . . safety valve to the Twain tension upon rib
and lung.[5]

Implicit in some criticisms was the belief that Cable gave tone
to a performance that otherwise might have suffered from an
overdose of Twainian nonsense.

Mark Twain praised his partner. In *Life on the Mississippi* he
called Cable "the South's finest literary genius . . . a masterly
delineator of its interior life and its history." In Hartford, he said,

Cable has been . . . creating worshipers on all hands. He is a marvelous
talker on a deep subject. I do not see how even Spencer could un-
wind a thought more smoothly or orderly, and do it in a cleaner,
clearer, crisper English.[6]

In 1883, after Cable had been training with an expert in New
York, Mark Twain called him "just a rattling reader—the best
amateur I ever heard; & with 2 seasons of *public* practice I guess

he'll be the best professional reader alive."[7] Such approval made the partnership seem happy. The two had much in common: a large sense of justice, sympathy for the underdog, fierce contempt for frauds and shams. Cable had moral courage. Having advocated prison reform and abolition of the vicious contract labor system, he went further in a controversial essay, "The Freedman's Case in Equity," published in the *Century* in January, 1885. A bold argument in favor of full civil rights for the Negro, it brought down upon him a storm of denunciation, chiefly from the South. Mark Twain, admiring Cable's fight for justice, said that he was a better humanitarian than novelist.

The two were in accord on many points. Yet anybody associating with such an unpredictable man as Mark Twain or such a stubborn one as Cable was likely to have an uneasy time. One was a creature of moods somber and explosive, careless, worldly, an outspoken skeptic; the other was proper, rather mousy, a fanatical believer. Bedeviled by concern for the will of God, Cable strictly interpreted the Scriptures and relentlessly observed the ritual of piety. Daily he read his Bible—even reading it to Mark Twain until brusquely stopped after a few trials—and rigidly he kept the Sabbath holy by avoiding Sunday work and travel. With an evangelist's zeal he nagged Mark Twain about his religious duty and fretted over his lying slothfully abed on Sundays instead of going to church. "Would to God," said Cable, "I might prevail to take him there."[8] Mark Twain seems to have enjoyed arguing with a zealot over the state of his soul, but he did not give up his unreligious habits.

Fearful of worldly contamination, Cable had once been fired by the New Orleans *Picayune* for refusing to report theatrical performances. In 1883 he was still so disturbed by the iniquitous theater that in New York he could not bring himself to see Salvini or Joe Jefferson. After much soul-searching, he attended a performance of a minor play, but only because its leading man was a noble and sincere Christian. In these ways Cable was poles removed from his impious partner. The New Orleans *Picayune* defined the differences between the pair by saying: "Twain will . . . do the funny business for the show, while Cable keeps up the prayer-meeting end and scoops in the churches."[9]

Unassuming though he was, Cable had a strong will that was no doubt annoying, and a keen insight into the danger of being devoured by the literary lions of Nook Farm. When he heard that Mark Twain and Livy had been house-hunting for him and his wife in Hartford in the spring of 1884, he sent Pond instructions to quash that scheme because he did not care to live where he would be subjected to the exhausting emotional demands of Mark Twain. That sort of resistance must have been irksome to a man who liked to manage affairs and to have his own way with friends.

Between two individualists friction was almost a certainty. Mark Twain sensed it, for on the eve of the tour he said that he did not relish the prospect of the ensuing winter. He must also have expressed his doubts freely to Livy, for he had been gone only two weeks when she urged him not to be annoyed by Cable. He is your friend, she wrote, and an advantage to you.[10] Three days later she cautioned him to be guarded in public comments about Cable, even those made in fun.[11] That warning had little effect on her garrulous husband. Introducing Cable at Philadelphia, he said: "If it weren't for that fellow Cable this company would have some chance of paying its board bill before it leaves town."[12] Underlying that facetiousness was a genuine belief, which became more pronounced as the tour wore on, that Cable was not worth his pay, that he bored audiences, and that he was besides an insufferable Sabbatarian, a penny-pinching sponger, and a supercilious traveler toplofty with servants. These shortcomings Mark Twain confided to his notebook, and indiscreetly broadcast in letters.

Cable, to his credit, made no uncomplimentary remarks about his partner. Hence, the story of their four months together is a one-sided account heavily weighted against him. To redress the balance, it must be said that he, too, had trials in daily exposure to a fitful temperament. Raging and sulking, sunny and gloomy, erratic, difficult, the swiftly changing moods of Mark Twain tried the patience and strained goodwill. If neither man was completely tolerant of the other's idiosyncrasies, Cable, on the whole, made the more amicable adjustment. A non-smoker, he did not remonstrate against Mark Twain's continual pipes and cigars, cheerfully rode in smoking cars enveloped in blue haze, and amiably accepted his companion's nervous inability to sit still. When Mark Twain had finished his cigar, he got out of the fog to the chair car. After a half hour there, he bolted back to the smoker. So it went all day, this shuttling from car to car, Cable trotting along. Pacifically he endured outbursts of temper, and did not complain of sulphurous language. The relationship was friendly, sometimes animated by noisy camaraderie. At Cincinnati, where they registered as "J. B. Pond and two servants," an *Enquirer* reporter found them engaged in a mock battle in the hotel dining room, Cable brandishing Mark Twain's ale bottle at him, Mark Twain threatening Pond. "We fight all the time," said Cable. "I think that in four three minute rounds with soft gloves I could knock him out; he's not much on science."[13] There was no ill will in that sort of horseplay.

Yet the peculiarities of his partner's character puzzled Mark Twain. He called the tour "a curious experience." It taught him, he said, to admire Cable's

gifts of mind. . . . I like him; he is pleasant company; I rage and swear at him sometimes, but we do not quarrel; we get along mighty happily together; but in him and his person I have learned to hate all religions. He has taught me to abhor and detest the Sabbath-day and hunt up new and troublesome ways to dishonor it.[14]

For such a strangely-matched pair, "curious" was a good word.

Pond had shrewdly advised Mark Twain to travel alone, but he held out for a joint tour. "I wanted somebody," he said, to keep me in countenance on the stage, and to help me impose on the audience. But more than that, I wanted good company on the road and at the hotels. A man can start out alone and rob the public, but it's dreary work and a cold-blooded thing to do.[15]

This gregarious man was lonesome in his own company. Cable was a sociable talker, and the two whiled away voluble hours on long train rides. In adjoining hotel rooms they chatted and sang, almost every night the old Mississippi River song, "Jan and Gan." They sang in carriages, so tunefully that Pond prolonged the concert by telling the driver to take the long way around to railroad station or hotel. At talking, the manager was an articulate third. A hearty man of endless yarns, he kept his conversational "mill" continually going. "Of course," Mark Twain casually told one audience, "he is a liar, like all other managers."[16] That failing enhanced his skill as story-teller, and surely endeared him to Mark Twain, who also had considerable facility at stretching the truth. Like Dr. Johnson, he preferred a man who talked, on no matter what, to a glum citizen who had nothing to say.

Pond arranged a schedule with, or despite, the assistance of Mark Twain. As usual the latter dispatched a flurry of instructions: under no circumstances were Elmira and Hartford to be on the list (but Elmira was on); an advance publicity agent was essential; programs must be so printed, probably on cardboard, that they would not rattle, and of such a size that they could not be used as fans; nothing should be said about new pieces written for these readings, for that would be a confession that the readers' names had not in themselves enough drawing power; it was imperative that six to ten tryouts in small places precede the first appearance in a city. As adept as Redpath in dealing with Twainian crotchets, Pond produced a schedule of fifteen weeks and 104 performances in sixteen states, the District of Columbia, and Canada. Every week was solidly booked, usually with one or two matinees besides six evenings. Mark Twain disliked matinees, probably because audiences were small and mostly feminine. In his notebook he once observed that men, no matter how stupid, were more responsive than women, no matter how bright.[17] But there they were in a dozen cities. The only respites were Sundays and a ten-day Christmas holiday beginning December 19.

Mark Twain said that he was ready to go on for twenty weeks, but that Livy had objected. He had settled for fifteen on her tentative promise that he might read again the next year if he did not stay out so long this time. But he publicly announced that this trip was to be his very last forever, then made fun of his resolution. "They say," he remarked in New York,

lecturers and burglars never reform. I don't know how it is with burglars—it is so long now since I had intimate relations with those people—but it is quite true of lecturers. They . . . say they are going to leave the lecture platform, never to return. They mean it, they mean it. But there comes, in time, an overpowering temptation to come out on the platform and give truth and morality one more lift. You can't resist.[18]

He weathered the hard tour vigorously, boasting of good health. There were long slow train rides, "sockdolagers for length," he said: eight to twelve hours a day, sometimes without food, and an evening's reading at the end of the grind. Going from Grand Rapids to Toledo took eighteen hours; from Pittsburgh to Dayton, fifteen. Leaving Rockford, Illinois, on a freight train at 11 P.M., they changed to a Pullman at 12:30 but could not turn in because of another change at 2:40 A.M. Arriving at Rock Island about seven, they trudged across the Mississippi toward Davenport, carrying their bags, until picked up by a sleigh. Mark Twain sometimes felt so seedy after these tiresome journeys that only strong black coffee enabled him to get through a program. At Rockford and Milwaukee he tried the expedient of a bath just before reading time, but that only dulled his mind. The wear and tear affected both and made each aware, at times, that he was not at his best on the stage.

Still, Mark Twain believed that rigorous travel made life more cheerful. Indicative of well-being, he told Livy about a colossal dining car dinner en route to Toronto: sirloin steak with mushrooms, sweet and Irish potatoes, trout, tomato soup, a whole apple pie, two plates of ice cream, an orange, and three cups of coffee. Still hungry after that feast, he said that only the expense stopped him from ordering more. Whatever his complaints of trouping, he throve on it, though not without protest. At Quincy he was so wrathful over getting up at nine o'clock that he smashed a window shutter. When Cable refused to leave Davenport on Sunday to make a Chicago engagement on Monday, Mark Twain heatedly damned his partner's scruples, and threatened to expose him to the Chicago audience if he did not get there. Cable got there by leaving Davenport on Monday. Strict Sabbath-keeping made Mark Twain explode to Livy: "I don't believe he 'lays over' Sundays gratis: I believe he keeps an account against God."[19]

Besides the hardships of travel they suffered the oddities of audience behavior and other distractions that always annoyed Mark Twain. At Springfield, Massachusetts, the uproar of a political rally outside almost defeated the speakers within. At Baltimore the principal of a female college led forty girls across the auditorium immediately in front of the stage while he was speaking. With a bored look he stopped his reading, waited till they had rustled by, then remarked: "Time to catch a train, I expect. . . . You can't always tell the custom of the country."[20] At Buffalo the steam pipes started banging. This time he kept on talking, though on the tip of his tongue was a request to the janitor not to grit his teeth so loudly. At South Bend, Indiana, when the gaslights almost went out, he pleased everybody by gravely looking from side to side and solemnly asking, "Is—is this a habit?"[21] At Hamilton, Ohio, a man in squeaking shoes started to tiptoe out. Mark Twain called, "Take your shoes off, please; take your shoes off."[22]

Throughout the tour he was a business man trying to direct affairs at Hartford by remote control. Back to Charles Webster flowed instructions by mail and telegraph about Pond's accounts, Canadian copyright, the American Publishing Company, the patent bed clamp, the perpetual calendar, the history game, buying and selling stock, lawsuits pending and contemplated. Business, travel, and readings gave him a full program.

There were ameliorations. Surprised at the changes wrought during his long absence from the speaking circuit, he remarked upon the brilliance of cities electrically lighted. In Detroit, he said, "the night was as beautiful as the day" with "clusters of coruscating electric suns floating in the sky . . . and casting a mellow radiance upon the snow-covered spires and domes and roofs." Hotels were more comfortable than the gloomy barns of unlamented memory. "They have dry towels . . . now, instead of the pulpy-damp rag of former days, which shuddered you up like a cold poultice," also electric call bells "instead of those crooked bell handles which always tore your hand and made you break a lot of the commandments." The telephone had replaced "the petrified messenger boy." One innovation seemed excellent: "six fat green bottles in a wire frame hanging on the wall by my door. Gratis refreshment for the weary instructor in place of having to go to the bar and lie." After his "missionary work on the platform," he brought out lemons and sugar for a sociable evening. Then, examining the labels "to see what brand of sourmash it was," he was chagrined to find that the bottles contained only water "to put out another kind of fire."[23] Removing the labels, he carried all six to his prohibitionist partner.

Good hotels were useful on weekends. Since the schedule allowed them to lie over Sundays, each was a free agent one day a week. While Cable sought spiritual refreshment in Sunday School and church, Mark Twain sought repose. One interviewer was embarrassed to find him still in bed at four in the afternoon. Mark Twain, wearing an embroidered robe and puffing an old corncob pipe, was not at all abashed. He explained that on Sunday he often did not get up until Monday. The reporter found the room

in an alarming state of disorder. Articles of clothing, books, letters and various other things were scattered about it in the most promiscuous fashion. The humorist's capacious valise, which lay open upon a center table, looked as though it had been struck by a cyclone.[24]

When off-duty he reverted to the careless bachelor ways that not all the drilling of his tutors had reformed. On the stage he was meticulously correct. One observer said that he appeared "in evening dress rather more pronounced than Mr. Cable's."[25]

On November 5 they opened at New Haven, then filled the month with performances at eastern towns and cities, including Boston, New York, Philadelphia, Brooklyn, Washington, and Baltimore. They read alternately, Cable first, after being introduced by Mark Twain. He might say, "Lays sun gen'l'men, I introduce to you Mr. Caaa-ble,"[26] or in a more sprightly mood:

Allow me to introduce to you, ladies and gentlemen, one whom I regard, the world regards and you regard, as the greatest modern writer of ancient fiction, and likewise the greatest ancient writer of modern fiction the world has ever known. One who has all the talent, all virtues and vices blended together to make the perfect man—Mr. Geo. W. Cable.[27]

Sometimes Cable walked on alone, introducing himself by saying, "I'm not Mark Twain."

At one point Mark Twain was maliciously pleased to note that since the audience was still filing in at eight o'clock, only about half of it heard the first number, a good thing because Cable took a disproportionate part of the evening anyway. He told Pond that Cable's reputation drew only a small fraction of the audience, though he used over half the time on the two-hour program. Like all prima donnas, Mark Twain wanted his full share of the spotlight, and then some. At Cincinnati, Cable simply sat down until about two hundred people had clattered to their seats, then dryly observed that he had never tried to read to a parade.

He usually read from *Dr. Sevier* about Kate Riley and Ristofalo, Narcisse and the Richlings; frequently from *The Grandissimes* about Aurora and Clotilde, and Raoul Innerarity announcing his marriage, also exhibiting his "pigshoo" of "Louisihanna riffusing to hanter the Union." For encores he sang weird Creole songs of Place Congo, sometimes Confederate Army songs, like "Brave Boys are They." He disliked the singing so much that he had to force himself to do it, but critics always praised his clear tenor voice. One recitation, "A Sound of Drums," had ladies swabbing their eyes, and an even more emotional number was his prize piece, "Mary's Night Ride," from *Dr. Sevier*. A dramatic story of mother and child riding through Confederate lines to a dying husband and father, it made women weep and swoon— in the first two months four vaporous casualties had to be carried out in a dead faint—and rarely failed to win the plaudits of audience and press. For awhile Mark Twain himself thought highly of it. But when Cable capitalized on its popularity by gradually extending the reading time from six minutes to fifteen, annoyance mounted.

Mark Twain's selections varied. Usually he read from his new book, *Huckleberry Finn*, about King Sollermun and "How come a Frenchman doan' talk like a man?" For others he drew upon his growing repertoire: tragic tale of the fishwife, a trying situation, encounter with an interviewer, Buck Fanshaw's funeral, the jumping frog, Tom and Huck rescuing Jim, Tom Bowline and the governor-elect of Massachusetts. He might tell an audience that its printed programs were useless, then substitute the stories of his struggle with the German language, the trials of editing an agricultural paper, Colonel Sellers, the whistling stammerer. A standard reading was the ghost story of the golden arm, which moved an audience literally. When he quaveringly repeated the eerie question, "Who-o-o-o's got my go-o-o-olden arm?" then, after a well-timed pause, leaped into the air and shouted, "You got it!" everybody jumped, and impressionable girls yelped.

At the outset, trying to imitate Dickens by merely reading from a book, he was startled to find the results "ghastly." So he learned his pieces, and after a week he laid the book aside in favor of what he called "flexible talk, with all their obstructing preciseness and formalities gone out of them for good."[28] It was better, he said, to fail without a book than to go on with one. Like a stock company actor, he continually memorized lines, finding it uphill work when he was worn out by travel. Cable paid tribute to his partner's craftsmanship, remarking upon the careful study to achieve the right vocal effect, also upon the concern that a program be increasingly entertaining as the evening went on. Diligent study did not prevent betrayal by the faulty Twain memory, but he was not disconcerted. At Fort Wayne, Indiana, he got lost in a favorite anecdote, disarmingly admitted his forgetfulness, and brought down the house.

Pond everywhere advertised "Mark Twain's world-famous wit; Mr. Cable's exquisite humor and pathos" as "A combination of genius and versatility that appeals freshly to the intelligent public." The New York *Times* slyly observed:

The management . . . neglected to say which of the gentlemen had the genius and which the versatility. Some . . . may have felt justified in . . . the conclusion that Mr. Cable represented both these elements, while Mr. Clemens was simply man, after the fashion of the famous hunting animal one-half of which was pure Irish setter and the other half "just plain dog."[29]

The differences between the "literary Siamese twins" provoked comment: Mark Twain lounging loosely, Cable "now here, now there, now standing, now sitting"; Mark Twain thoughtfully pulling his mustache or shoving a hand into his pocket, Cable using "appropriate flowing gestures"; Cable "although the possessor of a fine sense of humor . . . serious and earnest . . . Mr. Clemens

. . . droll, in everything he says and does"; the audience "dropping abruptly . . . from such delightful people as Narcisse, Ristofalo and Kate Riley to such earthy creatures as Huckleberry Finn."

Critics made stock observations about Mark Twain: his apparent timidity, his awkwardness—"as though nature . . . had, somehow, gotten the joints mixed"—his quizzical or lugubrious expression. Most reporters were more enthusiastic about him than about Cable, but they did not neglect that half of the team. He "impressed everyone,"said the Springfield *Republican,* "as a romantic figure, a sort of knightly ideal, with his broad . . . forehead, his brilliant eyes, and his long mustache over his full brown beard."[30] He was in "admirable voice," said the Boston *Globe,* "and some of the touches reminded one of some of the best passages of Dickens."[31] "It would be difficult to say," observed the New York *World,* "which effort of either was the most appreciated by the audience."[32] "Mary's Night Ride" brought out an assortment of compliments: strong, beautiful, intense, dramatic, powerful, vivid, graphic, impressive.

Social interludes eased the hard schedule. On Thanksgiving Day they dined and stayed overnight in the home of Thomas Nast in Morristown, New Jersey. Mark Twain distinguished himself by doing away with five helpings of oysters on the half shell; then, annoyed by the loud ticking of several clocks in the night, he got up and stopped them all. In his letter of thanks he told Nast to be "piously grateful" that he could stay home with his family:

and do all your praying now, for a time is coming when you will have to go railroading and platforming, and then you will find that you cannot pray any more, because you will have only just time to swear enough.[33]

Mark Twain always had time to swear. One thing that fretted him was small audiences. Although newspapers gave the impression of large crowds, they are not confirmed by the figures in Pond's cash book.[34] At only eleven performances during the first four weeks were gross receipts $500 or better; at nineteen they were less than $450, and at the little town of Berlin, Connecticut, only $88. The average was about $440, out of which expenses took from a third to a half. Matinee attendance was slim, Providence yielding $185, Boston $168. That was hardly enough to pay hall rent, hotel bills, and Cable's salary. In small towns tickets sold at 25¢ for the gallery to 75¢ for a reserved seat in the dress circle; in cities like New York prices were 75¢ to $1. On that basis, the paying part of the house at only four places—Philadelphia ($918), Washington ($789), Brooklyn ($983), and possibly Baltimore ($754)—was over one thousand. All others were in the lesser hundreds, a number that does not seem extraordinary.

Mark Twain thought it was not. He was so distressed by small turnouts, even in Boston, that he urged Pond to put out more blatant advertising, else they might as well shut up shop. He wanted every town on the schedule placarded with large red posters; he suggested a patrol of sandwich men draped in billboards proclaiming the coming attraction.[35] Apparently Pond did not adopt that suggestion, but he did produce a poster about a foot and a half square headed "Report Along the Line," and made up of good press notices. Later he published a similar one entitled "Yes! They Are Coming Here!" Possibly they had some effect, for attendance improved slightly, but at no time was it of the great size of popular report. During the entire tour the receipts of only one performance, at Chicago, topped the thousand mark with a gross of $1216.

On December 1 they read in North Adams, Massachusetts, then went on to Troy, Ithaca, Syracuse, Utica, and two performances each in Rochester, Toronto, and Buffalo. Moving west, they appeared in Ann Arbor on the 12th, thereafter in Grand Rapids, Toledo, Detroit, and Cleveland. On December 18 they finished the year in Elmira, then departed for home and a welcome ten-day vacation. In the Middle West Cable was described as a "ministerial-looking person" with mustaches "of the St. John (not the Evangelist but the Prohibitionist) type." He received good notices for "remarkable powers as an elocutionist" and for gestures that were "the perfection of grace and dramatic intensity." Mark Twain was "A little grayer, a little more top-heavy and perhaps a little funnier than when he was on the lecture stage."[36] His hair, like "bleached brick-dust . . . had evidently been gone over with a harrow to make the stubborn crop of hirsute delirium tremens stay down for an hour."[37] Half-closed eyes suggested "an expression of doubt, as though their owner were balancing in his mind whether . . . he had better deliver the lecture or go to bed."[38]

At Albany they called upon President-elect Cleveland, who regretted that a political dinner would prevent him from hearing the readers. Mark Twain offered to trade places with him, then casually sat down upon a battery of push buttons and summoned a squad of secretaries. At Rochester he whiled away much of the night entertaining local Elks at their monthly social. At Toledo the pair dined with Nasby. Cable acutely described him as

a big man with disheveled hair, knotted forehead, heavy middle and dowdy dress. An easy talker, a coarse man of the harder world, successful and unsatisfied.[39]

Part of that was apropos of Mark Twain, who was also successful and dissatisfied.

At the midpoint Pond said that, despite hard times, the venture was a success because the old stagers of the lecture circuit were off the platform. He was so well pleased that he proposed to Mark Twain a tour in England, without Cable, beginning in April, 1885. Probably the idea was tantalizing, but a surmise is that Livy's verdict was a firm No. At any rate, nothing came of it. The joint tour was a success in terms of pleased audiences, but financially it was not spectacular. Cable's weekly $450 took a sizable portion of receipts, and Mark Twain was not an economical traveler. Like Shaw's character, Adolphus Cusins, in *Major Barbara*, he was quite content with the best of everything. His share of net profits so far amounted to about $7500, which meant that for each performance he received about $165. That was not a large fee for one who had once vowed never to "yell" again for less than five hundred.

On December 29 they were back in harness again at Pittsburgh, which was a jumping-off point for a long series of engagements in the Middle West, Ozias Pond having replaced his brother as traveling factotum. During the Christmas holidays Mark Twain must have unburdened himself freely about his partner's quirks, for soon after he left home Livy sent him another cautionary reminder. She wished, she said rather sadly, that he were less ready to do battle with somebody.[40] The remark was well taken, for in the second half of the tour he complained more sharply of Cable's penury and Sabbath-keeping. He said that "K" had saved a trunkful of laundry to be put on the expense account; that he borrowed stationery or helped himself freely at hotels rather than buy his own; that shortly before midnight at a Saturday reception, to avoid breaking the Sabbath, he wanted to walk out in the middle of somebody's story. Of this "idiotic Sunday-superstition," said Mark Twain, "I would throttle a baby that had it,"[41] and to Pond he blew off about "a Christ-besprinkled psalm-singing Presbyterian."[42]

There was "a thundering sight too much" of Cable on the program. "Mary's Night Ride" grew to be such a trial that one line from the story, "Cover the child! cover the che-ild!," became in the Clemens household a stock comment for minor crises. The vagaries of his partner made Mark Twain express strong judgments to Livy: "this paltry child"; "the pitifulest human louse I have ever known." Yet he also said: "I speak but the truth when I say I like K better & better," and "He is in many ways fine & great, & splendid." As Alice said in Wonderland, curiouser and curiouser. Still, they enjoyed their swing through the cornbelt. If Mark Twain's temper erupted, it soon subsided, and no acrimony marred offstage talk and song. To add to the entertainment, he took the trouble to recast in dialogue form episodes of the raft journey down the Neckar from *A Tramp Abroad,* so that he and Cable might read them for the amusement of themselves and Ozias Pond.

He was much pleased with Paris, Kentucky. Only a southern audience, he said, could bring out the best in a speaker. The people there

laugh themselves all to pieces. They catch a point before you can get it out—& then, if you are not a muggins, you *don't* get it out; you leave it unsaid. It is a great delight to talk to such folks.[43]

In sharp contrast to that pleasure in arousing laughter was his outburst at some point: "Oh, Cable, I am demeaning myself. I am allowing myself to be a mere buffoon. It's ghastly. I can't endure it any longer."[44] Nevertheless, he studiously worked upon the humorous effects of manner and speech, and he was chagrined if he could not make a solemn crowd laugh. Apropos of his fondness for southern audiences, he did not meet many, for he never spoke below the border states of Kentucky, Missouri, and Maryland. Possibly he felt that, as a sort of renegade southerner who was a nominal, but not hidebound, Republican, he might not be warmly welcomed in the unreconstructed deep South.

Middle western audiences were lively and somewhat larger than heretofore. Matinees improved. Cable's drawing power increased when he became the center of heated argument over his *Century* article on equity for the Negro. Damned by Democrats and by "the living representatives," as one northern paper put it, "of that old time bourbonism which has 'forgotten nothing and learned nothing,'" he was praised by freedom-lovers everywhere. As a controversial figure, he was more provocative than a mere author. If occasionally criticized for thin voice and overdone gentility, he did his part well. In Burlington, when Mark Twain was delayed by a slow train after remaining in Keokuk to visit his mother, Cable went on alone for an hour and a half. He had "to lift a stone-dead audience out of the grave," he said, "& put life and mirth in them & keep their spirits rising."[45] He was proud to report that he did it, so that when Mark Twain belatedly arrived, he faced a warmed-up crowd.

In the mid-country Mark Twain was usually considered the star of the show, but he did not escape censure. At Quincy, Illinois, a querulous critic who did not care much for either reader, not even for "Mary's Night Ride," complained that he took the sparkle off his humor by stringing out his stories far too long. It was a nice point, for he was sensitive to timing. He wanted an audience always to be emotionally coming to him for more, never receding because it was bored. Continually tinkering with his readings, he cut the Jumping Frog to thirteen minutes for Chicago —"shortest time on record," he said—and reduced from forty-five minutes to twenty-five the story of Tom and Huck aiding Jim to escape. Notwithstanding the apparent leisureliness of his drawling manner, he knew the value of compression.

Friendly press comments in this territory showed that he was among home folks. As awkward as the countrymen he liked to describe for Livy and as unpolished, or pretending to be, he seemed in tune with the lives of these people. The trip through familiar country was a nostalgic journey back to old scenes and old acquaintances, all weathered by time. Of Hannibal, he said: "you can never imagine the infinite great deeps of pathos that have rolled their tides over me. I shall never see such another day. I have carried my heart in my mouth for twenty-four hours."[46] At Quincy, meeting Pet McMurray, a farmerish-looking ancient with long bushy whiskers, he reflected sadly that thirty-five years before, this "Last Leaf" had been a plug-hatted dandy with a red goatee, "a most mincing, self-conceited gait," and

a red roll of hair, a recumbent curl . . . (between two exact partings) which extended from his forehead rearward over the curve of his skull, & you could look into it as you would into a tunnel.[47]

Hospitable Chicago gave the readers three good audiences and a good press that stimulated both. Cable said that they inspired each other. The *Tribune* of January 17 observed that the "wide diversity in the manners, methods and styles of the two men . . . brings out in stronger relief the merits of both." The *Daily Inter Ocean* praised "Mark Twain's quaint style . . . and George W. Cable's pathos, descriptive powers, and fund of wit." After one number Mark Twain provided unscheduled humor when, failing to find the exit, he wandered around the stage trying several doors before he found one that got him off, the audience roaring at his antics. The *Daily News* commended Cable's stand on the Negro question, citing him as an example of "northern progressiveness" preferable to "the mossbacks of the south." The matinee crowd on the 17th was better, and that night the turnout was the largest of the three, a good-natured gathering of about twelve hundred. Mark Twain was at his best. "We've had an immense time here," he said, "with these three big audiences in this noble Central Music Hall. . . . you should have seen that alert & radiant mass of well-dressed humanity, rising tier on tier clear to the slope of the ceiling." With engaging lack of false modesty he admitted that "I was the greatest triumph we have ever made." His revised readings

went with a long roll of artillery-laughter all down the line, interspersed with Congreve rockets & bomb shell explosions, from the first word to the last.[48]

After stopping at Evanston, they took off for Wisconsin and Minnesota. The forty-below northern temperature did not chill their spirits. At St. Paul the whole party tramped nine blocks through a snowstorm to see a so-called ghost house that had a cloudy image on a window, variously interpreted as the head of a pretty girl, or a devil, or a mysterious divine message. Mark Twain, who saw nothing but a smudge, observed that "a lot of idiot spiritualists" believed the image to be a heaven-sent confirmation of their doctrine. "If all the fools in this world should die," he said, "lordly God how lonely I should be."[49]

The pace finally told on Ozias Pond. Having suffered a heart attack at Madison, he had to give up at Milwaukee. Bedridden, and nursed by Mark Twain and Cable, he paid tribute to their thoughtful care. Of Cable, he said that he had never known "a kinder, nobler, manlier man." Mark Twain, he said, had "a heart as tender as a child's. . . . I shall never forget his quaint, kind ways, and shall always love him as one most desiring *the love of his friends*."[50] When Ozias had to be left behind, Major Pond rejoined the troupe, reluctantly because, he remarked, his small commission was sadly out of proportion to the labor of keeping this show on the road. "I have never," he said plaintively, "done so much for so little money . . . as I have the past Seven months."[51] That is an interesting comment on the hazards of doing business with Mark Twain.

February began with return engagements at Chicago, continued with stops in Indiana and Ohio, then took the readers to Detroit and across Canada to Montreal. The return engagement was not successful. On the whole tour they returned to twelve places after an interval of a few days to three months. At nearly all of them audiences were much smaller the second time. At Madison and Toronto, the second crowd was less than half the size of the first, at Detroit a third smaller. At Philadelphia and Boston in November and at Indianapolis in February, the matinee and evening crowd combined was not so large as the single one of the first appearance. The Indianapolis *Journal* explained the difference by saying: "if the evening seemed less full of zest than the previous one, it was because the novelty had somewhat worn off, and not that the performance was below standard."[52] That was probably correct. Since much of the attraction lay in the readers and their individual manner, one viewing and hearing damaged the freshness. Mark Twain needed a large area of unexploited territory. He could not count on repeaters hearing him as often as they would a favorite opera.

Chicago, a brilliant exception to the rule, gave the troupers the best house of the entire season on February 3. Both were in good form, both were repeatedly encored. At one point Mark Twain, nervously stepping on the stage too soon, ran into applause still pattering for one of Cable's songs. "I'll go back and get him," he said, and the crowd laughed. Returning without the singer, he drawled, "He's sung all he knows," and the audience roared again. It was that kind of house, friendly, laughing easily.

Small towns had no such audiences, and, as often happened in uncitified places, they were more critical. At South Bend, Indiana, the *Daily Times* of February 5 said that Cable's numbers "possessed a sameness that made them . . . monotonous." Even Mark Twain, when he began "in his drawling, devil-may-care way . . . caused an inward fear to creep through the minds of many . . . that it was their fate to be bored." Fortunately, that fear proved unfounded. One event at South Bend was a brief reunion with Charles Warren Stoddard, Professor of Literature at the University of Notre Dame. Probably they talked about those pleasant London days of almost twelve years before, but the only item Mark Twain mentioned was Stoddard's remark that professors of literature do not need to know how to spell. At Fort Wayne, the *Daily News* of February 6 also complained of Cable monotony, adding with unconscious humor that "there was not enough variety—too much domesticity to hold the interest of the audience." The Lafayette *Daily Courier* of the 7th called him "insipid," "very tiresome after the first five minutes." The readings from *Dr. Sevier* were

a very severe test of the patience of the audience. . . . Only the utmost Christian charity . . . could have prompted them to applaud the dreary barrenness of Mr. Cable's efforts. . . . he makes Twain appear like a god by contrast.

The tables were turned five days later at Oberlin, Ohio, where the *Weekly News* said on February 13 that Cable "proved himself the peer of his companion in the humorous, while he excelled in the pathetic at which Twain made no attempt." The *Oberlin Review*, the college paper, remarked that "Twain's humor was distasteful" to many, then delivered a neat back-handed slap by saying that "the younger part of the audience enjoyed the entertainment immensely."[53] A week later a letter in the *News* from a disgruntled citizen said that the audience had been humbugged.

No doubt there are but few persons who do not admire Mark Twain's writings, but as a lecturer, I think that at least four-fifths of the people who heard him in Oberlin will agree . . . that he is not a success. . . . I like to laugh, but I am provoked . . . that so many laughed when there was nothing to laugh at.[54]

Evidently he was not acclimated to the intellectual atmosphere of this college town. Perhaps its condescension nettled him, for it has been conjectured that when he wrote about a smug, self-righteous community in "The Man That Corrupted Hadleyburg," he was using Oberlin as a model.

Detroit preferred him, but in Canada the London *Advertiser* awarded honors to Cable as "the most artistic. . . . a real actor." Of Mark Twain the paper observed that too often he strained for effect, and that he gloried too much in being grotesque:

one can't help feeling that he is in the position of a man who is capable of playing high comedy, but who knows there is more money in doing a song and dance. He is entertaining, but he is not doing his best work.[55]

Whether or not he did his best work, he certainly labored at it, so hard that only after three months on the road could he say that he had learned his "trade." It was the best of its kind, yet his momentary distress over being a buffoon suggests that he recognized unsounded deeps he did not plumb because the reward of hearty laughter was too precious to forego. Over and over the record shows his delight in a roaring crowd. At Columbus, for example, he said that "before a full Opera House of the handsomest people you ever saw," he "made them shout, & tore them all to pieces till half past 10, & not an individual deserted till the thing was over."[56]

That was the sort of experience that warmed the heart of Mark Twain. He never remarked upon the pleasure of making his hearers think, of appealing to their minds. That broad comedy paid he was no doubt aware. The profit-motive was conspicuous in his character, but it was mixed with sheer delight in talking, in tearing an audience all to pieces. He was fully as pleased at Columbus as at Chicago, where profits were over twice as great. As a humorous story-teller he was the best going. Yet the *Advertiser* may have been right in saying that he was capable of something more subtle and thoughtful. But no critical attitude is so pointless as lamenting what a man is, and imaginatively reconstructing him according to what one wishes he might have been.

The trip across Canada was a carnival of entertainment. At London, invited to visit the Helmuth Female College, they were momentarily abashed by massed femininity. "Mark and I," said Cable,

are certainly a pair of hardened old tramps, but it surely taxed our power of face to enter and stand in silence before that ranged battery of seventy-odd pairs of young girls' eyes.[57]

Soon recovering their aplomb, they went tobogganing with the girls and sleigh-riding in twenty-below weather, Mark Twain hurrahing, waving his hat, and blowing kisses to the young ladies. At Montreal, the Tuque Bleu Snowshoe Club whisked the troupe out to its clubhouse and there initiated them into honorary membership. At the command, "Bounce 'um!" the young men seized Mark Twain, Cable, and Pond in turn, and tossed them into the air four or five times. Mark Twain made a speech, Cable spoke and sang, there were boisterous choruses and great good fellow-ship. "Put Montreal down," said Cable, "as one of the brightest, liveliest and most charming cities—at least in winter—that can be."[58]

They headed back to the States, reading in Saratoga on Febru-ary 20. Then followed Brooklyn, New Haven, Orange, Newark, Philadelphia, and Baltimore. On the last day of the month two performances in Washington ended the long tour. At Saratoga their exposure to Canadian winter stood them in good stead, for the Town Hall was so cold that the audience shivered through the evening wrapped in ulsters and capes. At Brooklyn, New Haven, and Orange, houses were smaller than they had been in November. Philadelphia did fairly well, and Baltimore gave them a good turnout of about one thousand.

Thus the strange adventure of the strangely-matched partners came to an end. According to Pond's cash book, total gross re-ceipts were $46,201, out of which Cable's salary and other ex-penses took more than twenty thousand. Cable received $6750, Mark Twain an uncertain amount somewhere in the neighbor-hood of $15,000. Pond's commission was a modest $2500 to $3000, for which he had expended the tremendous labor of making ar-rangements, supervising publicity, paying bills and keeping ac-counts, being companion and nursemaid, and serving as after-hours billiardist for Mark Twain, sometimes until two A.M.

Reverberations from the tour resounded for almost twenty years. Two months after it ended, the Boston *Herald,* on May 7 and 9, publicized Cable's alleged shortcomings as "Personal Pe-culiarities of a Well Known Author." When ill at Hartford, he was said to have lived on champagne for three weeks, and to have been so parsimonious that he refused to pay for a telegram that "should not have been received." He was alleged to have com-plained of "hoggishness on the part of Twain in getting a dis-proportionate share of the glory," to have ordered five-dollar breakfasts on the road, and to have charged to expenses "so highly

luxurious a thing as champagne and so lowly a one as the blacking of his boots." Pond asserted, said the *Herald*, "that the bills
rendered by Cable are greater curiosities of literature than the best
of his Creole dialect." His refusal to travel on Sunday was cited
as stubborn observance of a ritual regardless of inconvenience to
others. Throughout the *Herald's* story ran the implication of bad
feeling between the partners.

The champagne part must have been the invention of malicious
fancy. Otherwise, as Arlin Turner, Cable's most recent biographer,
points out, the data on close-fistedness, expense account and
Sabbatarianism probably reached the paper by a grapevine that
grew from the indiscreet remarks of Mark Twain and possibly of
Pond.[59] When Cable protested to the editor that the story was
"slanderous and libelous," the *Herald* published a retraction and
an apology. By telegraph Cable appealed to Mark Twain: "All
intimations that you and Pond are not my Beloved Friends are
false and if you can say the same of me do so as privately or as
publicly as you like."[60] Mark Twain did not answer this message,
nor did he make a public statement. Then Cable appealed by
letter: "If you care to know it, I esteem you more highly since
our winter's experience than I ever did before & should deeply
regret if scandal mongers were to make an estrangement between
us."[61] Mark Twain responded with a brief note that merely advised Cable not to give himself "any discomfort about the slander
of a professional newspaper liar—we can*not* escape such things.
I do assure you that this thing did not distress me. . . . Why, my
dear friend, flirt it out of your mind—straight off."[62] That was
not very reassuring from a man who was not offhand when
touched too nearly himself. In April, 1885, for instance, he was
so incensed over the banning of *Huckleberry Finn* from the Con-
cord library, and the criticisms of the book's coarseness and im-
morality that he planned a speech at Cornell attacking its critics.
Howells talked him out of it. It was too small a matter, he said,
for rancorous controversy.[63] Yet in a larger matter Mark Twain

could allow Cable's character to be traduced and their relationship to be slandered without a word of public protest.

Despite the *Herald's* retraction, rumors of friction between the two persisted, probably encouraged by the silence of Mark Twain. Not until ten years after the tour did he finally speak up. In a Seattle interview in 1895 he said:

There is no truth whatever in the story . . . going the rounds . . . that the lecture partnership in which Cable and I were at one time engaged was broken up by a quarrel between us. There is no foundation for such a story. . . . Mr. Cable and I entered into a specific agreement for four months, and it is a sufficient contradiction of the story about a quarrel to say that we did not miss a single engagement. We are of exactly opposite temperaments, and on that account perhaps became not only close friends, but the most congenial of traveling companions.[64]

It was high time for such a statement, which could have been made with better grace ten years earlier, in 1885.

As late as 1901 Elbert Hubbard's *Philistine* published a yarn about the two having become so vexed with each other that on the last three weeks of the tour they had not exchanged a word. Cable was said to have prayed that Mark Twain would "give his heart to Jesus," and to have "rastled" with him about smoking, "the folly of turning in at Three O'clock in the morning and eating breakfast at noon; the vice of profane swearing, and the heinous sin of telling tales that bring the blush of Shame to the cheek of Innocence." While Cable prayed, Mark Twain was represented as puffing away on his pipe and finally exclaiming, "Hell!" One evangelistic effort purportedly turned into a real wrestling match, which so angered both that only Pond's diplomacy held them together for the rest of the tour. Mark Twain was reported as feeling "no enmity . . . but he has ever refused to apologize, and thinks that George should apologize to him for trying to take away his religion, which consists of Every Man Minding His Own Business."[65]

That irresponsible tale was indicative of uninformed opinion in the air sixteen years after the tour, and in part still with us today. Mark Twain probably contributed to the legend. In letters to Livy, Howells, and Pond, he had aired his views of Cable's peculiarities, and of his ineffectiveness as a reader not worth his pay. Twelve years later he was still so irked that he entered in his notebook the old complaint that Cable had stolen far more than his share of platform time.[66] If he wrote such remarks, the chances are that he also spoke them, with elaborations upon Cable's idiosyncrasies, and thus aggravated gossip. Yet he could also say to Cable in 1895:

> Yes *sir!* I liked you in spite of your religion; & I always said to myself that a man that could be good and kindly with that kind of a load on him was entitled to homage—& I *paid* it. And I have always said, & still maintain, that as a railroad-comrade you were perfect— the only railroad-comrade in the world that a man of moods & frets & uncertainties of disposition could travel with, a third of a year, & never weary of his company.[67]

That was a friendly letter and a true one, just as true as the raging complaints. Mark Twain did like Cable as an agreeable companion, and no evidence shows that the serious disruptions alleged in gossipy stories had any foundation in fact.

Still, the friendship did not flourish. In 1890 Cable said wistfully that Mark Twain did not write often, and there were few letters thereafter. The aftermath of the tour, full of malice and unfavorable inferences about Mark Twain, did not damage Cable's admiration for his lecture partner. He did not air criticism of Twainian oddities, he praised his books, and at the seventieth birthday dinner he gave a warm-hearted reminiscence of their touring days. In the troubled combination of genius and versatility, Mark Twain may have had the genius, yet Cable, because he was the more versatile, was the more humane.

13
Another Retirement

THE YEARS from 1885 to 1895 were an agitated decade in the life of Mark Twain. More intensely than ever before he was businessman, public figure, and entrepreneur with many irons in the fire. Of this restless period he wrote no reminiscence about remaining quietly under shelter at home. Pursuing a mad program, he was in and out of Hartford attending to publishing company affairs, investigating new inventions that always attracted him, like the envelope-making machine, serving the voracious demands of the ever-imperfect typesetter, and occasionally giving readings and after-dinner speeches. It is a frantic story. Hither and yon, changing trains, directing several enterprises, attending dinners—generally accompanied with champagne, always with much talk and many cigars until well after midnight—entertaining the usual crush of visitors at Hartford, reading the poetry of Browning to select groups—taking hours, he said, to prepare for one reading: to survey the record of compulsive action is to be staggered by this so-called lazy man's furious energy. Truly, as he said in his seventieth birthday speech, he achieved longevity "by sticking strictly to a scheme of life which would kill anybody else."

He had little time—perhaps no great inclination—to be a

writer. By 1885 his best work was done, and what followed was of lesser moment. In 1886 he began *A Connecticut Yankee,* but there were so many interruptions that it did not see print for three years. *The Prince and the Pauper,* dramatized by Abby Sage Richardson, reached Broadway in 1890. It occupied some of his unused moments by requiring testimony in a bitter lawsuit brought by his old friend, Ned House, who alleged a prior claim. Affidavits, hearings, and injunctions made a stir in New York papers as the case dragged on, accompanied by a voluminous correspondence between lawyers and litigants.

There were few hours in which Mark Twain could be a writer. Besides, prosperity seemed more certain and more lush in other ways. The Webster Publishing Company's success with *Huckleberry Finn* and Grant's Memoirs led him to make the jubilant remark that whatever he touched turned to gold. It was fool's gold. Poor investments and bad editorial judgment, added to the unwisdom of draining publishing company funds to subsidize the Paige Compositor Manufacturing Company, with a payroll of over $800 a month, pushed him into such a financial morass that he could not extricate himself. To save money, he gave up the expensive Hartford house in 1891, and took the family to Europe —then spent some of the savings in nervously commuting back and forth across the Atlantic.

As a speaker he was, if not voluble, not silent. Now and then he underscored his dislike of the platform, his determination never to return to it, and so forth. These statements meant no more than they ever had. To one correspondent he made a new point: that he avoided lecturing because he could not think of a lecture worth delivering; furthermore, after twenty years of platforming, it was time to subside.[1] He did not really believe that, for he did not subside and never would. In April and May, 1886, he read to the cadets at West Point, having a jolly time in the company of Twichell. Refusing Pond's request that he introduce Henry M. Stanley at Hartford, he said he was so well known there that the audience would merely look at him in stony silence. Never again, he vowed, would he speak in Hartford.[2] Yet in February, 1889, he did read there, the results being about as he had feared, chiefly because a hushed church atmosphere inhibited people. The audience wanted to whoop, but it was afraid to. It was odd that, having shattered churchly reserve elsewhere, he should be unable to do so in his home town. In November, 1887, he gave for Union veterans of Baltimore a variant of his Civil War experience, this time telling of a "battle" in which he saw action. In January, 1889, he read again in Baltimore in collaboration with Thomas Nelson Page.

In late February, 1889, when he went to Boston to hear the combined readings of James Whitcomb Riley and Bill Nye, Pond waylaid him in the Parker House and persuaded him to introduce the pair. As an unexpected addition, he exhilarated the large audience of three thousand. People stood up, waved handkerchiefs, clapped and shouted, while the organist of Tremont Temple added to the din by sounding off fortissimo. Mark Twain, described by one paper as "a frowsy-headed, round-shouldered man, as gray as a rat, yet still vigorous in spite of his years,"[3] made quite an occasion of the introduction, which turned out to be his last public appearance in Boston. He remarked that he had first known the readers when Mr. Barnum had them as the Siamese twins, Chang and Eng. "Mr. Chang Riley," he said, "had a high . . . an abnormally high and fine, moral sense," but

no machinery to work it; whereas Mr. Eng Nye, who hadn't any moral sense at all and hasn't yet, was equipped with all the necessary plant for putting a noble deed through, if he could . . . get the inspiration on reasonable terms outside. . . . Laboring together, they could do miracles. . . . They must travel together, conspire together, beguile together, hoe, and plant, and plow, and reap, and sell their public together, or there's no result.[4]

The success of this innovation led Pond to propose a tour of twenty large cities in the company of Nye and Riley, Mark Twain to do nothing but introduce the "Twins of Genius," and receive two-thirds of the profits. The junket would be, said Pond, "Ostensibly a pleasure trip for you. . . . it will be the biggest thing that can be brought before the American public."[5] Probably it would have been a big thing, and no doubt Mark Twain was tempted, but nothing happened. Other abortive speaking ideas bobbed up. Looking toward California, as he had off and on for many years, he sounded out Pond on a Pacific Coast tour. It did not come off, perhaps because the press of his affairs in the East prevented a journey so far from the nerve centers of business. In 1891 Pond proposed a season in fifty large cities with a troupe composed of Mark Twain, Riley, Warner, and Page. But no troupe assembled, and no tour got under way.

Mark Twain did read with Riley on February 26 and 27, 1894, in Madison Square Garden at $250 a night. Telling the stories of the jumping frog, of the miner docked for lost time when he was blown up, of the whistling stammerer, and other familiars, he frankly acknowledged that all of them were fully adult, aged twenty-five years or older. On the 27th the New York *Times* observed in a bored way that when people were determined to laugh,

nothing can turn them from it—not even Mark Twain. Last night's audience . . . turned out to look, hear, and laugh. It executed that intention thoroughly, while Mark Twain loitered through several of his back numbers.

That reluctant approval testifies to his skill at making good with old material. Unashamedly he used back numbers, which stimulated as much hilarity, the *Times* grudgingly admitted, as if they "had come off the humorist's reel for the first time."

In a sense they were coming off the reel for the first time. Substance remained more or less the same, but manner and detail continually varied. One of the best expositions of his storytelling method is the paragraph about the narrative gifts of the

Paladin in Chapter VII of *Joan of Arc*. This garrulous swash-buckler, says his creator, did not bore everybody by repeating his stories over and over in precisely the same words. His

art was of a finer sort; it was more stirring and interesting to hear him tell about a battle the tenth time than it was the first time, be-cause he did not tell it twice the same way, but always made a new battle of it and a better one, with more casualties on the enemy's side each time, and more general wreck and disaster all around, and more widows and orphans and suffering in the neighborhood where it happened.

Fascinated listeners urged him to " 'Tell about the surprise at Beaulieu again—tell it three or four times!' That is a compliment which few narrative experts have heard in their lifetime." Mark Twain was himself like the Paladin, and in the laughter induced by the fanciful variations of his many-times-told tales he heard the compliment often.

Some of his most entertaining inventions appeared in after-dinner speeches. At the Brander Matthews dinner in December, 1893, he spoke upon the resounding name of the guest of honor:

his blighting and scathing name—Bran-der Matthews! his lurid and desolating name—BRAND-er MATH-thews! B-r-r-an-der Matthews! makes you think of an imprisoned god of the Underworld mutter-ing imprecations . . . . B-r-ran-der Math-thews! . . . makes the most abandoned person resolve to lead a better life. . . . when the veteran profane swearer finds all his ammunition damp . . . how fresh and welcome is the dynamite in that name—B-r-r-RANder M-M-ATHthews! You can curse a man's head off with that name if you know where to put the emphasis.[6]

Everybody praised that speech—Howells, Gilder, and Matthews himself—but Mark Twain thought it had no "meat" in it. He said he brought it off only because he delivered it with assurance, and that showed the value of platform training.

One of his most agreeable speaking experiences occurred on

February 22, 1894, at the dedication of Mrs. Rogers' gift of a town hall to Fairhaven, Massachusetts. There was a satisfactory assembly of dignitaries, a special train, champagne. As the star attraction, he was number eleven and last on a long program of overture, prayer, chorus, presentation address, presentation of keys, address by the governor, and so forth. Mark Twain's topic was "Advice." Praising the building as "Chief of all the speakers, and the most eloquent," he said that he approved of a memorial while the donor was still alive, for after death "you get credit for the *intention* and the lawyers get the money." Some people, he mused, "do seem to get duller and duller the deader they get." Washington's birthday led him to acknowledge the debt he owed to the moral example of that great man. Then he took off on the watermelon story:

> The first time I ever stole a watermelon—I think it was the first time—it was the thought of Washington that moved me to make restitution, and made me morally whole again. When I found out that it was a green watermelon, I was sorry; not superficially, but deeply and honestly sorry.

After wrestling with the problem, asking himself what Washington would have done, he "rose up spiritually refreshed and strong," carried the watermelon back to the farmer's wagon, told the farmer he should be ashamed to peddle green ones, and demanded a ripe substitute. The abashed farmer, admitting his error, made the exchange and was a better man thereafter. The credit for this moral victory, said Mark Twain, "was not mine, but Washington's."[7]

That was the first telling of the watermelon story, which became a favorite. Often using it later, particularly on the world tour, he worked it over many times. In his notebooks are a number of variants showing a buildup of suspense, also experimentation with pauses and repetitions of words. The drafts of that story, indicating concern for achieving the best effect, are an excellent illustration of his craftsmanship.

In other ways 1894 was a bad year. When the Webster Company failed in April and when, eight months later, the typesetter had to be given up as hopeless, Mark Twain's fortunes ebbed. The two enterprises having been intertwined, publishing company money, including more than $60,000 from Livy, had gone into both the book business and the Paige machine. But precisely how badly off the failures left him is unclear even at this late date. The New York *Times* of September 19 reported that publishing company liabilities were $94,191, its net actual assets $54,164. Bainbridge Colby, a lawyer, said that in the crash Mark Twain lost everything, and Paine speaks of "reduced circumstances." Yet the normally restless pace of his life does not appear to have been much slowed down; his movements do not seem to have been restricted by the flat purse of a man who is really on his uppers. He sailed for Europe in May, returned to America in July, went back to Europe in August, and on both continents gadded around about as usual. He did not act like a bankrupt who has lost all. Still, it is clear that what he called his "ten-year dream" of the big money had ended in disillusion. He was eminently modern in rejecting the modest, steady return in favor of the spectacular plunge and the huge profit. That had gone with the wind.

Seizing the moment, the sympathetic Pond proposed a lecture tour, beginning in November. Mark Twain might have accepted had not Henry Rogers advised that he stand by to assist in salvaging financial wreckage. There was no more speaking for a time. Yet in his notebooks for the decade memoranda about lectures and after-dinner speaking show that his mind was often on these subjects. He entered an imaginary advertisement for lyceums: a philandering preacher, hero of numerous love affairs, offering to lecture about his amorous experience, with stereoptican slides, at $600 a night.[8] What wayward clergyman inspired that item? Beecher perhaps? There was the story of a man who got up to make a speech to an audience that had been tired out by many previous speeches. He spoke one sentence, then fell dead. The weary audience was much gratified.[9]

He drew up a list of rules for after-dinner speaking: the chairman should be a clever man, who should give each speaker a text, preferably stated as a question; each speaker should learn his speech by heart; positive means should be used to stop a dull fellow from boring everybody by rambling on and on.[10] These rules were born of hard experience. He had sat through lively dinners and dead dinners, and he would endure a good many more before he stopped dining out. There had been smart chairmen and clumsy chairmen, but so few of the former that when he looked back some years later, he could remember only five perfect introductions. The tiresome speaker is so common a handicap to any function that the rule about suppressing him deserves applause. Mark Twain eventually devised his own method of avoiding boredom by skipping the dinner and most of the speaking, and arriving only when it was his turn.

He drafted a Patent Adjustable Speech, which he delivered to the Boston Congregational Club on December 20, 1887. This talk, he said, was good for any sort of gathering: Granger meeting, wedding breakfast, "theological disturbance," "political blowout," inquest, funeral. It included the apologetic remarks of one supposedly called on by surprise: "I am called up suddenly, sir, and am indeed not, not prepared to—I was not expecting to be called up, sir, but I will, with what effect I may, add my shout to the jubilations of this spirited, stirring occasion." Then there was a ringing statement: "Agriculture, sir [or matrimony or religion or politics] is after all, the palladium of our economic liberties." High-flown generalities urged "songs of praise perennial, outpourings of Thanksgiving for that most precious boon, whereby we physically thrive and are made rich and strong, grand and aspiring, imbued with the mighty, far-reaching and all-embracing grace, and beauty, and purity and loveliness." The speaker need only "change three or four words in that speech, and make his delivery anguishing and tearful or chippy and facetious, or luridly and thunderously eloquent." Mark Twain illustrated by shifting from gayety to thunder to crocodile tears. Practise, he said, should make anybody so skillful with that talk that "by the time he has delivered it 15 or 20 times he could go to any intellectual gathering in Boston even and he would draw like a prize fight."[11]

14

Around the World

In late April, 1895, Mark Twain signed a contract with Carlyle G. Smythe, an Australian agent, for a six- to nine-months speaking tour around the world. The agreement called for engagements in the principal cities of the Sandwich Islands, Australia, New Zealand, Ceylon, India, Mauritius, South Africa, and England. The decision to make the long trip had cost, he said, "a hellish struggle" over "the horrible idea, the heart-torturing idea. . . . I, with patience worn to rags, I was to pack my bags and be jolted around the devil's universe for what? To pay debts that were not even of my making."[1] The American lectures on the way were an afterthought. In early May he said that he was considering a few readings before sailing for Australia, and by the end of the month he had engaged Pond to manage twenty-three performances in twenty-two cities of the United States and Canada. As originally planned, the tour included San Francisco. Mark Twain wanted a week of readings there, six nights and three matinees, all tickets one dollar, fifty cents extra for reserved seat. He suggested advance publicity by such prominent San Francisco journalists as Ambrose Bierce and Arthur McEwen, also a press banquet preceding the lecture series. The homecoming, after twenty-seven years, was to be a gala occasion.

For some reason this plan miscarried. Mark Twain offered the curious explanation that San Francisco would be unprofitable because too many people were out of town in midsummer. Possibly he could not find a hall that suited him; perhaps somebody's less than eager response out there offended him. The upshot was that the itinerary avoided California by taking a northern route across Michigan, Minnesota, Montana, and Washington. He proposed to make a sociable affair of the transcontinental journey. Pond would go along, of course, and in addition he hoped to have Henry Rogers, Judge and Mrs. Duff, Livy, and Clara—enough people, he said, to charter a private car.[2] That was Mark Twain all over: hard up, undertaking the tour to repay a heavy debt, yet thinking of private cars. The large party did not materialize. Major and Mrs. Pond accompanied the tourists as far as Vancouver; then Mark Twain, Livy, and Clara embarked for Australia, where Smythe took over as manager.

Mark Twain's platform zeal reappeared. Pushing sixty, not so spry as he once was, beset by rheumatism and disillusion, worn down by the strain of critical months that had ended disastrously, he nevertheless forgot the "horrible idea" as he prepared with great industry. In his notebooks are at least one hundred titles of possible readings, most of them from *Huckleberry Finn, Roughing It,* and *The Innocents Abroad,* some from *A Tramp Abroad,* and several from *Joan of Arc.* On the tour he used about forty selections. The most frequent numbers were the watermelon story, the German language, grandfather's old ram, the stabbed man, the Nevada duel, the Mexican plug, punch-brothers-punch-with-care, the whistling stammerer, the christening story, the golden arm, encounter with an interviewer, and a poem about the Ornithorhyncus he composed on shipboard. Others, less often read, were about his first meeting with Artemus Ward, Aunty Cord, Baker's blue jays, acting as courier, the jumping frog, King Sollermun, the incorporated company of mean men, the two raft bullies, Buck Fanshaw's funeral, and so forth. To the end of the long tour he worked over his material, rephrasing and varying the timing, and rehearsing to make each program an hour and a half. If he missed that limit by a few minutes either way, he was concerned. To the end, also, he introduced new anecdotes, like that of his Waterbury watch: setting it up and back to conform to an erratic Pretoria clock that struck ten at nine-thirty, then ten again at ten, and strange numbers at other times.

He considered several devices he did not use. One was an illustrated lecture, showing a number of pictures of himself and each time giving the photograph a different name. What evolved was a series of stories loosely held together by transitional sentences. Reflections on the human disposition to trust strangers led to the Mexican plug; a drift to comments on the wandering mind introduced grandfather's old ram; ruminations on the nobility of a good heart in a moral emergency brought him to the story of Huck and Jim. Mark Twain did not take his assignment lightly. As if he were not a seasoned campaigner, he worked as hard preparing for this tour as any novice uncertain of his reception.

Contemplating several tryout performances, he had to give them up because of a painful carbuncle. Facing the prospect of starting cold in Cleveland on July 15, he wrote Henry Rogers:

Nothing in this world can save it from being a shabby, poor disgusting performance. I've got to *stand*. I can't do it and talk to a house, and how in the nation am I going to sit? Land of Goshen, it's *this night week!* Pray for me.[3]

Yet he did manage two rehearsals. On July 12 he tried his program on the 700 boy inmates of the House of Refuge on Randall's Island. ". . . by the way it takes here," he said, "I will be able to tell how it will take on the other side of the world." The New York *Sun* said that the performance " 'took,' and the boys were in a roar . . . from the time they found . . . that it wasn't against the rules to smile until the speaker sat down."[4] Mark Twain thought that the talk was a failure because it was too adult for boys. On July 14, before the less juvenile inmates of the Elmira Reformatory, he said he was a "roaring success."

Then the tour got under way at Cleveland. In the Music Hall a tremendous audience of 2600, cheerfully sweltering in ninety-degree heat, made the evening look like a triumph. He started with a preface about morals. Since the Australians wanted lectures on "any kind of morals," he said he intended "to teach morals to those people. I do not like to have them taught to me, and I do not know of any duller entertainment than that, but I know I can produce . . . goods that will satisfy those people." Stating the principle that, to achieve moral superiority, one should commit all the 462 possible crimes, he remarked:

When you have committed your 462 you are released of every other possibility and have ascended the staircase of faultless creation, and you finally stand with your 462 complete with absolute moral perfection, and I am more than two-thirds up there.

Proceeding from principle to illustration, he launched into the watermelon story. Another theory, "that when you do a thing do it with all your might," introduced Baker and the blue jays:

You never saw a bluejay get stuck for a word. He is a vocabularized geyser. . . . A bluejay hasn't any more principle than an ex-Congressman. . . . A bluejay is human. . . . He likes especially scandal; he knows when he is an ass as well as you do.[5]

The audience was rollicking, but Mark Twain was disgusted. A program of flute and violin solos, with several encores, had delayed his entrance forty minutes, by which time he must have been fuming. Behind him on the stage two hundred newsboys squirmed and scuffled, distracting everybody and so annoying the speaker that he brought his talk to a fast close by skipping a third of it. Cleveland papers were complimentary, but he called the evening a defeat.

Embarking on the luxurious Great Lakes liner *Northland*, the party sailed away to Sault Ste. Marie and Mackinac. At both, he said that he satisfied the audience and his family but not himself because he did not have his whole program well in hand. Using spare time to memorize readings, he found the job difficult while nursing that stabbing carbuncle. At the summer resort town of Petoskey he did well, reporting with pride that "We had $548 in the house, which was $300 more than it had ever had in it before. I believe I don't care to have a talk go off better than that one did."[6]

On the *North West* they set out across Lake Superior for Duluth. The ship was delayed, and when she reached port well after lecture time, there was a great bustle of scrambling into carriages and galloping to the First Methodist Church. "I am glad," said Mark Twain as he ambled in an hour late, "that my strenuous efforts did succeed in getting me here just in time."[7] The crowd laughed, and kept on laughing at the jumping frog, the dead man story, the christening story, and others. The Duluth *Commonwealth* of the 23d remarked that "The lecturer was especially popular with the women," an interesting observation in view of his distrust of a feminine audience. On the disconcerting mop of gray hair, the paper said:

It . . . seems to be only in the way and of no use except to stamp its owner as a crank with a peculiar right to something nobody wants. . . . his most ardent admirers wouldn't call it becoming.

The *Evening Herald* said that the hair "makes one believe Twain is trying to rival Paderewski."

At Minneapolis he filled the Opera House; the evening, said Pond was "about as big a night as Mark ever had to my knowledge."[8] Of his hair, the Minneapolis *Progress* observed that it "has adopted silver as its standard, and . . . it adds much to the picturesqueness of the wearer."[9] Mark Twain evidently thought it was picturesque. In allowing it to grow wild, possibly he was, as the *Herald* surmised, trying to rival other artists in a day when long hair was the hallmark of the maestro.

After his performance at St. Paul the *Pioneer Press* of the 25th, noting the changes in the speaker since his previous visit in 1885, made this surprising comment: "His delivery is not so animated as it used to be, but it lacks none of the former charm on that account." If delivery were less animated than before, it must have been extraordinarily slow. On that point he twice entered in his notebook the curious caution about remembering to talk slowly.[10] It seems strange that this lazy man of the long talk should have needed such a reminder, unless during his platform days he had deliberately over-exaggerated the drawl for humorous effect. Apparently the pace did vary. A listener who once heard him read from Browning's *The Ring and the Book* remarked that during this exercise the humorist was completely suppressed by the serious literary man, then said: "I had wondered what he would do with the drawl, but for the most part it simply disappeared."[11]

Winnipeg, despite the heat, turned out large numbers for two rousing nights. To a *Free Press* reporter he made wryly humorous capital of his carbuncle. On the platform, he said, a good thing to have was an alert expression.

Perhaps I have that naturally, or perhaps it's the carbuncle. Yet, although we are at present inseparable, we are hardly friendly, and I shall not be sorry . . . when we part.[12]

Then the route dipped down to Crookston, Minnesota. Seldom giving the same program twice, he introduced here a new reading from the diary of Adam, which the *Polk County Journal* called "the drollest of all his writings. This kept the audience in a continual uproar . . . and put them in excellent humor for 'The Golden Arm,' which wound up the entertainment at 10:30."[13] Using American towns as testing grounds, he tried about twenty stories on this transcontinental trip, both to give himself practise and to learn which ones went well. Despite the success of the Adam's diary story, it apparently did not please him, for he rarely used it thereafter.

The party set out across Minnesota and Dakota, pausing no more until it reached Montana for performances at Great Falls, Butte, Anaconda, Helena, and Missoula. A stranger to this western region, Mark Twain yielded to its vast serenity that had "the peace of the ocean about it," he said,

and a deep contentment, a heaven-sent sense of ampleness, spaciousness. . . . The scattering, far-off homesteads, with trees about them, were so homelike and remote from the warring world. . . . The most distant and faintest under the horizon suggested fading ships at sea.[14]

Wearing a nautical cap perched high on the bush of hair, he was himself like a mariner voyaging across an ocean of tremendous plains and great rolling hills.

In the copper country he was pleased to find an unexpected sophistication. At Butte he remarked upon a "Beautiful audience. Compact, intellectual and dressed in perfect taste. It surprised me to find this London-Parisian-New York audience out in the mines."[15] On August 2 the Butte *Miner* said: "If anyone attended with the expectation of hearing . . . flaming eloquence or ponderous logic he was disappointed." Those who looked for "quaint humor and native wit . . . went away feeling that they had been in the presence of one of the most admirable characters which the struggles and eccentricities of American life have produced." After the performance, mining veterans of the Comstock Lode carried him off to a club for champagne and stories till midnight. Next day he and Pond caught the train to Anaconda only by one of those adroit expedients familiar to the seasoned trouper. When their trolley car broke down on the way to the railroad station, they jumped out and hailed a wagon driver, who asked ten dollars to taxi them to the train. Pond told him where he could go, then commandeered a grocery wagon for a dollar, and they clattered pell mell to the station, where they hopped aboard as the train was pulling out. At Anaconda the audience was so small that the local manager lost money. Pond had no qualms about pocketing all the receipts and leaving the poor fellow in the hole, but when Mark Twain heard about it he insisted on sending the Anaconda man $100. "I'm not going around," he said, "robbing poor men who are disappointed in their calculations as to my commercial value."[16]

At Helena, where people did not care much for lectures, the house was only half-full. Yet the *Daily Herald* of August 5 called it a "culture audience," which "enjoyed the easy style and unaffected manner of the speaker quite as much as the stories he told." Afterward the usual crush of people shook hands, and there was the customary reception, this time at the Montana Club. Mark Twain had stamina. Feeling his age, putting great energy into his readings, and partly disabled by the carbuncle, he yet bore up under a hardy regime both on and off the platform. Besides social events, he faced a steady parade of interviewers. All of them, he said, asked the same questions he had answered

so many millions of times already: "First visit? . . . Where do you go from here? . . . Have you enjoyed the trip? . . . Are you going to write a book about the voyage? What will be the character of it?" (tempted to say hydrophobia, seamanship and agriculture.)[17]

He disliked interviews, yet he seemed to enjoy talking to reporters, often subsiding into the nearest easy chair as he did so, and he never rebuffed them. Neatly he confounded one inexperienced journalist of Anaconda, who confronted him while he was waiting for a train. Without giving the reporter a chance to open up, Mark Twain began asking questions about Montana and so leading this novice on that by train time the young man discovered that he had been doing all the talking, having got from Mark Twain nothing but questions, a farewell handshake, and a cigar.

At Missoula, Pond was impressed by much military brass and braid from nearby Fort Missoula. "As most of the ladies who marry army officers," he said snobbishly, "come from our best Eastern society, it was a gathering of people who appreciated the occasion."[18] That was ironical praise for an old Comstocker like Mark Twain, who was as western as sagebrush, and some of whose best stories were flavored with sourmash and alkali.

The party moved on to Washington. At Spokane, a small crowd did not half-fill the splendid new Opera House, the *Spokesman-Review* was cool, and Mark Twain profanely expressed his dissatisfaction. Portland, Oregon, made up for several indifferent performances by an overflow audience, but Olympia gave him a poor reception. When the local *Washington Standard* deplored this lack of enthusiasm, one of those indignant letter-writers retorted that such scant attention was deserved. People "had a laughing time of it," he said, "but . . . where the 'intellectual treat' came in . . . is hard to say." Comparing the inferior literature of Mark Twain with the masterpieces of Homer, Virgil, Milton, and Byron, he snorted over "bouncing into notoriety upon the back of his 'Jumping Frog'!" As for me, he said,

I had rather . . . eat oatmeal with Bobby Burns in his poverty than to have written a hundred "Jumping Frogs" and be the recipient of all the seven hundred thousand dollars that Mark Twain received from his publishers.[19]

That blast was the most entertaining outburst of the tour. This humorless critic seems not to have sensed that on the superiority of Homer and his literary peers Mark Twain would probably have been the first to agree.

At Tacoma the *Morning Union* made illuminating comments: "The thing that Mark Twain looks like least is a funny man. He looks more like Hamlet, the melancholy Dane. . . . his hair . . . dressed . . . like Ophelia's . . . after she loses her mental reckoning."[20] Close up, his eyes "did not look so wild as they did at a distance. Twenty feet away they look not unlike burned holes in a blanket . . . out of joint with Mr. Clemens' calm and slightly ashy face." He got on the subject of his various doubles who had been lecturing under his name. One of them, he said, panhandled fifty cents in San Francisco. "He got the money in a saloon, and I think he was a mighty sharp fellow to raise a half dollar in that way."[21] After the Tacoma performance he talked about after-dinner speaking at a Press Club dinner that lasted until one-fifteen. "As a rule," he said,

a chairman at a banquet is an ass, but your chairman is not an ass. His plan is the best I have . . . encountered. It gives the irresponsibles an opportunity to be heard before the guest of the evening. . . . As a rule . . . the guest of honor is introduced . . . first . . . and the more he is lauded, the more difficult it is for him to speak. Every compliment ties his tongue.[22]

The over-effusive chairman stood high on his list of dinner handicaps. Good-natured insults and outrageous lies, though not malicious ones, were better, he believed, than fulsome compliments.

Seattle was a sellout. "There is but one Mark Twain," said the *Post-Intelligencer* of August 14:

He is not classic, and . . . just as far from . . . conventional; but people like him . . . all the more because he is himself . . . . a crowded audience heard . . . with unwearying enjoyment . . . one of those strange medleys of humor and philosophy which have . . . the sound of a great literary improvisation.

During the reading about the German language a voice called from the gallery, "Haf you been to Heidelberg?" Yes, was the reply, "I studied German there, and I learned many other things there also, among them how to drink beer."

To a Seattle interviewer he mentioned the business reverses responsible for the long tour, and pointed out the parallel between himself and Sir Walter Scott. At a similar age Scott, when his publisher failed, had set out to pay off a heavy debt by writing. He killed himself by overwork, said Mark Twain, and added:

if I have to pay my debts by writing books . . . I might easily kill myself in five years as he did. But I have the advantage of this lecture bureau system. . . . Instead of killing me, it builds me up physically. The fatigue of travel by easy stages is not great. . . . My health is a hundred per cent. better already than when I started out from home in July.[23]

The labor of writing might seem to be less exhausting than constant traveling, packing and unpacking, speaking, late hours, handshaking—but not for Mark Twain, whatever his blasphemies. Meeting his nephew, Sam Moffet, in Tacoma, he had spent some minutes whole-heartedly cursing the tiresome vexations of the entire trip, remarking, according to Pond, "that if everything had been made and arranged by the Almighty for the occasion, it could not have been better or more comfortable."[24] Still, thriving on conflict as always, he was in lively spirits, and his health was so much improved that even the carbuncle, a nagging handicap all the way from Elmira, was about to disappear.

At the small town of New Whatcom an indifferent crowd kept straggling in until nine-thirty, to the great annoyance of the speaker. The *Reveille* said on the 16th: "He probably never told his stories more effectively, though a New Whatcom audience is not . . . enthusiastic over humorous lectures, and would boycott Bill Nye were he to reappear." That is another comment on the lukewarm response to humor in a western country where humor was supposed to flourish. Nevertheless, people were so eager to meet the distinguished visitor that at the reception afterward a mob surged in. Mark Twain, instead of allowing the long queue to file by him, moved along the line shaking hands like a political candidate.

Expecting to sail for Australia on August 16, he was delayed a week when his ship, the *Warrimoo,* ran aground on her way into the harbor. He filled in the time with two extra performances, at Vancouver and Victoria, B. C. En route to Vancouver he noted that in "A stretch of 18 miles . . . there is not a single place named Victoria. . . . This shows that we are not under the British flag."[25] Yet in western Canada a trace of British tradition was a faint reminder of London. At the Victoria reading the Governor-General, his lady and son, in Highland costume, arrived fifteen minutes late, the audience standing, the orchestra playing "God Save the Queen." "I wish they would always be present," said Mark Twain, "for it isn't permissible to begin till they come; and by that time the late comers are all in."[26]

This appearance ended the American part of the world tour. The financial result is, as usual, vague. In his notebook Mark Twain recorded figures for every stop; the total was slightly over $5300, but whether that sum was gross or net is not clear. Paine says that from the West Coast he forwarded five thousand dollars to Henry Rogers to be applied to the publishing company debt. That meant that he was receiving over $200 a performance, a better return than he had averaged on previous tours. In a Seattle interview he said that he expected to take four years to pay off the debt: two American lecture seasons and one British besides the world tour. At the rate the money was coming in, he would not need so long a time.

Eight days out from Vancouver, the *Warrimoo* anchored in Honolulu roadstead, where the tourists were sadly dashed to learn that an outbreak of cholera in the Islands prevented a landing. Five hundred people who had bought tickets for the Honolulu lecture were disappointed, yet much worse was the destruction of Mark Twain's dream of returning to this paradise after almost thirty years. All he could do was to gaze longingly at lush tropical beauty: "Oahu—Just as silky and velvety and lovely as ever." And say to his notebook: "If I might I would go ashore and never leave."[27]

At sea again on a two weeks' voyage to Sydney, he worked up a jingle that became one of his most frequently-used readings in Australia, India, and South Africa. The story, as he told it on the stage, was about his struggle to find rhymes for the names of peculiar animals of the antipodes. Beginning with "Land of the Ornithorhyncus,/Land of the kangaroo,/Old ties of heredity link us," he was stuck for a rhyme. Starting again with "Land of the fruitful rabbit,/Land of the boomerang," he bogged down once more. Then he recited twenty lines that may or may not have been his own: about the Ornithorhyncus with "cordial claw," "fin of fish," and "beaver trowel tail"; and the kangaroo with "body tapered like a churn."[28] Possibly he lifted these lines, for he admitted, truthfully, that they sounded as if composed by Julia A. Moore, the Sweet Singer of Michigan. He wandered around in this foolery about fifteen minutes, promising his audience that the masterpiece would probably be finished in another year if he had time, and inspiration held out. The so-called "poem" was popular with everybody except the literal-minded. In Bombay a pedantic reporter said that "the poetry was beautiful, but unfortunately the description of the points of the Ornithorhyncus turned out to be quite wrong."[29] Undoubtedly.

In Sydney nine days, he spoke four times to audiences resplendent in full dress and patent leather shoes, the social aspect enhanced by advertising performances as "Mark Twain At Home." People came in from points distant over a hundred miles. Two faithful listeners everywhere were Livy and Clara, who acted as scouts reporting on the varying effect of readings, and of pauses in the stories of the golden arm and grandfather's old ram. Mark Twain was exacting about those pauses; they had to be just right, not by a fraction of a second too long or too short. He was amused by response to the watermelon story. People who knew his books accepted it as the tall tale it was. Others were puzzled, wondering whether he was serious, somewhat aghast at the nonchalant theft and upside-down morality. Their sense of humor must have been more British than Britain's.

The Sydney *Bulletin* complimented him: "He wears a cleaner collar than Talmage, and lacks the funereal aspect of most humorists this paper, has known."[30] Another paper, like the press of long-ago London, remarked upon "that characteristic nasal sound" and a manner of speaking full of quaint Americanisms,

and showing an utter disregard for the polished diction of most lecturers. "It was not" is always "twarn't" . . . and "mighty fine" and
"my kingdom" and "they done it" and "catched."[31]

He praised the Australians. "There could not be," he said,

a choicer audience or more satisfactory one to me, and I have found
the same characteristics here as in England and Canada, that they
adopt a friendly and uncritical attitude at the beginning, whereas it
frequently happens in America that they only get into that attitude
after one is fairly at work. The American audience is delightfully responsive and sympathetic, but not always in the very beginning.[32]

Nevertheless, having established an intermission about halfway
through, he confided to his notebook that an audience was likely
to be rather stiff before the break. New, untried pieces were not
advisable then, but afterward people were so relaxed—after visiting the bar?—that he could spring anything on them with a good
chance of success.

Social events filled the days—dinners, receptions, touring the
beautiful harbor—and interviewers dogged his steps. To a man
from the Sydney *Argus* he expressed himself strongly about Bret
Harte. "I detest him," he said,

because I think his work is "shoddy." His forte is pathos, but there
should be no pathos which does not come out of a man's heart. He
has no heart, except his name, and I consider he has produced nothing
that is genuine. He is artificial.[33]

That opinion was probably influenced by personal dislike, yet
modern critics would surely agree that much of Harte's work is
artificial. Mark Twain's sweeping judgment provoked an international controversy that brought forth indignant rejoinders from
Harte partisans. One burlesque interview represented him as
talking about his favorite lecture, called "The Homologation of
the Ideal, or the Transcendentalism of the Present with the Obtra-
sion of the Previous." The story ran that Smythe had objected to
this dissertation because "right-thinking persons might imagine it

was something . . . neurotic . . . and Australia fairly stinks with right-thinking persons just at present." Whereupon Smythe, urged to write a proper series of lectures himself, did so,

and now the great secret is out, and Smythe's blood be upon his own head—yes, even upon my own night-shirt, which he had retained in the hope of being asked to a ball at Government House.[34]

On September 25, the party entrained for Melbourne, where the stay was protracted for over two weeks by another carbuncle that kept him in bed most of the time. Yet he read five nights before Melbourne audiences. He said that, though pronounced almost a sick man,

when I come out at night and get a welcome like this I feel as young and healthy as anybody, and as to being on the verge of being a sick man, I don't take any stock in that. I have been on the verge of being an angel all my life, but it's never happened yet.[35]

The cordial greeting, he said, "which an American lecturer gets from a British colonial audience is a thing which will move him to his deepest depths, and veil his eyes and break his voice."[36] At one performance, the moment he appeared on the stage a stentorian voice called from the gallery, "Is he dead, Mark?" Not understanding the relevance of the question, he was for once nonplused, apparently having forgotten the old guide-baiting routine of the doctor and the boys in *The Innocents Abroad*.

In the audiences was a large quota of the most respectable and right-thinking. "That gentleman in the higher stage box," said the Melbourne *Argus*, "who laughed till his face was scarlet and banged the end of his walking-stick on the floor was an arch-deacon, and close to him was a rural dean, backed by a number of the minor clergy, all cackling like school-boys." The cloth was well represented, "several Presbyterians laughing really hard. . . . It is suspected that there were even some particular Baptists present, but on such a point one must speak with reserve."[37] Mark Twain was always pleased to win over clergymen. Later he told a reporter that he "made it a point to go about much with them, as it caused both parties to look more respectable."[38] Yet he was disgusted with the dour Australian Sabbath: no real Sunday papers, no cable cars running in the forenoon. Commenting on the popularity of horse-racing, he said: "When people get to be as good as this no amount of horse-racing can damn them."[39]

On October 11 the tourists left Melbourne for five days in Adelaide. The carbuncle, said Mark Twain to an interviewer, "sits on me like the nation; it keeps quiet awhile, but at times it gathers itself together and gives an almighty hard twist."[40] Adelaide, he told another, "possessed advantages over America in the fact that the city government was honest." Speaking of scenery, he said that he "recognized the grass, but the trees were new to him." Having received much information about flora and fauna, he remarked that he did not care whether it was correct, "for all he wanted was information and plenty of it."[41] Avoiding the usual tourist gush about natural beauty, he entered in his notebook the private opinion that Australia was an "unpretty country," of which "the native Australian is as vain . . . as if it were the final masterpiece of God, achieved by Him from designs by that Australian."[42]

In four "At Homes" in Adelaide he introduced several new stories: of the man who fell into a carpet-making machine and was returned to his widow as fourteen yards of three-ply carpet that was buried "in a second-hand tunnel set up end ways"; of the trouble that occurred when Miss Sophie lent her glass eye to Miss Wilkinson, "seeing that Miss Sophie wore a No. 5 eye and Miss Wilkinson was excavated for a No. 7"; and a variant of the old ram story as Uncle Lem and his "composite" dog, "composed of a sort of syndicate of dogs." He started the morals disquisition by regretting that the apple, not the serpent, had been forbidden in Eden, else Adam would surely have eaten the serpent. The Adelaide *Register* said:

He has a habit of carefully holding the one side of his head up with his right hand and propping his elbow with his left palm, as though the great straggling thatch of hair had caught the wind and canted his massive head over.[43]

Perhaps he felt too bad to hold his head up without support. Yet no twists of a mere carbuncle blighted his readings, kept him away from notables who crowded around, or prevented his staying out until well along in the early morning matching wits and yarns with other long-distance talkers.

Brief pauses at Horsham, Stawell, Ballarat, Maryborough, Bendigo, and Geelong ended the main part of the Australian tour by the last of October. In two performances at Ballarat he introduced the punch-brothers-punch jingle, the story of the champion liar of the Sandwich Islands, and an anecdote of Artemus Ward who once palmed off on him as a whiskey cocktail a mixture of water and Worcestershire sauce, then went on with the garbled explanation of silver mining that made Mark Twain believe that the drink had affected his mind.

At Bendigo the old ram story turned into the wandering narrative of a man who lost a dime in the field where the ram was, the narrator maundering along without ever revealing whether the man found his dime or got butted. The performance there was not profitable. "Unfortunately," said the local *Advertiser,* "the prices of admission were not so popular as 'Mark Twain,' and the result was a moderate attendance."[44] The paper had a point. If not immoderate by city standards, prices were steep for small towns, ranging from two shillings sixpence for a gallery seat to three and four guineas for a box. Yet he had good houses nearly everywhere. In early October he sent more than £400 to Henry Rogers, in early December £200, and from Adelaide later about £800. Considering the heavy expense of a journey like this one, that surplus was handsome. Abroad, he talked for much better fees than he had at home.

At sea on November 1, they put in at Hobart in Tasmania— described as "the neatest town that the sun shines on . . . also the cleanest"[45]—then proceeded to New Zealand. In about six weeks there the route touched all important places and some lesser ones: Invercargill, Dunedin, Tamaru, Omoru, Christchurch, Nelson, New Plymouth, Auckland, Gisborne, Napier, Palmerston North, Wanganui, Hawera, and Wellington.

Dunedin was a dry town, but Mark Twain was happy to find that it had excellent Scotch. That was not surprising, for the place had been settled by Scotsmen who, he observed, had "stopped here on their way from home to heaven—thinking they had arrived."[46] When a reporter for the Dunedin *Otago* asked him which of his books he liked best, he replied that he could not say because for many years he had not read any of them. Often asked that question, he once nominated *Huckleberry Finn,* at another time *Joan of Arc,* at still another *The Prince and the Pauper.* Perhaps he did not take the tiresome inquiry seriously; possibly the various answers were only a way of playing games on reporters, or of diversifying sales. At Omoru the performance was enlivened by a dogfight. Plenty of dogs wandered in to all his lectures, he said, but at Napier there was discrimination: "Dogs positively forbidden in the dress circle." Evidently, he concluded, that rule gave them "Tacit permission to fill up the rest of the house."[47] In Napier he was laid low by carbuncle number three, which forced cancellation of the second engagement there. Illness, coinciding with his sixtieth birthday, made him momentarily gloomy over the onset of old age.

At Palmerston North he had another sort of painful time. The Club Hotel was a jerry-built place of thin partitions and small rooms, "parlor the size and shape of a grand piano." The fat, red-faced landlord, who kept his hat on, could not find room keys, and noisy drunks racketed in the bar. In the early morning a baby began whimpering, "pleasantly," said Mark Twain, "—didn't mind baby," but then the "tin kettle" of a piano started up,

played by either the cat or a partially untrained artist . . . straight average of three right notes to four wrong ones, but played with eager zeal and gladness . . . and considering it was the cat—for it *must* have been the cat—it was really a marvelous performance. It convinces me that a cat is more intelligent than people believe, and can be taught any crime.[48]

On December 17 the travelers returned to Sydney for a week, then retraced the route to Melbourne and Adelaide, Mark Twain speaking in each. On New Year's Day, 1896, they embarked on the *Oceana* for a long voyage through the Indian Ocean to Ceylon. Yielding easily to the subdued rhythm of shipboard life, Mark Twain became a much calmer man than his restless self ashore. At sea he lived up to the characterization Smythe gave one interviewer: "the laziest man in the United States. Everything makes him tired; even sleeping."[49] A long voyage, said Mark Twain, brought "Peace, everlasting peace, and tranquillity. . . . it is infinitely comfortable and satisfying."[50] He read novels, even resolving to tackle *The Vicar of Wakefield* again and Jane Austen, noted the increasing heat as they steamed north, the beautiful blue of the ocean, the playful porpoises. After a short stay at Colombo, where he took to his bed with a bad cough, they were off again for Bombay.

There the pace abruptly accelerated. The family met an eager young man named Gandhi, lunched with the governor and his lady at Government House, visited Prince Kumar Shri Samatsinghi —who, in true princely fashion, bestowed rich gifts—attended the knighting of the Prince of Pulitana, a bejeweled figure resplendent in ropes of pearls and, as Mark Twain called them, "green rubies." He found Bombay "A bewitching place, a bewildering place, an enchanting place—the Arabian Nights come again!"[51] Three "At Homes" attracted full houses fashionable and glittering, dignitaries British and Indian. So many carriages, attended by dark footmen in white turbans, rolled up that in India, he said, "The vicinity of a lecture-hall looks like a snowstorm, and makes the lecturer feel like an opera."[52] If not an opera, he was a good show. "I like the platform," he told a Bombay reporter, "when I am there, but the

thought of it makes me shudder; the prospect of it is dreadful."
Collapsing into a chair, he went on about his method of preparing
for a lecture. No speaker could succeed, he said, unless he had

gone over every sentence again and again until the whole thing is
fixed upon his memory. I write my lectures, and try to memorize them,
but I don't always succeed. If I had a better memory it would be
worse in some respects, for when one has to fill up an ellipsis on the
spot, there is a spontaneity about the thing which is a considerable
relief.[53]

He never stopped going over the sentences. Constant drill had
given him such command of his material that by this time he could
shift easily from one story to another, or introduce an unscheduled
new one at the last moment without destroying continuity. So
skillfully could he cover a lapse of memory that an audience was
not aware of the slip. He had been known to get lost in the middle
of one story, switch to the middle of another and carry on without
anybody's being the wiser, not even Livy, who knew his stories
as well as he did. Of his casual piecing together of unrelated
yarns, the Bombay *Gazette* remarked: "the transition is so . . .
naturally effected that the . . . lecture fits . . . together as a complete whole, albeit it is but a medley of quaint anecdote, humour-
ous sketch and keen reflection strung together by the . . . slightest
of threads."[54] The thread might be slight, but it was there, and
it was enough. He was a professional who could make good with
slender substance. The christening story, for instance, one of his
favorites: about a Scotch clergyman who rhapsodized at length
about the fine boy he was to baptize, the upstanding young man
he would become, the great poet or warrior or statesman, only to
discover that the name of the child was Mary Ann. Very simple
and obvious, yet, stringing out that tale for ten or twelve minutes,
he made people all but roll in the aisles.

After ten tumultuous days in Bombay, other Indian cities followed: Poona, Baroda, Allahabad, Benares, Calcutta, Darjeeling,

Mazaffarpur, Lucknow, Cawnpore, Agra. He marveled at native vegetation and architecture—though he could not make the Taj Mahal live up to its reputation—swarming cities, the patience of servants, the fatalism of the people, the conjunction of man and nature, both producing with teeming abandon. In *Following the Equator* he called India

the land of dreams and romance . . . of splendor and rags . . . palaces and hovels . . . famine and pestilence . . . genii and giants and Aladdin lamps . . . tigers and elephants, the cobra and the jungle, the country of a hundred nations and a hundred tongues, of a thousand religions and two million gods, cradle of the human race . . . the land that *all* men desire to see, and having seen once, by even a glimpse, would not give that glimpse for the shows of all the rest of the globe combined.

It was the India of Kipling, he observed, but said nothing about the white man's burden. Rather, he accepted native life as he found it, and commented on the irony of a small minority of Christians hoping to convert hundreds of millions of Asiatics.

All along the line there was sumptuous entertainment by Indian princes, British officials, and army officers: drives, luncheons, receptions, dinners. Jammed houses were the rule. At Calcutta he interpolated another jingle, saying that he had got the suggestion from "an old hand at poems": "Here is Jebong,/Where the righteous belong./And there is Panam,/Where they don't care a —." On the last line he scrabbled through his notebook as if looking for the concluding word, then announced that he was unable to find it. Although he seldom gave a joke a local application, he did so here. "It pains me," he said,

to hear people cast slurs on Adam—for family reasons . . . as he was a distant relative of mine. . . . I have never in all my travels up and down the world seen any place whatever where that apple Adam ate would have been safe—except Calcutta.[55]

Apropos of the morals dissertation and the 352 possible sins, a number that continually varied, the Calcutta *Englishman* remarked upon "the semi-pastoral tone which Mark Twain can so well assume."

In Jeypore on March 1, he was there for two weeks, struck down again by illness. The relapse was not dull, for British friends rallied around to give him what he called "the charmingest times . . . . All over India the English—well, you will never know how good and fine they are until you see them."[56] By the 15th he was ready to go, to Delhi, Lahore, and Rawalpindi, then back to Calcutta. In Delhi, impudent monkeys invaded his bedroom. One brushed his hair before the mirror, another behaved in a most insulting manner by crying over humorous items in the notebook. In Lahore he rode on an elephant, which grandly shuffled down the middle of the street, all other traffic giving way. Tom Sawyer would have enjoyed that. Mark Twain said that he liked the immunity from collisions, the dignity of high place, and the fine view from up there.

After more than two months in India, the party embarked for Ceylon on the *Wardha,* another of those "frantic little ships," as he called them. Pausing at Madras, then at Colombo, where he lectured twice, they were at sea again for a long voyage to Mauritius. Again he relaxed, resuming his salt water calm, his reading, his notebook speculations on matters scientific and religious. The ship might be small and slow, but he adapted himself to it as readily as the plodding craft rode the long lazy swells of the Indian Ocean. Seventeen days out from Calcutta he remarked upon "a tranquil sea and a cloudless sky. . . . 17 days of heaven, and in 11 more it will end. There will be one passenger who will be sorry."[57]

They landed at Port Louis on the island of Mauritius, then removed ten miles south to the small town of Curepipe, where they remained about two weeks. It was a rest period. Apparently there were no lectures on the island, nor the usual heavy schedule of social affairs. Mark Twain talked to the people and looked at the country. It was "pretty enough," he said, "charming," though "not imposing; not riotous, not exciting; it is a Sunday landscape . . . . a garden and a park combined," lacking "Spaciousness, remote altitudes, the sense of mystery which haunts . . . inaccessible mountain domes and summits reposing in the sky. . . ."[58] His chief complaint was of dampness that ruined all brands of matches. Out of sixteen, he said, only one gave him a light.

Then they were at sea once more on an eight days' run to Durban, South Africa. During ten days there he lectured twice to the packed houses that had become routine. The Durban *Natal Mercury* perceptively observed that "this experienced man of the world and in public appearances is as nervous as a child when he goes on the platform."[59] Like all seasoned actors, he was apprehensive before a performance. But an audience did not suspect tension, for on the stage no nervousness marred his languorous stance. Papers everywhere noted the conversational tone, the slow, weary speech, the easy, almost unmoving pose. In South Africa he relished the climate and luxuriant foliage. Grassy slopes and clumps of trees reminded him of New England; rutted tracks made him think of American prairie roads. The Negroes seemed like those at home: same clothes, same faces. But tall palms destroyed the illusion, spike-like plants, the flat-roof tree, and sometimes

a gang of unmodified Zulus . . . festooned with glass beads and with necklaces made of the vertebrae of snakes, the men's hair wrought into a myriad of little wormy forms, gummed with tar, the women's greased with red clay.[60]

While Livy and Clara remained in Durban, he went on to Pietermaritzburg, Johannesburg, Pretoria, Bloemfontein, Queenstown, King Williams Town, East London, and Port Elizabeth, where the family was reunited about the middle of June. At Johannesburg, when he sauntered upon the stage carrying a glass of water, the gallery gods whistled "Yankee Doodle." He read here one of his seldom-used pieces, about the fantastic confusion resulting from his attempt to act as courier for the family in Europe, elaborating upon a succession of awkward blunders for twenty-seven minutes. Talking of silver mining in Nevada, he said that towns of the Comstock Lode were different from his native village, "where half the people were alive, the other half dead, and it took an expert to tell them apart."[61]

At Pretoria, stolid Boer audiences were, he said, "hard to start, but promptly and abundantly responsive after that."[62] While there he visited the imprisoned Jameson raiders, and gave them an impromptu speech. "This jail is as good as any other," he said, "and, besides, being in jail has its advantages. A lot of great men have been in jail. If Bunyan had not been in jail, he would never have written 'Pilgrim's Progress.' Then the jail is responsible for 'Don Quixote.' "[63] He went on to say that they were better off in jail, that they probably would have got there anyhow, that they should prefer the easy life to working for a living, and that he would use his influence to have their sentences doubled. Not all the prisoners appreciated these absurdities, and they so annoyed President Kruger that he ordered more stringent restrictions for the captives. Whereupon Mark Twain explained that it was all a joke, which even Oom Paul—"hat, beard, frock coat, pipe, and everything else"—eventually understood, and relaxed the severity.

The family spent a week at Port Elizabeth, then five days at Grahamstown, paused at Cradock, stopped two days at Kimberley, and ended the long tour with a week at Cape Town. At Kimberley, Mark Twain was fascinated by diamond mines, going into statistics of carats and values like the *Enterprise* reporter of boom days in Virginia City. He commented on the country, on towns "well populated with tamed blacks; tamed and Christianized too, I suppose, for they wear the dowdy clothes of our Christian civilization."[64] For the Boers he could pump up no great enthusiasm, representing them as rather cloddish people dressed in outfits that "For ugliness of shape, and for miracles of ugly colors inharmoniously associated . . . were a record."[65] In Cape Town he saw everything: Table Rock, Table Bay, St. Simon's Bay, the Parliament, old Dutch mansions—in fact, when he reached the Cape, he said he had seen "each and all of the great features of South Africa except Mr. Cecil Rhodes."[66]

Three "At Homes" attracted houses described as "crowded and brilliant." Through with innovations, he used standard readings given many times before: the morals homily, called "a gigantic system of moral regeneration by the inoculation of a mysterious sort of a moral vaccine"; the Nevada duel, the first meeting with Artemus Ward, Virginia City newspaper experiences, Huck and Jim, the horrors of the German language. One reporter, observing that the lecture was "not of a strictly orthodox character," said that it was "a delightful revelation to those who have been familiar with the books of the whole-hearted, smile provoking, pure-minded humourist."[67]

On July 15 the party set sail on the *Norman* for a two-weeks' voyage to Southampton. To Henry Rogers, Mark Twain wrote that he had become very tired of the platform toward the end, particularly of the demands of a heavy schedule that had forced upon him a regime of rest and self-denial. He hoped that need would never again drive him back to lecturing.[68] Summing up the experience in *Following the Equator,* he said: "I seemed to have been lecturing a thousand years, though it was only a twelve-month." He had given about a hundred readings in fifty-three cities of five countries. How much money he sent back to Henry Rogers is unknown. On the basis of fragmentary evidence, a conjecture is that the tour yielded a net of twenty thousand to twenty-five thousand dollars. It was not enough to discharge the debt, but Mark Twain had not expected to do that.

Regardless of platform fatigue, he looked forward to several weeks of speaking in England in September, and at least two seasons in the United States. These plans were shattered—as the family was shattered—by the death of Susy Clemens on August 18, 1896.

15

Emeritus

FOR MONTHS after the death of Susy the Clemens family lived in seclusion in London. Finding work an anodyne for grief, Mark Twain spent the grim winter writing *Following the Equator,* and by late spring of 1897 it was ready for the press. His being out of the public eye gave rise to rumors that he badly needed money, and that, under the strain of debt, travel, and tragedy, his health had given way. He still owed about $50,000 of publishing company debts, but he was not hard up, and he did not remotely resemble a broken-down invalid.

Nevertheless, on June 1, 1897, the New York *Herald* headlined his parlous state, physical and financial, and on the 13th initiated a relief fund for Mark Twain, the paper heading the list with a subscription of $1000. Thereafter for almost two weeks a daily story reported progress: Editors and Others Endorse Twain Fund, Ingersoll on Twain, English Press on Twain Fund, Carnegie Gives $1000 for Twain. This publicity stimulated a minor flurry. One subscriber organized ten-cent clubs. Solomon Selig, the Boy Orator of the Hudson, called for a contribution from every American boy who had ever laughed at one of Mark Twain's stories. "Selberry Mullers" gave up cigars to contribute one dollar a week. By June 26 the *Herald* had collected $2928.01.

Other New York dailies, ignoring the campaign of a rival, made their silence imply disapproval. *Town Topics* forthrightly spoke up:

It is almost incredible that a newspaper of the prestige . . . of the *Herald,* for the sake of . . . self-advertising, should so ruthlessly invade the private affairs of a man of Twain's rank and achievements and subject him to cruelest humiliation.[1]

On the same page as that editorial was a stronger comment in the form of a burlesque "Charity Extraordinary," sponsored by the "New York *Daily Lunatic,*" with a list of contributions: *Daily Lunatic,* $1000; man who gave streetcar transfer; Prominent Citizen, $0000.02; Vox Populi, $0000.05. The irony was that Mark Twain was not humiliated by this invasion of his private affairs. He made no move to stop the money-raising scheme, and he carefully guarded the news from his family. In a letter to an unknown correspondent he said he was so tired of being in debt that he would welcome the assistance of friends, for such aid was better than a memorial after death. Others thought differently. Henry Rogers cabled that the *Herald* fund was a mistake, and advised polite rejection. Bliss cabled that the fund was damaging Mark Twain's prestige, and advised declining. These opinions might have had no effect had not his family taken the same view. When Livy heard about it, as she was bound to, she immediately and emphatically disapproved.

Acceding to her wishes, Mark Twain, in a letter to the *Herald,* declined the relief fund. Admitting his error in not having taken his family into his confidence, he said:

Now that they know . . . about the matter, they contend that I have no right to allow my friends to help me while my health is good and my ability to work remains. . . . I am persuaded that they are right. . . . I was glad when you initiated that movement, for I was tired of the fact and worry of debt, but I recognize that it is not permissible for a man whose case is not hopeless to shift his burdens to other men's shoulders.[2]

Commenting on those statements, one editorial writer said that Mark Twain had revealed

in a most unseemly way . . . what a nasty time family pride had . . . conquering his own lack of scruples. We have tried in vain to look upon Mr. Clemens's communication as . . . humorous . . . little suited as humor seemed to the occasion. The only refuge seems to be . . . that his health is . . . broken, that he has lost his grip on himself, and that his . . . false position is due to an act for which he is as little accountable as a sick child. . . . We should like to believe . . . that the real man in health and happiness is . . . more sturdy than the . . . flaccid and groveling figure we are trying not to see to-day.[3]

That rebuke might have served for another relief device that originated about the same time. In the spring of 1897 some friend, possibly Frank Fuller, conceived the idea of a grand benefit lecture at the Waldorf. A dozen wealthy men would be asked to contribute large sums; tickets would be priced at $5 to $100, also sold at auction. Informed of this scheme, Mark Twain played the role of innocent prepared to manifest grateful surprise at the proper moment, and once again kept the secret from his family. Plans went so far that he made elaborate notes for a lecture. Proposing to tell the story of his Cooper Union debut in 1867, he let his imagination run as he invented details about newspaper advertising he and Fuller had devised, the barrels of handbills, and a long list of distinguished and notorious Americans and Europeans who had been invited: generals, poets, statesmen, tycoons, political bosses, Sing Sing convicts, an Emperor who was three years old at the time. He sketched an exaggerated biography of Fuller, wrote an account of the 1867 occasion—somewhat like that in the *Autobiography*, but with more fanciful trimmings—and planned to show portraits of well-known people on a screen, accompanying each with an anecdote.[4] He was as ready to accept the benefit lecture as he had been to take the *Herald*'s relief fund. But Livy found out about this one, too. Summarily rejecting the plan, she said firmly that if he lectured, he had to do so at legitimate prices. The benefit scheme died forthwith.

These episodes show a curious lack of sensitivity in Mark Twain. We may wonder why he was willing, even eager, to appear before the world like a beggar passing the hat. His own explanation was the worry of being in debt. Yet that burden was not overwhelming nor was it everlasting, for he was steadily reducing it. By the end of 1897, having made another partial payment of 25% to creditors, he had liquidated 75% of the whole. As the world tour had shown, he could make plenty of money legitimately. His books produced a good income that, in the capable hands of Henry Rogers, would in a few years restore the affluence of Hartford days. Mark Twain was so far from poverty-stricken that the burden of debt was not crushing; it did not in the least restrict his goings and comings, or force drastic retrenchment upon his way of life.

The best defense of his asking for handouts is perhaps his strong, though mistaken, conviction that the publishing company debts were not of his making. To the end of his life he believed that he had been victimized by others. Yet the evidence in Samuel Charles Webster's *Mark Twain, Business Man* shows not only that he shared responsibility for failure, but also that at times he was the least sensible man in the business. Nevertheless, aggrieved over the supposed bungling of Charles L. Webster and his successor, Fred Hall, and feeling therefore no real obligation to make their mistakes good, Mark Twain was probably ready to get out from under by any means. If so, his position was so shaky that it was well Livy was there to prevent the error of accepting one or both of these charities. It was not the first time she had shown better judgment.

At this propitious moment Pond appeared in London with an offer of $50,000 for 125 nights in America. Mark Twain was so much in favor that, as he told the story, he at once drew up the terms of a contract, then labored all night with Livy to persuade her to agree. Remembering the illnesses that had dogged their trail around the world, she was reluctant. "You'll have pneumonia, she said. "I'll go with you, the girls'll go with you, we'll all die."[5] At four A.M. she gave in. But later that day she changed her mind, and the lecture tour was shelved.

Spending the summer of 1897 in Switzerland, the family then moved to Vienna for two winters. In the Austrian city Mark Twain admirably performed the duties implicit in his title of "self-appointed ambassador-at-large of the United States of America—without salary." A social lion and privileged character, known to everybody from royalty to policemen, he dined with dukes, visited princesses, and entertained gatherings of the famous and witty. He could not take a walk without being pointed out, hailed, made much of. Like Tom Sawyer he loved it. "The fact is," he said to an interviewer, "I am so used to being stopped and greeted that I am just spoiled, spoiled, and expecting it, and discontented and disagreeable when it does not happen."[6]

He gave a few readings there and in Budapest, "merely for fun, not for money. . . . I like to talk for nothing, about twice a year; but talking for money is *work,* and that takes the pleasure out of it."[7] He believed that in Vienna he finally learned the art of reading: walking on with a book, he read a few sentences, then switched to an improvised introduction, and worked into the story while the audience was still expectantly waiting for the sketch to begin. By memorizing only the substance of a piece, he discovered that

one flashes out the happiest suddenly-begotten phrases now and then! . . . Such a phrase has a life and sparkle about it that twice as good a one could not exhibit if prepared beforehand, and it "fetches" an audience in such an enthusing and inspiring and uplifting way that that lucky phrase breeds another one, sure.[8]

To depend upon finding the sparkling phrase at the right moment might not be wise for the slow-witted, but it was valid for this imaginative man. One talk, for the Concordia, a Socialist club, was a mixture of German and English that dealt with reforming the unwieldy German language. He recommended removing its parentheses, moving the verb forward, and abolishing the separable verb. Schiller

has the whole history of the Thirty Years' War between the two members of a separate verb in-pushed. That has even Germany itself aroused, and one has Schiller the permission refused the History of the Hundred Years' War to compose—God be it thanked![9]

In early 1898, when the debts were finally paid, friends and press applauded the feat. The London *Daily News* praised "a fine example of the very chivalry of probity" that "deserves to rank with the historic case of Sir Walter Scott."[10] But Mark Twain had no sooner obliterated reminders of previous bad business guesses than he was fascinated by the profitable potential of a carpet-making machine designed by the Austrian inventor, Szczepanik. Visionary millions again floated before his mind's eye as he dreamed of organizing a huge company to corner the carpet-weaving industry of the world. As a speculator he was incurable. Fortunately, this time the harder-headed Henry Rogers firmly restrained his impulsive friend, and there was no reckless jumping into the carpet business.

Periodically, he expressed his abhorrence of the platform. Yet he kept on trying to persuade Livy to let him lecture when they returned home, and he was continually turning down tempting offers from Pond and others. In 1899, he even advised Howells to try a tour. Pond, he said, was neither truthful nor sensible, yet for those reasons he was probably more companionable than a wiser man. When Howells took to the road, Mark Twain said gloatingly:

Oh, I know how you feel! I've been in hell myself. You are there tonight. . . . Nothing is so lonesome as gadding around platforming. I have declined 45 lectures to-day—England and Scotland. I wanted the money, but not the torture. *Good* luck to you!—and repentance.[11]

Mark Twain did not repent, nor had he found platforming such hellish torture as he let on. Some years later he defined his attitude more accurately when he said: "I love to hear myself talk, because I get so much instruction and moral upheaval out of it, but I lose the bulk of this joy when I charge for it."[12]

In the early summer of 1899, the family returned briefly to London. During about a month there, he made a Fourth of July speech, and was feted by the Authors' Club, the Whitefriars, Savage, New Vagabonds, and Beefsteak, speaking at all of them, also at a dinner for Sir Henry Irving. In the Fourth of July speech to the American Society, he told of picking up by mistake the hat of Canon Wilberforce, and of being for five hours under so strong a clerical influence that he could not tell a lie. To the Savages he said that he had "not professionally dealt in truth. Many when they come to die have spent all the truth that was in them, and enter the next world as paupers. I have saved up enough to make an astonishment there."[13] At the Irving dinner he spoke of having been a dramatist for thirty years, always striving "to overdo the work of the Spaniard who said he left behind him 400 dramas when he died. I leave behind me 415, and I am not yet dead."[14]

After a summer in Sweden, the family was back in London and vicinity for a stay of a year. It was a repetition of Vienna, a whirl of social events, lionizing, and distinguished associates. Setting sail for America on October 6, 1900, they arrived in New York on the 15th, home again after a long absence of nine years. In August, Pond had forehandedly offered $10,000 for ten nights. Mark Twain, admitting the splendor of the sum, declined it, saying that he was now out of circulation and not likely to re-enter the lecture arena. At long last that statement was true. He made no more lecture tours, nor did he ever again accept pay for talking. Yet as the dean of American speakers, the elder statesman of the platform, he was not allowed to be silent, nor did he wish to be. He spoke on behalf of charitable causes, for organizations, schools, and churches. "I shan't," he said, "retire from the gratis-platform

Mark Twain in 1902.

Mark Twain in his study, 1903.

until after I am dead and courtesy requires me to keep still and not disturb the others."[15] He did not quite make that assertion good, but he probably would have done so had not ill health forced him to give up public appearances ten months before his death.

Barely settled at 14 West 10th Street, he became a busy diner-out. At numerous dinners he was the principal speaker and main attraction. A banquet, he once said, was "a dreadful ordeal," "the insanest of all recreations." It began with a wearisome preliminary half hour when everybody got tired standing around bandying inanities with fellow-diners. Then they marched into the dining hall, to be greeted sometimes with a blare of music, that din soon augmented by a great clatter of china and silverware and the shouts of guests trying to talk to each other above the noise. The uproar was so great, said Mark Twain, that "there is nothing to approach it but hell on a Sunday night."[16] After an hour of pandemonium, speeches followed for another two hours or more, and then the banqueter crept home with exhaustion in his bones and a loud buzzing in his ears. Nevertheless, Mark Twain, trying to taper off on dining engagements but being no more successful than a hard drinker, sallied forth night after night.

The Press Club honored him, the Society of American Authors, Lotos Club, St. Nicholas Society, Twentieth Century Club. At the Press Club dinner the chairman made the mistake of lavishly complimenting the guest of honor, who responded by saying that he

felt like using a gun on anybody who treated me that way. . . . I don't mind slanders. The facts are what I object to. I don't want any of my true history getting abroad. I appeal to you journalists to keep it from the public.

He also remarked upon the intelligence of one guest, who "said he had read all of my books. He fairly oozes intelligence."[17] At the Society of American Authors dinner, another effusive chairman poured on too much praise. "It seems a most difficult thing," said Mark Twain,

for any man to say anything about me that is not complimentary. Sometimes I am almost persuaded that I am what the Chairman says I am. . . . Nothing bites so deep down as the facts of a man's life. The real life that you and I live is a life of interior sin. Every one believes that I am just a monument of all the virtues. Some day there will be a Chairman who will be able to give the true side of my character.[18]

At the Lotos Club he himself praised the ninety-five creditors who had been kind and considerate during his financial distress, all but one, whom he called "a Shylock." That was probably Thomas Russell and Sons. Having filed suit to recover $4623 when the Webster Company failed, this firm was the only one to invoke legal action. For the St. Nicholas Society, responding to the toast, "Our City," he dwelt ironically upon the "fragrant" municipal government of New York, and the great moral improvement he had observed since his return. "Some think," he said, "it's because I have been away."[19]

When Winston Churchill, fresh from dramatic experiences among the Boers, spoke at the Waldorf on December 12, Mark Twain introduced him. Howells and Henry Van Dyke had refused to allow their names to be used as endorsers of Churchill, and Mark Twain's introduction was no endorsement either. Mr. Churchill, he said, knew a great deal about war, but nothing about peace. War might be interesting to anybody who enjoyed that sort of pastime, but he had never found it entertaining himself. Taking the anti-British position prevalent in the United States at the time, he condemned intervention in South Africa as a damnable sin, matched only by the crime of American meddling in the Philippines. "England and America," he concluded, "are kin in almost everything; now they are kin in sin."[20]

He returned to the anti-imperialism theme in an after-dinner speech for the City Club in early January, 1901. Half-flippantly proposing an "anti-Doughnut party" to prevent the election of any future candidate like Bryan or McKinley, he became suddenly earnest by saying that he did not vote for Bryan because he was wrong on the money question. As for McKinley, "I knew enough about the Philippines to have a strong aversion for sending our bright boys out there to fight with a disgraced musket under a polluted flag, so I didn't vote for the other fellow."[21] A stronger statement of his protest against American imperialism was his article, "To the Person Sitting in Darkness," in the February *North American Review*. Discussing another subject in a vein more serious than funny, he talked about woman's suffrage at the Hebrew Technical School for Girls. "Why," he said, "I have been in favor of woman's rights for years. . . . The suffrage in the hands of men degenerates into a couple of petrified parties."[22]

⁀ The humorist becoming a sober commentator on political and social questions, turning moralist, affronting the flamboyant patriotism whipped up by our far eastern adventure, disconcerted people. "Mark is on a spree," said the New York *Sun;* "for the moment he is in a state of mortifying intoxication from an overdraught of seriousness, something to which his head has not been hardened."[23] The *Times,* calling his Philippines remarks "Certainly False, but Probably Funny," observed:

Mr. Clemens, unfortunately, has suggested several times of late that . . . fame as a humorist does not content him, and that he aspires to add to his own abundant laurels those which lesser men acquire by . . . consistent gravity. This has now and then proved confusing, even to some of his most ardent admirers.[24]

One distressed ardent admirer was Livy. "Why," she wailed, "don't you let the better side of you work? . . . You go too far, much too far in all you say. . . . Does it help the world always to rail at it. There is great & noble work being done, why not sometimes recognize that?"[25] Thus he paid the humorist's penalty he had spent many years imposing upon himself. As skeptic and cynic, oppressed by a deepening sense of the injustices of life, of the baseness and ignorance of men, he had to learn that unflattering opinions of what he called "the damned human race" were acceptable only if disguised by wit or humor.

He was both facetious and serious as chairman of the Lincoln birthday celebration at Carnegie Hall. It was a love feast. Henry Watterson, another well-known former rebel, was there, also Union General Miles and Confederate General Wheeler. Introducing Watterson, Mark Twain, referring to his own brief service in the Confederate Army, said: "It was my intention to drive Gen. Grant into the Pacific Ocean. If I could have had the proper assistance from Col. Watterson it would have been accomplished. I told Watterson to surround the Eastern armies and wait until I came up."[26] He paid high tribute to Lincoln and remarked upon the healing of old wounds in the merging of North and South under one name, Americans. But that was over a generation before the reopening of old wounds in the struggle over racial integration.

For the Eastman Club of Poughkeepsie he gave a generalized account of his disastrous business experience, and of the large sums he had lost in unwise ventures. "I cannot say," he observed, "that I have turned out the great business man that I thought I was when I began life. But I am comparatively young yet and may learn. . . . My plan is to get another man to do the work for me. There's more repose in that. What I want is repose first, last, and all the time." He phrased a cynical motto, "Honesty is the best policy—when there is the most money in it," and concluded with an axiom: "to succeed in business, avoid my example."[27]

That was sound advice, which he could not follow himself. He promoted a company to sell plasmon, a health food he had discovered in Sweden, invested an unknown amount, and according to his own story was royally swindled by a man with the unbelievable name of Butters. He put money into a patent cash register that looked promising, but that, like the Paige machine, never advanced beyond promise. He invented a spiral hatpin that was supposed to attract women buyers because it was guaranteed to keep a lady's hat on in any gale, but all he got out of that was souvenirs for feminine visitors. Mark Twain belied the old adage about the teaching value of experience, yet he generally took the consoling position that mistakes and losses were not his fault. Somebody else was usually the villain. Once he made up a list of swindlers who had cheated him: Butters, Bliss, Paige, and a long roster of some thirty others, most of them probably imaginary, yet for all that no less indicative of ever-ready suspicion of double-dealing.

In 1901, money tossed away on bad investments produced no crisis like that of 1894. Within a year his annual income, climbing back to former heights, became $60,000 from books, $100,000 from all sources. Life resumed the bustle and splendor of the old days. When the family moved into a spacious home at Riverdale, with a dining room thirty feet by sixty, an unending procession of visitors made the place a hostelry like that of Nook Farm. Paine says that in a run-of-the-mill week there were guests three nights out of seven, and for seventeen meals out of twenty-one. It was Hartford over again. Similar to this resurgence was Mark Twain's tremendous spurt of nervous energy.

He joined the Acorns, a political club organized to break the corrupt Tammany control of New York City. On October 17, 1901, he delivered a fiery denunciation of Boss Croker, who had contemptuously referred to the club as "The Popcorns." Yet reform succeeded in the November election, sweeping Seth Low into the mayor's office by a plurality of 30,000. Mark Twain got out of a sick bed to join the jubilee parade up Broadway, and to spout soapbox eulogies of the "dear departed" of Tammany Hall:

Van Wyck, the gentle peddler of life-saving ice at 60 cents per hundred. . . . And Devery. That indescribable. . . . His character is so black that even Egyptian darkness would make white spots on it. . . . farewell to Croker forever, the Baron of Wantage, the last, and I daresay the least, desirable addition to English nobility.[28]

He went to Yale for an honorary degree, and junketed on Henry Rogers' yacht to Florida and Nassau. In 1902, going out to Missouri for another LL.D., he bore up vigorously under a hard program that might have exhausted most men, but not this one. Arriving in St. Louis on May 29, he was up, without grumbling, at the extraordinary hour of six. After talking for hours with reporters, he lunched at the Merchants' Exchange, where he made a five-minute speech, then talked with all sorts of people for two more hours until he entrained for Hannibal. There, on May 30, the schedule was similar: from eight A. M. until midnight hours of talking, taking part in a long afternoon of Decoration Day speeches, dining with John Garth, attending the high school commencement, speaking there and giving out diplomas, then more talking and handshaking, and withstanding all day long a vast deal of unnerving adulation. Afterward he called it merely "a rushing day," and insisted that he "felt no fatigue & feel none now."[29] To this lazy man, perhaps the most fatiguing experience was inaction, or silence.

At the University of Missouri, he again handed out diplomas, and made a fairly long talk. He told the watermelon story, then satirically praised himself. "Since I have been in Missouri," he said,

I have distributed more wisdom than ever before, and I am sure that much good will result. . . . I have had many honors conferred upon me, but I deserved them all. . . . I . . . am always willing to accept anything in the way of honors that you have to offer.[30]

Being funny on a solemn cap-and-gown occasion might have been out of place for anybody other than Mark Twain, but for him all rules were suspended. He alone was permitted the license of extravagant humor wherever and whenever he chose. Stopping at St. Louis on his way home, he attended the christening of a new harbor boat, *Mark Twain,* which was properly splashed with champagne by the Countess de Rochambeau. Taking a turn at the wheel, he also made a short speech, in which he commended

French explorers of the Mississippi valley. La Salle, he said, "opened up this great river and by his simple act was gathered in this great Louisiana territory. I would have done it for half the money."[31]

At the 67th birthday dinner at the Metropolitan Club on November 28, the chairman, George Harvey, played a mild joke. He introduced Howells, who read a "double-barrelled" sonnet, then called for toasts to the guest of honor. Thomas B. Reed commented on Mark Twain's inaccuracy of statement; John Kendrick Bangs read a rhymed obituary; Chauncey DePew, Hamilton Mabie, Brander Matthews, Henry Van Dyke and others damned with faint praise. As this succession of ironical toasts went on and on, the chairman gently restrained Mark Twain from jumping up to reply. Finally given the floor after a fidgety delay, he retaliated with stories about various diners. On the Rogers yacht in heavy weather, he said, Tom Reed had come lurching into the "poker chapel" in pajamas, complaining that his berth was wet. "Why, you old thing," said Mark Twain, "you ought to be ashamed of yourself—scared to that extent." He talked of growing up with John Hay in Missouri: "So we grew, John and I, and now John is Secretary of State, and I am a gentleman."[32]

His dinner assignments he took as seriously as he had taken his paid lectures. He wrote his speeches, memorized them, and depended upon ready wit, aided by experience, to furnish extemporaneous additions. Notwithstanding his remarks on the insanity of banquets, he was a sturdy principal at dinners. From 1902 to 1905, however, he was mostly absent from the speaking scene. The chief reason was the serious illness of Livy, which caused the family to move to Italy in October, 1903. After her death in Florence on June 5, 1904, he was back home again by early July, and in the fall established residence at 21 Fifth Avenue.

New York was an appropriate home for Mark Twain. He was better attuned to the feverish life of the raucous, rowdy city than he had ever been to the traditional reserve of New England. New

York gave him scope, took him to its heart as its chief citizen, dubbed him "the Belle of New York," indulged eccentricities like the white suits, and showered more affectionate attention than he had ever received in Boston. After a subdued interval of a year on Fifth Avenue, his life speeded up as he again became a public speaker. Modifying his dinner habits, he conserved energy by staying away from the turmoil of eating and music, and arriving only when the speechmaking had got down to his place on the list. That "judicious habit," he said, "has saved my life, I suppose."[33]

At the seventieth birthday dinner he was there from start to finish. Given by George Harvey at Delmonico's on December 5, 1905, it was a splendid occasion at which 170 guests, including most American writers of note, paid homage to Mark Twain. Mixing humor and pathos, he talked of his first birthday when he had no hair, of his lifelong unhealthful habits of eating and drinking, of constant smoking, especially in bed, and lack of exercise. He spoke of the first moral he ever got:

It was an old moral, an old second-hand moral, and didn't fit anyway. But if you're careful with a thing like that, and keep it in a dry place, and save it for processions, and Chautauquas, and World's Fairs, and so on, and give it a fresh coat of white-wash once in awhile, you will be surprised to see how long she will keep sweet, or at least inoffensive.[34]

Closing with the familiar words about "the Scriptural statute of limitations," he dwelt upon the privileges of a man who has reached threescore and ten. He was so much moved by the whole affair that three weeks later, addressing "Harvey the Magnificent," he said that he was only slowly recovering

from its emotions and its splendors—the most satisfying and spirit-exalting honor ever done me in all my seventy years, oh, by seventy times seventy! By George, nobody but you could have imagined and carried out that wonderful thing.[35]

Although he said that being seventy permitted a man to decline invitations and to "nestle in the chimney corner," he kept going: presiding at a Players' Club dinner, at a huge meeting in Carnegie Hall on behalf of Booker T. Washington, at another large gathering in aid of the blind, speaking to the girls of Barnard College and to the Freundschaft Society. When he spoke for the Y. M. C. A. in March, 1906, at the Majestic Theater, such a jam assembled outside that the police gathered in riot force. Inside, he was disgruntled by a dull program: a poor speaker, a poor singer, another poor speaker, a poor band, and a poor Bible-reader.

When not otherwise engaged, he listened to himself talk by dictating fragments of autobiography. He was much taken with the method because, he said, it took the stiffness and artificiality out of sentences. Talking made them more limber and casual than written words. He was right about the easy informality of his dictated sentences, yet his haphazard method of talking, without plan, on whatever was in his mind made the dictations add up to no orderly whole.

On April 19, 1906, he gave what he called his farewell lecture, appearing in Carnegie Hall on behalf of the Robert Fulton Memorial Association. The fee of $1000 he donated to the Fulton monument fund. Trying to give the old Washoe humor a final fling, he had proposed advertising announcing that Mark Twain would take "PERMANENT LEAVE (very large) of the platform (very small type)."[36] But the association rejected that idea in favor of a sober "Farewell Lecture" statement that guaranteed the presence of the Old Guard military organization, and music by the Old Guard band. The hall was festooned with bunting and crowded with cheering notables. Mark Twain started with an earnest plea for aid to stricken San Francisco, which had been devastated a few days before by the great earthquake and fire. Then he took off on nonsense. He said he had been studying "a biographical sketch of Robert Fulton, the inventor of—er—a— let's see—oh, yes, the inventor of the electric telegraph."[37] After further burlesque history, he wandered into the interviewer story, then into the yarns about grandfather's old ram, Miss Sophie's glass eye, and the man who fell into a carpet-making machine. The audience had a very good time, and so did he.

The farewell was a technicality. On May 6 he spoke at the opening of the Actors' Fund Fair in the Metropolitan Opera House. To the Associated Press on September 19—what he called the "Dinner of Associated Liars"—he appealed for simplified spelling. When his daughter, Clara, made her musical debut in Norfolk, Connecticut, her father was naturally called upon. He told the story of his stage fright before the first San Francisco lecture in 1866, and thanked the audience for appreciating Clara's singing. Her talent, he said, was hereditary. For small, secluded gatherings he read selections from the great poets.

When he went abroad for the Oxford degree in June, 1907, the warmth of his reception in England exceeded all previous welcomes. *Punch* wished him long life, happiness, and perpetual youth. He appeared to possess the youth, the years dropping away as he gamboled through a tumultuous month. The toast of London, cheered in the streets, he met everybody from King and Queen down, and spoke a number of times: at a Pilgrims' Club luncheon, at the Lord Mayor's dinner, for the American Society on the Fourth of July, at the Savage Club, *Punch* dinner, the Lord Mayor's banquet in Liverpool. In the Liverpool speech, his last in England, on July 10, he closed with the moving "homeward bound" farewell. Besides the honor of the Oxford degree there was

another lofty honor, a continuous honor, an honor which has flowed serenely along, without halt or obstruction . . . the heart-felt grip of the hand, and the welcome that does not descend from the pale-gray matter of the brain, but rushes up with the red blood from the heart.

For one hour out of twenty-four this whole-souled greeting made him humble, like the skipper of the insignificant coaster, *Mary Ann*. During the other twenty-three he rode "high on the crests of your approval" like a proud Indiaman, "the *Begum*, of Bengal, 142 days out from Canton—homeward bound!"[38] T. P. "Tay Pay" O'Connor, remarking upon Mark Twain's unnoticed oratorical gifts and his skill at shifting from gay to grave, said: "It is only a great litterateur that could conceive such a passage; it is only a great orator that could so deliver it." He commented on "management of voice which has a great gamut of melodies—a voice the most perfect singer or actor might envy."[39] Mark Twain was at his best for the British, using all the artistry gained in forty years of study of the speaker's craft.

At New York metropolitan reporters met him in numbers proper to the reception of an ambassador-at-large. Answering many questions, he diplomatically evaded others, such as whether British women were better-looking than American. He said that he did not mind being seventy-two. "Every year that I gain furnishes a new privilege, and all I want to dodge is second childhood."[40] After the turbulence of England, he found the quiet of Tuxedo lonesome, something of a letdown. As if trying to recapture exhilarating excitement, he spent a good deal of time dictating accounts of British functions that had honored him. Like an innocent who had never got over astonishment at moving in exalted circles, he made these memoranda sound like society pages replete with names of the titled and famous. They are among the least interesting of the autobiographical dictations.

On September 23 he spoke on Fulton Day at the Jamestown Exposition. Using again the technique of garbled history, he had Admiral Harrington on the stage as confederate, whom he pretended to ask about facts that had slipped his mind. "No doubt," he said,

you have heard . . . about Robert Fulton . . . but his little steamboat is suffering neglect. It was the most important steamboat in the world. I was there and saw it. . . . The boat was one—[whispering to Admiral Harrington] he said ten feet long. The breadth of that boat was [consulting the Admiral] two hundred feet.[41]

So he went on, with whispered conferences, telling of the initial trip of Fulton's steamboat from Jersey City to Chicago by way of Albany, and interpolating the jingle about the town of Param where they don't give a —.

He said that he had renounced the dinner habit, but he was on hand with a speech at the New York Engineers' Club dinner honoring Andrew Carnegie. Making game of Carnegie's simplified spelling, he advocated instead "a sane and healthy and competent alphabet instead of a hospital of comminuted cripples and eunuchs." Admitting some merit in Carnegie's system, he remarked that it was "well enough, but like chastity . . . it can be carried too far!"[42]

On January 11, 1908, he was chief guest and speaker at his last Lotos Club dinner. On the menu were Innocent Oysters Abroad, Roughing It Soup, Fish Huckleberry Finn, Joan of Arc Filet of Beef, Gilded Age Duck, Punch-Brothers-Punch, and White Elephant Coffee. Mark Twain was beginning to feel the strain of these affairs, for about halfway through, when Jumping Frog Terrapin came on, he had to retire for a nap. Coming back to speak, he gave an unabashed recital of compliments paid him. "Other people," he said, "collect autographs, dogs, and cats, and I collect compliments. I have brought them along." He told the story of the long-ago Red Dog introduction, and read laudatory words by Howells, Hamilton Mabie, and others. The most satisfying praise had come from a little girl in Montana, who said of a photograph of Mark Twain: "We've got a John the Baptist like that. Only ours has more trimmings." "I suppose," said he, "she meant the halo."[43]

After an interval in Bermuda, he had a busy spring, speaking at a Pilgrims Club dinner for Whitelaw Reid, at a cartoonists' dinner, at the dedication of City College, at its alumni meeting, at the American Booksellers dinner, and the Victoria Day dinner of the British Schools and University Club. For the Pilgrims he played briefly upon the hands-across-the-sea motif, then said that removing "In God We Trust" from our coins had caused the financial panic of 1907. At the dedication of City College he was a spectacular figure, brilliant in the scarlet gown of Oxford, and the center of whooping attention. For the alumni, at the Waldorf, he returned to the coin motto. It was a gross overstatement, he said. "In the unimportant cases, perhaps, we do trust in God— that is, if we rule out the gamblers and burglars and plumbers, for of course they do not believe in God."⁴⁴ Then he told the christening story.

In June he took part in the dedication of the Thomas Bailey Aldrich Museum at Portsmouth, New Hampshire. The weather was hot, the trip laborious, the procession of speakers wearisome, and Mrs. Aldrich, according to Mark Twain, less than gracious. Becoming impatient with the "funeral" as "Mourner after mourner crept to the front and meekly and weakly and sneakingly read the poem which he had written for the occasion," he discarded his prepared spech in favor of impromptu nonsense. That, he said, would have pleased Aldrich better than all the lugubrious gloom. Dictating an amusing and exasperated account of the affair, he said: "It was dreary; it was devilish; it was hard to endure; there were two sweltering hours of it, but I would not have missed it for twice the heat and exhaustion and Boston and Maine travel it cost, and the cinders I swallowed."⁴⁵

Settled at Stormfield by late June, he held open house for the people of Redding, entertained many visitors, and played billiards with Paine until two, three, or four A.M. Recalling Oxford, he planned to return there in 1910 to add his own vivid red splash to the shining pageant. He kept on talking. When he opened the Mark Twain Library of Redding, he said: "I like to talk. It would take more than the Redding air to make me keep still, and I like to instruct people. It's noble to be good, and it's nobler to teach others to be good, and less trouble."⁴⁶

The man seemed indestructible, his vitality exhaustless. Yet time was running out, and his speaking days were drawing to an end. On April 3, 1909, he was in Norfolk, Virginia, for a dinner in honor of Henry Rogers. Mark Twain told the story of the Webster Company in 1894, and paid affectionate tribute to the man who had pulled him out of a bad hole:

You see his white mustache and his hair trying to get white (he is always trying to look like me—I don't blame him for that). These are only emblematic of his character, and that is all. I say, without exception, hair and all, he is the whitest man I have ever known.[47]

If that description flattered overmuch the ruthless Standard Oil operator, it was appropriate to the friend. On May 7 he attended his last dinner in New York, in honor of District Attorney Jerome. Introduced as the final authority on public questions and public men, Mark Twain praised the probity of Jerome, then regretted that, since he had moved away from New York, he could no longer vote for so reputable a public servant. "I am a farmer," he said,

. . . up in Connecticut, and winning laurels. Those people already speak with such high favor, admiration, of my farming, and they say . . . I am the only man that has ever come to that region who could make two blades of grass grow where only three grew before.[48]

On June 8 he set out for Catonsville, Maryland, to speak at the commencement exercises of the girl graduates of St. Timothy's School. Stopping overnight in Baltimore, he provoked remark by his white suit, met the press, and discoursed amiably on the unique excellence of Baltimore fried chicken, the stimulating influence of Baltimore's pretty girls, and getting old. "I am just as young now as I was 40 years ago. Why, I don't see any reason why I shouldn't live for another hundred years. There's nothing funny about that."[49] There was an ominous reason. The night before, he had complained of an odd, persistent pain in the chest. It was the first symptom of the angina that caused his death about eleven months later.

At Catonsville, he amused the girls with a short list of useful precepts:

There are three things . . . which I consider excellent advice. First, girls, don't smoke—to excess. I am 73½ years old and have been smoking 73 of them. But I never smoke to excess—that is, I smoke in moderation, only one cigar at a time. Also, never drink—to excess. Third, don't marry—to excess.[50]

He illustrated the old adage, "Honesty is the best policy," with a story of being stranded in New York and in need of three dollars: so he appropriated a wandering dog, which he sold for that sum. Then, finding the rightful owner who offered a reward of three dollars for the lost dog, he hunted up the man to whom he had sold it, retrieved the dog, and ended with the three dollars he needed. Prolonged with drawling detail and mock seriousness, this story delighted the audience. He gave out diplomas, and afterward, adjourning to the lawn where he lighted a black cigar, docilely posed for snapshot after snapshot: alone, with one white-clad graduate bearing flowers, with two graduates bearing flowers, with bevies, with the whole class. Approached by one more interviewer, he said:

No, I have nothing to say worth while. People are constantly expecting me to say . . . clever and brilliant things. But that is . . . hard to do unless one has some inspiration. . . . You can't always say beautiful things at random. This morning I got the inspiration for my address from the beautiful girls and the flowers and the harmonious surroundings.[51]

Perhaps. Yet as a seasoned campaigner he had probably given some thought to his address much earlier.

The commencement speech at St. Timothy's, on June 10, 1909, was the last public appearance of Mark Twain. Thereafter his talk was conversational, the chief beneficiary being his biographer, Paine. There were long chats on books, religion, science, mankind, and the universe in general. The younger man was so dazzled by this extraordinary talker that he could only say: "For me, of course, nothing can ever be like it again in this world. One is not likely to associate twice with a being from another star."[52] James M. Barrie called it "witching talk." In a reminiscence that may serve as a symbolical summary of Mark Twain's speaking career and of his character, Barrie said: "I see myself getting closer and closer to him as he neared the point of what he was saying; then his voice fell and he turned his face away from me and his one hope seemed to be that I should not catch his meaning. He always appeared to be pained in a gentle lovable way if his listeners smiled, and it almost broke him up if we laughed."[53] He was, said Brander Matthews, "a born actor, a born speech maker, a born story teller."[54]

Notes

Abbreviations in Notes (full references in Bibliography):

Autobiography—Mark Twain's Autobiography
Berg—Henry W. and Albert A. Berg Collection
*Biography—*Albert Bigelow Paine, *Mark Twain: A Biography*
*Enterprise—*Virginia City, Nevada, *Territorial Enterprise*
*Fairbanks—*Mark Twain, *Mark Twain to Mrs. Fairbanks*
Letters—Mark Twain's Letters
LL—The Love Letters of Mark Twain
*MFMT—*Clara Clemens, *My Father, Mark Twain*
*MTE—*Mark Twain, *Mark Twain in Eruption*
*MTP—*Mark Twain Papers, University of California
*Notebook—*Mark Twain, *Mark Twain's Notebook*
O.L.C.—Olivia Langdon Clemens
S.L.C.—Samuel L. Clemens
Speeches—Mark Twain's Speeches

1. YOUNG SAM CLEMENS

1. Fort Wayne, Indiana, *Daily News,* February 6, 1885.
2. S. L. C. to O. L. C., February 7, 1885, MTP.
3. S. L. C. to Miss Noyes, February 23, 1882, MTP.
4. S. L. C. to Mary Rogers, August 4, 1906, typescript copy, MTP.
5. C. J. Armstrong, "Sam Clemens Considered Becoming a Preacher," *The Twainian,* Vol. 4, No. 8 (May, 1945), 1.

6. *MTE*, 390.

7. *Ibid.*, 392

8. *Letters*, I, 122.

9. *Ibid.*

10. Brooklyn *Daily News*, February 8, 1873.

11. Baltimore *American*, November 29, 1884.

12. S. L. C. to Mrs. Ogden, October 13, 1909, longhand copy, MTP.

13. Emerson's son told Mark Twain that Emerson once bewildered a country audience that mistook him for Artemus Ward. After a solemn hour the verdict was that, though moderately funny, he had been less hilarious than expected. Notebook No. 38, 1905, MTP.

14. Fred W. Lorch, "Mark Twain in Iowa," 421.

15. *Enterprise*, May 3, 1863.

16. The Houghton Library, Harvard University, which found it among the papers of Senator Sumner. He probably got it from Governor Nye when Nye was lobbying for Nevada statehood in Washington.

17. See Mark Twain, *Mark Twain of the Enterprise*, 102; also Claude M. Simpson, Jr., "Captain Jim and the 'Third House.'"

18. *Enterprise*, n. d. Reprinted in Virginia City *Bulletin*, December 28, 1863.

19. *Biography*, I, 245.

20. St. Louis *Republican*, March 24, 1867.

21. Keokuk, Iowa, *Gate City*, April 7, 1867.

22. January 30, 1864.

2. FIRST SAN FRANCISCO LECTURE

1. Marysville, California, *Daily Appeal*, October 7, 1866.

2. G. E. B., "Mark Twain as He Was Known During His Stay on the Pacific Slope," San Francisco *Call*, April 17, 1887. Paine says that the editor was Col. John McComb, of the *Alta California*. In *Roughing It*, Mark Twain refers merely to "an editor." Allowing for the vagaries of memory after twenty-one years, the *Call's* story is as plausible as any other.

3. September 29, 1866.

4. October 2, 1866.

5. September 30, 1866.

6. October 2, 1866.

7. October 2, 1866.

8. Marysville, California, *Daily Appeal*, October 7, 1866.

9. For a more detailed analysis of this parallelism, see Paul Fatout, "Mark Twain's First Lecture: a Parallel."

10. October 3, 1866.

11. October 3, 1866.

12. October 7, 1866.

13. October 6, 1866.

14. Walter Francis Frear, *Mark Twain and Hawaii*, Appendix D2, 431-36.

15. San Francisco, California, *Call*, April 17, 1887.

16. Oakland, California, *Daily News*, October 10, 1866.

3. TOURING SPEAKER

1. Unless otherwise noted, comments by Mark Twain in this chapter are from his "Interior Notes," Nos. 1 and 2, San Francisco *Evening Bulletin*, November 30 and December 6, 1866.

2. Sacramento, California, *Union*, October 13, 1866.

3. October 11, 1866.

4. October 14, 1866.

5. Como, Nevada, *Sentinel*, June 4, 1864.

6. Virginia City *Daily Trespass*, April 27, 1868. See also the formula for the "west-sou'-wester," Letter No. VI, San Francisco *Alta California*, March 17, 1867.

7. October 11, 1866.

8. October 21, 1866.

9. Nevada City, California, *Gazette*, October 19, 1866.

10. *Autobiography*, I, 161.

11. *Biography*, I, 295.

12. Notebook No. 38, 1905, MTP.

13. October 19, 1866.

14. October 29, 1866.

15. October 30, 1866.

16. Steve Gillis to A. B. Paine, c. 1907, *The Twainian*, January-February, 1956, 3.

17. *Letters*, I, 121.

18. Sacramento *Union*, November 6, 1866.

19. Autobiographical dictations, August 31, 1906, MTP.

20. November 14, 1866.

21. November 12, 1866.

22. November 18, 1866.

23. S. L. C. to James Redpath, January 22, 1871, Will M. Clemens, "Mark Twain on the Lecture Platform."

24. Walter Francis Frear, *Mark Twain and Hawaii*, 209.

25. Bradford A. Booth, "Mark Twain's Comments on Holmes's *Autocrat*," 461.

26. Autobiographical dictations, August 10, 1906, MTP.

27. November 29, 1866.

28. December 1, 1866.

29. December 11, 1866.

30. Notebook No. 32, June 2–July 24, 1897, MTP.

31. San Francisco *Alta California*, December 8, 1866.

32. December 10, 1866.

33. December 10, 1866. Walter Frear believes that this letter was an expression of genuine distress. Surely not. The manner is too much like that of earlier extravagance on the *Enterprise*.

34. San Francisco *Alta California*, December 15, 1866.

35. Will M. Clemens, "Mark Twain on the Lecture Platform."

36. *Autobiography*, I, 351.

4.   WESTERNER IN THE EAST

1. Letter No. XXV, San Francisco *Alta California*, August 11, 1867.

2. *LL*, 352.

3. Letter No. XIII, San Francisco *Alta California*, May 19, 1867.

4. *Ibid*.

5. Vancouver, British Columbia, *News Advertiser*, August 20, 1895.

6. T. P. McMurray to S. L. C., July 16, 1872, MTP.

7. Fort Madison, Iowa, *Democrat*, January 21, 1885.

8. *Reminiscences of Senator William M. Stewart of Nevada*, 219.

9. *Letters*, II, 449.

10. "Utah's War Governor Talks of Many Famous Men," New York *Times*, October 1, 1911.

11. *Letters*, I, 124.

12. *Autobiography*, I, 355.

13. *Ibid*.

14. Brooklyn *Union*, May 10, 1867.

15. Letter No. XIX, San Francisco *Alta California*, June 30, 1867.

16. S. L. C. to Frank Fuller, August 7, November 24, December 2 and 5, 1867, typescript copies, MTP.

17. *Fairbanks*, 8.

18. *Enterprise*, January 31, 1868.

19. San Francisco *Alta California*, February 19, 1868.

20. *Ibid*.

21. *Fairbanks*, 16n.

22. San Francisco *Alta California,* February 5, 1868. It has been conjectured that the young lady was Olivia Langdon. Aside from the question of whether or not he had yet met her, it is doubtful that he would have referred to her in these terms.

23. A forerunner of the Brigham Young story as told by "Johnson" in Chapter XV of *Roughing It.*

24. *Letters,* I, 143. Probably the lecture represented by fragmentary notes on the Ms. entitled "Lecture Notes for Innocents Abroad," DW 16, MTP.

25. Washington, D. C., *Daily Morning Chronicle,* January 11, 1868.

5. RETURN TO CALIFORNIA

1. April 12, 1868.
2. *Fairbanks,* 26.
3. Virginia City *Daily Trespass,* April 27, 1868.
4. April 18, 1868.
5. San Francisco *Call,* May 20, 1868.
6. April 16, 1868.
7. Joel Benton, "Reminiscences of Eminent Lecturers," 610.
8. Chicago *Evening Post,* December 20, 1871.
9. April 24, 1868.
10. April 28, 1868. Adah Isaacs Menken, the delectable Mazeppa of flesh-colored tights, had once been given a gold bar worth $2000 by the miners of Virginia City. Artemus Ward had received a gold chain so heavy that he found it uncomfortable to wear.
11. Will M. Clemens, *Mark Twain, His Life and Work,* 69. He gives the date as 1867 (when Mark Twain was not in the West), says that the subject was "The Future of Nevada," and makes the scene the Episcopal Church. Otherwise, the story is plausible.
12. Grass Valley, California, *Daily National,* May 20, 1868.
13. San Francisco *Daily Dramatic Chronicle,* June 13, 1868.
14. *Fairbanks,* 33.
15. San Francisco *Alta California,* July 3, 1868.
16. July 4, 1868.
17. *Fairbanks,* 34.

6. THE LECTURE CIRCUIT

1. Sacramento, California, *Rescue,* November 1866.
2. Notebook No. 10, 1868, MTP.
3. J. G. Holland, *Plain Talks on Familiar Subjects,* 117.

4. *Fairbanks*, 146n.

5. *Letters*, I, 429. See also remarks on Talmage in "Extract From Captain Stormfield's Visit to Heaven."

6. N. d. Reprinted in Indianapolis *Journal*, December 25, 1868.

7. *Autobiography*, I, 159.

8. Autobiographical dictations, April 11, 1906, MTP.

9. March, 1872, 489.

10. *Enterprise*, January 3, 1869.

11. N. d. Reprinted in Galena, Illinois, *Gazette*, November 9, 1869.

12. *Fairbanks*, 44.

13. Cleveland *Herald*, n. d. Clipping, MTP.

14. Chicago *Daily Tribune*, January 8, 1869.

15. Cleveland *Leader*, December 18, 1884.

16. Mark Twain, *Mark Twain, Business Man*, 102.

17. S. L. C. to Mrs. Fairbanks, November 26, 1868, Berg.

18. Chicago *Daily Tribune*, January 8, 1869.

19. LL, 24.

20. Newark, New Jersey, *Press*, n. d. Reprinted in Ottawa, Illinois, *Republican*, January 21, 1869.

21. San Francisco *The Golden Era*, January 14, 1866. From Mark Twain's correspondence to the *Enterprise*.

22. *MFMT*, 52.

23. S. L. C. to O. L. (C.), February 26, 1869, MTP.

24. "Josh Billings' Philosophy About Lekturing," unidentified clipping, Mark Twain's Scrapbook, 1869-1873, MTP.

25. Decatur, Illinois, *Republican*, January 14, 1869.

26. LL, 49.

27. January 20, 1869.

28. *Ibid.*

29. Cleveland *Leader*, January 23, 1869.

30. *Fairbanks*, 70.

31. *Ibid.*, 75.

32. Booth, "Mark Twain's Comments on Holmes's *Autocrat*," 162.

33. *Autobiography*, I, 149.

34. *Fairbanks*, 85n.

7. SECOND-EASTERN TOUR

1. LL, 108.

2. *Notebook,* 172.

3. LL, 121.

4. Exeter, New Hampshire, *News-Letter*, November 13, 1871.
5. *Letters*, I, 168.
6. Geneseo, New York, *Geneseo Valley Herald*, March 11, 1869.
7. *Fairbanks*, 113.
8. Providence, Rhode Island, *Herald*, November 10, 1869.
9. *Letters*, I, 168.
10. Boston *Daily Advertiser*, November 11, 1869.
11. *LL*, 116.
12. Notes for "Roughing It" lecture, DV 78, Paine 115, MTP.
13. *Autobiography*, I, 152-53.
14. New Britain, Connecticut, *Record*, December 17, 1869.
15. Troy, New York, *Times*, January 12, 1870.
16. *LL*, 121.
17. *Ibid.*, 129.
18. *Ibid.*, 130.
19. *The Twainian*, Vol. IV, No. 2 (November, 1944), 6.
20. December 17, 1869.
21. *Autobiography*, I, 151.
22. *LL*, 41.
23. *MFMT*, 209.
24. *LL*, 140-41.
25. *Autobiography*, I, 162.
26. *LL*, 138.
27. S. L. C. to James B. Pond, February 12, n. d., Berg.
28. December 4, 1869.
29. N. d. Reprinted in *Enterprise*, December 17, 1869.
30. New Haven, Connecticut, *Daily Palladium*, December 28, 1869.
31. Jamestown, New York, *Journal*, January 28, 1870.
32. *Letters*, II, 527-28.
33. *LL*, 137.
34. Pawtucket, Rhode Island, *Gazette and Chronicle*, December 17, 1869.
35. December 17, 1869.
36. New Haven *Daily Palladium*, December 28, 1869.
37. Oswego, New York, *Commercial Advertiser and Times*, January 17, 1870.
38. Cohoes, New York, *Cataract*, January 13, 1870.
39. *MFMT*, 70.
40. February 5, 1870.

8. INTERLUDE

1. *Fairbanks,* 114.
2. *Ibid.*
3. *Letters,* I, 172.
4. *Ibid.,* 173.
5. "The Josh Billings Papers," clippings, 1871, MTP.
6. January 7, 1870.
7. San Francisco *The Golden Era,* May 29, 1870.
8. *Fairbanks,* 145n.
9. Springfield, Illinois, *Illinois State Journal,* December 20, 1871.
10. Will M. Clemens, "Mark Twain on the Lecture Platform."
11. *Autobiography,* I, 157.
12. Kingston, New York, *Argus,* December 22, 1869.
13. Logansport, Indiana, *Democratic Pharos,* January 17, 1872.
14. "Mark at Home," San Francisco *The Golden Era,* November 27, 1870.
15. *Fairbanks,* 152.

9. MOST DETESTABLE LECTURE CAMPAIGN

1. S. L. C. to James Redpath, June 10, 1871, MTP.
2. *Letters,* I, 190.
3. *Fairbanks,* 159.
4. *Ibid.,* 158.
5. *Ibid.,* 155.
6. LL, 161.
7. Austin, Nevada, *Reese River Reveille,* November, 9, 1871.
8. LL, 162.
9. November 1, 1871.
10. November 3, 1871.
11. LL, 162.
12. November 13, 1871.
13. November 11, 1871.
14. *MFMT,* 45.
15. LL, 163-64.
16. *Ibid.,* 163.
17. November 16, 1871.
18. Brooklyn *Daily Times,* November 22, 1871.
19. Easton, Pennsylvania, *Daily Express,* November 24, 1871.

20. *LL*, 165-66.
21. W. H. Merrill, "When Mark Twain Lectured," 199.
22. N. d. Reprinted in *Lyceum Circular*, Boston Lyceum Bureau, January 1, 1872.
23. December 16, 1871.
24. December 22, 1871.
25. December 18, 1871.
26. *LL*, 170.
27. *Ibid.*, 171.
28. December 28, 1871.
29. January 4, 1872.
30. *MFMT*, 9-12. ·
31. *Letters*, I, 193.
32. "The Rambler," *The Book Buyer*, Vol. XXII, No. 3 (April, 1901), 179.
33. *Ibid.*
34. *MFMT*, 52.
35. *LL*, 172.
36. *Ibid.*, 173.
37. January 19, 1872.
38. New York *Herald*, January 25, 1872.
39. *Fairbanks*, 160.

10.   ERSTWHILE INNOCENT ABROAD

1. *Fairbanks*, 160.
2. *Biography*, II, 473.
3. *LL*, 181.
4. *Fairbanks*, 166.
5. *Letters*, I, 199.
6. Will M. Clemens, "Mark Twain on the Lecture Platform."
7. Unidentified clipping, Mark Twain's Scrapbook, 1872, MTP.
8. *Letters From the Sandwich Islands*, 222.
9. S. L. C. to Will? March 20, 1873, MTP.
10. New York *Herald*, July 9, 1873.
11. *Speeches*, 42-44.
12. Lafayette, Indiana, *Daily Courier*, January 14, 1874.
13. *Fairbanks*, 174.
14. October 14, 1873.
15. Clipping, n. d. MTP.
16. Basil Tozer, *Recollections of a Rolling Stone*, 40.

17. October 17, 1873.
18. London *Observer*, n. d., MTP.
19. October 25, 1873.
20. April 22, 1873.
21. Charles Warren Stoddard, *Exits and Entrances*, 69.
22. December 12, 1873.
23. Will M. Clemens, "Mark Twain on the Lecture Platform."
24. *Autobiography*, I, 140.
25. S. L. C. to O. L. C., December 13, 1873, MTP.
26. Stoddard, *Exits and Entrances*, 73-74.

11.   UNDER SHELTER AT HOME

1. Cyril Clemens, *Josh Billings, Yankee Humorist*, 124.
2. *Letters*, I, 311.
3. *MTE*, 215.
4. *Biography*, II, 520-21.
5. *Letters*, I, 319.
6. *Fairbanks*, 234.
7. Alton, Illinois, *Daily Telegraph*, December 22, 1871.
8. February 4, 1875.
9. March 14, 1875.
10. *Letters*, I, 328.
11. Notebook No. 14, February 26–September 8, 1879, MTP.
12. *Ibid.*
13. Typescript, "Spelling Match and Festival," 1877, MTP.
14. New York *Times*, October 7, 1877.
15. Frank Harris, *Contemporary Portraits, Fourth Series*, 162-73.
16. See Henry Nash Smith, "That Hideous Mistake of Poor Clemens's."
17. New York *Times*, November 13, 1879.
18. Documents, 1879, MTP.
19. *Letters*, I, 372.
20. *Ibid.*, 371.
21. *The Society of the Army of the Potomac. Twelfth Annual Reunion*, 62-63.

12.   GENIUS AND VERSATILITY

1. Lucy Leffingwell Bikle, *George W. Cable: His Life and Letters*, 134.
2. Brooklyn *Eagle*, November 23, 1884.
3. Springfield, Illinois, *Illinois State Journal*, January 8, 1885.

4. Utica, New York, *Morning Herald*, December, 6, 1884.
5. November 19, 1884.
6. *Letters*, I, 426-27.
7. Guy A. Cardwell, *Twins of Genius*, 65.
8. Arlin Turner, *George W. Cable*, 187.
9. July 28, 1884.
10. O. L. C. to S. L. C., November 21, 1884, MTP.
11. O. L. C. to S. L. C., November 24, 1884, MTP.
12. Philadelphia *Press*, November 22, 1884.
13. Turner, *George W. Cable*, 173.
14. *Letters*, II, 450.
15. Davenport, Iowa, *Democrat*, February 2, 1885.
16. Philadelphia *Press*, November 22, 1884.
17. Notebook No. 23 (I), July 1–November 1, 1888, MTP.
18. New York *Sun*, November 19, 1884.
19. *LL*, 237.
20. Baltimore *American*, November 29, 1884.
21. South Bend, Indiana, *Evening Register*, February 5, 1885.
22. Turner, *George W. Cable*, 183.
23. *Notebook*, 172-73.
24. Rochester, New York, *Herald*, December 8, 1884.
25. Springfield, Massachusetts, *Republican*, November 8, 1884.
26. Detroit *Free Press*, December 17, 1884.
27. Buffalo *Times*, December 11, 1884.
28. *MFMT*, 216-17.
29. November 19, 1884.
30. November 8, 1884.
31. November 14, 1884.
32. November 19, 1884.
33. Albert Bigelow Paine, *Thomas Nast, His Period and His Pictures*, 513.
34. James B. Pond, Holograph Cash-book, November 5, 1884–February 28, 1885, Berg.
35. S. L. C. to James B. Pond, November 15, 1884, Berg.
36. Rochester, New York, *Democrat and Chronicle*, December 7, 1884.
37. Detroit *Post*, December 17, 1884.
38. *Ibid.*
39. Turner, *George W. Cable*, 174.
40. O. L. C. to S. L. C., January 2, 1885, MTP.
41. *LL*, 234.
42. Cardwell, *Twins of Genius*, 55.

43. *LL*, 224.
44. *Ibid.*, 231-32.
45. Turner, *George W. Cable*, 180.
46. *LL*, 229.
47. *Ibid.*, 233.
48. *Ibid.*, 230-31.
49. *Ibid.*, 233.
50. Cardwell, *Twins of Genius*, 54.
51. *Ibid.*, 53.
52. February 8, 1885.
53. February 21, 1885.
54. February 20, 1885.
55. February 14, 1885.
56. *LL*, 235.
57. Bikle, *George W. Cable: His Life and Letters*, 139.
58. *Ibid.*, 141.
59. See Chapter XV, Arlin Turner, *George W. Cable*.
60. Arlin Turner, "A Professional Newspaper Liar," 27.
61. Cardwell, *Twins of Genius*, 108.
62. *Ibid.*, 109.
63. William Dean Howells to S. L. C., April 20, 1885, MTP.
64. Seattle, Washington, *Post-Intelligencer*, August 14, 1895.
65. Vol. 12, No. 5 (April, 1901), 146-49.
66. Notebook No. 32 (II), June 2–July 24, 1897, MTP.
67. Cardwell, *Twins of Genius*, 111.

13.   ANOTHER RETIREMENT

1. S. L. C. to John Garth, May 6, 1890, typescript copy, MTP.
2. S. L. C. to James B. Pond, November 18, 1886, Berg.
3. Unidentified clipping, MTP.
4. James B. Pond, *Eccentricities of Genius*, 231-32.
5. *Biography*, III, 877.
6. *MFMT*, 133.
7. New Bedford, Massachusetts, *Daily Mercury*, February 23, 1894.
8. Notebook No. 20, August 20, 1885–June 20, 1886, MTP.
9. Notebook No. 21, September 8, 1885–May 23, 1887, MTP.
10. *Ibid.*
11. *The Twainian*, Vol. 5, No. 1 (January-February, 1946), 2.

14. AROUND THE WORLD

1. *MFMT,* 179.
2. S. L. C. to Henry Rogers, April 2, 1895, Berg.
3. *Letters,* II, 627.
4. July 18, 1895.
5. New York *Times,* July 23, 1895.
6. *Letters,* II, 628.
7. Duluth, Minnesota, *Commonwealth,* July 23, 1895.
8. Pond, *Eccentricities of Genius,* 206.
9. July 27, 1895.
10. Notebook No. 28a (I), May 15–August 23, 1895; No. 30 (I), May 1–30, 1896, MTP.
11. M. B. C., "Mark Twain as a Reader," 6.
12. Winnipeg *Free Press,* July 27, 1895.
13. August 1, 1895.
14. *Biography,* III, 1003.
15. *Notebook,* 246.
16. Pond, *Eccentricities of Genius,* 210.
17. *Notebook,* 248.
18. Pond, *Eccentricities of Genius,* 214.
19. Olympia, Washington, *Washington Standard,* August 30, 1895.
20. August 9, 1895.
21. August 11, 1895.
22. Tacoma *Morning Union,* August 13, 1895.
23. Seattle *Post-Intelligencer,* August 14, 1895.
24. Pond, *Eccentricities of Genius,* 218.
25. *Notebook,* 248.
26. *Ibid.,* 249.
27. *Ibid.*
28. *Ibid.,* 264.
29. Unidentified clipping, January 28, 1896, MTP.
30. September 28, 1895.
31. Unidentified clipping, n. d., MTP.
32. Sydney *Sunday Times,* September 22, 1895.
33. September 17, 1895.
34. Sydney *Sunday Tribune,* September 22, 1895.
35. *Biography,* III, 1010.
36. Mark Twain, *Following the Equator,* I, 167
37. September 28, 1895.

38. Johannesburg *Times*, May 21, 1896.
39. *Notebook*, 252.
40. Adelaide *South Australian Register*, October 14, 1895.
41. *Ibid.*, October 15, 1895.
42. *Notebook*, 265.
43. October 14, 1895.
44. October 24, 1895.
45. Mark Twain, *Following the Equator*, I, 293.
46. *Ibid.*, 299.
47. *Notebook*, 261.
48. *Ibid.*, 259.
49. Pietermaritzburg *Natal Witness*, May 18, 1896.
50. *Notebook*, 266.
51. Mark Twain, *Following the Equator*, II, 23.
52. *Ibid.*, 160.
53. *Bombay Gazette*, January 23, 1896.
54. January 28, 1896.
55. Calcutta *The Englishman*, February 11, 1896.
56. *Letters*, II, 633.
57. *Notebook*, 289.
58. Mark Twain, *Following the Equator*, II, 327-28.
59. May 22, 1896.
60. *Notebook*, 292-93.
61. Queenstown *Representative*, June 8, 1896.
62. *Notebook*, 293.
63. New York *Times*, October 16, 1900.
64. Mark Twain, *Following the Equator*, II, 387.
65. *Ibid.*, 389.
66. *Ibid.*, 402.
67. Unidentified Cape Town clipping, July 11, 1896, MTP.
68. S. L. C. to Henry Rogers, July ? 1896, typescript copy, MTP.

15.   EMERITUS

1. N. d., clipping, MTP.
2. New York *Herald* n. d. Reprinted in *The Scrap-Book*, June, 1897, 151-52.
3. *Ibid.*, 152.
4. See DV 238, Ms. and notes (in three sections) on the New York Lecture, 1867, MTP.
5. William Ellsworth, *A Golden Age of Authors*, 227.

6. Unidentified clipping, August, 1901, MTP.
7. Pond, *Eccentricities of Genius*, 226.
8. *Letters*, II, 685.
9. *Speeches*, 173.
10. N. d. Reprinted in New York *Times Saturday Supplement*, March 12, 1898, 169.
11. *Letters*, II, 688.
12. *Ibid.*, 791.
13. *Notebook*, 371.
14. New York *Times Saturday Supplement*, July 7, 1899, 461.
15. *Letters*, II, 791.
16. *MTE*, 321.
17. New York *Times*, November 13, 1900.
18. *Ibid.*, November 16, 1900.
19. *Ibid.*, December 7, 1900.
20. *Ibid.*, December 13, 1900.
21. *Ibid.*, January 5, 1901.
22. *Ibid.*, January 21, 1901.
23. N. d. Reprinted in New York *Times*, February 7, 1901.
24. January 7, 1901.
25. *LL*, 333.
26. New York *Times*, February 12, 1901.
27. *Ibid.*, March 31, 1901.
28. *Ibid.*, November 7, 1901.
29. *LL*, 338.
30. New York *Times*, June 5, 1902.
31. *Ibid.*, June 7, 1902.
32. *Ibid.*, November 30, 1902.
33. *MTE*, 322.
34. New York *Times*, December 6, 1905.
35. Willis Fletcher, *George Harvey*, 448.
36. *Letters*, II, 793.
37. New York *Times*, April 20, 1906.
38. *Biography*, IV, 1401-1402.
39. *T. P.'s Weekly*, July 19, 1907.
40. New York *Times*, July 23, 1907.
41. *New York at the Jamestown Exposition*, 415.
42. *MTE*, 60.
43. New York *Times*, January 12, 1908.
44. *Ibid.*, May 15, 1908.
45. *MTE*, 303.

46. *Biography*, IV, 1472.

47. *Ibid.*, 1491.

48. New York *Times*, May 8, 1909.

49. Baltimore *News*, June 10, 1909.

50. Baltimore *Sun.*, June 11, 1909.

51. Baltimore *American*, June 10, 1909.

52. *Biography*, IV, 1505.

53. Mark Twain, *Who Was Sarah Findlay?*, 7-8.

54. Brander Matthews, "Mark Twain as Speech Maker and Story Teller," 24.

Bibliography

UNPUBLISHED MATERIAL

C. Waller Barrett Collection, New York, N. Y.
Henry W. and Albert A. Berg Collection, Public Library, New York, N. Y.
Lilly Collection, Indiana University, Bloomington, Indiana.
The Mark Twain Papers, University of California, Berkeley.

BOOKS AND ARTICLES

"About the Program of that 'Babies' Banquet." *The Twainian,* Vol. IV, No. 2 (November, 1944), 4-6.
Aldrich, Mrs. Thomas Bailey. *Crowding Memories.* New York, 1920.
Among the Humorists and After Dinner Speakers. Arranged by William Patten. New York, 1909.
Armstrong, C. J. "Sam Clemens Considered Becoming a Preacher," *The Twainian,* Vol. 4, No. 8 (May, 1945), 1.
Bainton, George. *The Art of Authorship.* New York, 1890.
"Belaboring the Brahmans Again," *Literary Digest,* Vol. LXIII, No. 1537 (October 4, 1919), 31.
Bellamy, Gladys Carmen. *Mark Twain as a Literary Artist.* Oklahoma, 1950.
Benson, Ivan. *Mark Twain's Western Years.* Stanford, 1938.
Benton, Joel. "Reminiscences of Eminent Lecturers," *Harper's,* Vol. XCVI, No. DLXXIV (March, 1898), 603-14.

Bikle, Lucy Leffingwell Cable. *George W. Cable: His Life and Letters*. New York, 1928.

Bode, Carl. *The American Lyceum*. New York, 1956.

Booth, Bradford, A. "Mark Twain's Comments on Holmes's *Autocrat*," *American Literature*, Vol. 21, No. 4 (January, 1950), 456-63.

Burnett, Ruth A. "Mark Twain in the Northwest," *Pacific Northwest Quarterly*, Vol. XLII (July, 1951), 187-202.

Cardwell, Guy A. *Twins of Genius*. Michigan State College, 1953.

Clemens, Cyril. *Josh Billings, Yankee Humorist*. Webster Groves, Missouri, 1932.

Clemens, Will M. *Mark Twain, His Life and Work*. San Francisco, 1892.

————. "Mark Twain on the Lecture Platform," *Ainslee's Magazine*, Vol. VI, No. 1 (August, 1900), 25-32.

Coleman, Rufus A. "Mark Twain in Montana, 1895," *Montana Magazine of History*, Spring, 1953, 9-17.

The Complete Works of Artemus Ward. New York, 1898.

Conway, Moncure Daniel. *Autobiography*. 2 Vols. London, 1904.

Dickinson, Anna E. *A Ragged Register*. New York, 1879.

Eggleston, George Cary. *Recollections of a Varied Life*. New York, 1910.

Ellsworth, William Webster. *A Golden Age of Authors*. New York, 1919.

Fatout, Paul. "Mark Twain's First Lecture: a Parallel," *The Pacific Historical Review*, Vol. XXV, No. 4 (November, 1956), 347-354.

————. "Mark Twain Lectures in Indiana," *Indiana Magazine of History*, Vol. XLVI, No. 4 (December, 1950), 363-67.

————. "The Twain-Cable Readings in Indiana," *Indiana Magazine of History*, Vol. LIII, No. 1 (March, 1957), 19-28.

Fletcher, Willis. *George Harvey*. New York, 1929.

Frear, Walter Francis. *Mark Twain and Hawaii*. Chicago, 1947.

Gabrilowitsch, Clara Clemens. *My Father, Mark Twain*. New York, 1931.

Gilder, Richard Watson. "Mark Twain: a Glance at His Written and Spoken Art," *The Outlook*, Vol. LXXVIII (December 3, 1904), 842-44.

Gilman, Arthur. "Atlantic Dinners and Diners," *Atlantic Monthly*, Vol. 100, No. 5 (November, 1907), 646-57.

Goodwin, C. C. *As I Remember Them*. Salt Lake City, 1913.

Gough, John B. *Platform Echoes*. Hartford, 1887.

Harper, J. Henry. *I Remember*. New York, 1934.

Harris, Frank. *Contemporary Portraits. Fourth Series*. New York, 1923.

Harris, Julia Collier. *The Life and Letters of Joel Chandler Harris*. New York, 1918.

Hart, Jerome A. *In Our Second Century*. San Francisco, 1931.

Hayes, Cecil B. *The American Lyceum*. Washington, D. C., 1932.

Hibben, Paxton. *Henry Ward Beecher: an American Portrait*. New York, 1942.

History of Nevada. Oakland, 1881.

Holland, J. G. "Lecture-Brokers and Lecture-Breakers," *Scribner's Monthly*, Vol. I, No. 5 (March, 1871), 560-61.

————. *Plain Talks on Familiar Subjects*. New York, 1865.

————. "Triflers on the Platform," *Scribner's Monthly*, Vol. III, No. 4 (February, 1872), 489.

Johnson, Robert Underwood. *Remembered Yesterdays*. Boston, 1923.

Landon, Melville De Lancey. *Eli Perkins (at large)*. New York, 1875.

————. *Kings of the Platform and Pulpit*. New York, 1895.

The Letters of Bret Harte assembled and edited by Geoffrey Bret Harte. New York, 1926.

Life in Letters of William Dean Howells. Edited by Mildred Howells. New York, 1928.

Livermore, Mary A. *The Story of My Life*. Hartford, 1898.

Logan, Olive. *Apropos of Women and Theatres*. New York, 1870.

Lorch, Fred W. "Cable and His Reading Tour With Mark Twain, 1884-85," *American Literature*, Vol. 23, No. 4 (January, 1952), 471-86.

————. "Lecture Trips and Visits of Mark Twain in Iowa," *The Iowa Journal of History and Politics*, Vol. 27, No. 4 (October, 1929), 507-47.

————. "Mark Twain in Iowa," *The Iowa Journal of History and Politics*, Vol. 27, No. 3 (July, 1929), 408-56.

————. "Mark Twain's Lecture From *Roughing It*," *American Literature*, Vol. 22, No. 3 (November, 1950), 290-307.

————. "Mark Twain's 'Morals' Lecture During the American Phase of His World Tour in 1895-96," *American Literature*, Vol. XXVI, No. 1 (March, 1954), 52-66.

————. "Mark Twain's Orphanage Lecture," *American Literature*, Vol. VII (January, 1936), 455.

————. "Mark Twain's 'Sandwich Islands' Lecture and the Failure at Jamestown, New York, in 1869," *American Literature*, Vol. XXV, No. 3 (November, 1953), 314-25.

————. "Mark Twain's Sandwich Islands Lecture at St. Louis," *American Literature*, Vol 18, No. 4 (January, 1947), 299-307.

Luther, Mark Lee. "Mark Twain and the First Nevada Legislature," *Land of Sunshine*, Vol. XV, Nos. 2-3 (August-September, 1901), 144-49.

Lutz, Alma. *Created Equal: a Biography of Elizabeth Cady Stanton*. New York, 1940.

M. B. C. "Mark Twain as a Reader," *Harper's Weekly*, Vol. LV, No. 2820 (January 7, 1911), 6.

Mack, Effie Mona. *Mark Twain in Nevada*. New York, 1947.

"Mark Twain: More Than Humorist," *The Book Buyer*, Vol. XXII, No. 3 (April, 1901), 196-201.

Matthews, Brander. *Essays on English*. New York, 1922.

————. "Mark Twain as Speech Maker and Story Teller," *The Mentor*, Vol. 12, No. 4 (May, 1924), 24-28.

Merrill, W. H. "When Mark Twain Lectured," *Harper's Weekly*, Vol. L, No. 2564 (February 10, 1906), 199, 209.

Moffett, Wallace B. "Mark Twain's Lansing Lecture on *Roughing It*," *Michigan History*, Vol. 34, No. 2 (June, 1950), 144-70.

Noffsinger, John S. *Correspondence Schools, Lyceums, Chautauquas*. New York, 1926.

O'Rell, Max. *Jonathan and His Continent*. Bristol, 1893.

Paine, Albert Bigelow. *Mark Twain: a Biography*. 4 Vols. New York, 1912.

————. *Thomas Nast, His Period and His Pictures*. New York, 1904.

Pond, Major J. B. *Eccentricities of Genius*. New York, 1900.

"The Rambler," *The Book Buyer*, Vol. XXII, No. 3 (April, 1901), 179.

Reed, Thomas B. *Modern Eloquence*. 4 Vols. Philadelphia, 1900.

Reminiscences of Senator William M. Stewart of Nevada. Edited by George Rothwell Brown. New York, 1908.

Reynolds, Cuyler. *New York at the Jamestown Exposition.* Albany, 1909.

Sachs, Emanie. *The Terrible Siren.* New York, 1928.

Scott, Arthur L. *Mark Twain: Selected Criticism.* Dallas, 1955.

Seitz, Don C. *Artemus Ward.* New York, 1919.

Simpson, Claude M., Jr. "Captain Jim and the 'Third House,'" *Western Folklore,* Vol. IX, No. 2 (April, 1950), 101-110.

Smith, Henry Nash. "That Hideous Mistake of Poor Clemens's," *Harvard Library Bulletin,* Vol. IX, No. 2 (Spring, 1955), 145-80.

The Society of the Army of the Potomac. Twelfth Annual Reunion Held in the City of Harford June 8th 1881. New York, 1881.

Stewart, George R. "Bret Harte Upon Mark Twain in 1866," *American Literature,* Vol. 13 (March, 1941—January, 1942), 263-64.

Stoddard, Charles Warren. *Exits and Entrances.* Boston, 1903.

Ticknor, Caroline. *Glimpses of Authors.* New York, 1922.

Tozer, Basil. *Recollections of a Rolling Stone.* London, 1923.

Train, George Francis. *My Life in Many States and in Foreign Lands.* New York, 1902.

Turner, Arlin. *George W. Cable.* Duke University Press, 1956.

————. "Mark Twain, Cable, and 'A Professional Newspaper Liar,'" *The New England Quarterly,* Vol. XXVIII, No. 1 (March, 1955), 18-33.

Twain, Mark. "Extract From Captain Stormfield's Visit to Heaven," *The Mysterious Stranger and other Stories.* New York, 1922, 223-78.

————. *Following the Equator.* 2 Vols. New York, 1899.

————. *Joan of Arc.* New York, 1926.

————. *Letters From the Sandwich Islands.* San Francisco, 1937.

————. *The Love Letters of Mark Twain.* Edited by Dixon Wecter. New York, 1949.

————. "The Love Letters of Mark Twain." Edited by Dixon Wecter. *Atlantic,* Vol. 180, No. 6 (December, 1947), 66-72; Vol. 180, No. 7 (January, 1948), 83-88.

————. *Mark Twain, Business Man.* Edited by Samuel Charles Webster. Boston, 1946.

————. *Mark Twain in Eruption.* Edited by Bernard DeVoto. New York, 1940.

————. *Mark Twain in Three Moods.* Edited by Dixon Wecter. San Marino, 1948.

————. *Mark Twain of the Enterprise.* Edited by Henry Nash Smith and Frederick Anderson. Berkeley, 1957.

————. *Mark Twain to Mrs. Fairbanks.* Edited by Dixon Wecter. San Marino, 1949.

————. *Mark Twain's Autobiography.* 2 Vols. New York, 1924.

————. *Mark Twain's Letters.* 2 Vols. Edited by Albert Bigelow Paine. New York, 1917.

————. *Mark Twain's Notebook.* Edited by Albert Bigelow Paine. New York, 1935.

————. *Mark Twain's Speeches.* Edited by Albert Brigelow Paine. New York, 1925.

————. *The Portable Mark Twain.* Edited by Bernard DeVoto. New York, 1946.

———— *Who Was Sarah Findlay?* With a Suggested Solution of the Mystery by J. M. Barrie. London, Privately printed, April, 1917.

Twichell, Joseph H. "Mark Twain," *Harper's,* Vol. XCII, No. DLII (May, 1896), 817-27.

Vaile, Charles. "Mark Twain as an Orator," *The Forum,* Vol. XLIV (July, 1910), 1-13.

Wecter, Dixon. *Sam Clemens of Hannibal.* Boston, 1952.

"When Mark Twain Petrified the 'Brahmins,' " *Literary Digest,* Vol. LXII, No. 2 (July 12, 1919), 28-29.

Index

Call: 35, 36, 59, 89; Chronicle: 40, 60; Daily Times: 60, 64, 66, 89; Evening Bulletin: 37, 40, 60, 66, 89; The Golden Era: 40, 57, 61, 87, 88, 142; News Letter: 41; Weekly Mercury: 89
San Jose, California: 61-62, 66
San Raphael, California: 89
Santa Rosa, California: 63
Saratoga, New York: 228
Sault Ste. Marie, Michigan: 244
Savage Club: 174, 272, 282
Sawyer, Tom: 15, 17, 18, 19, 21, 72, 73, 140, 179, 202, 215, 222, 262, 270
Scott, Sir Walter: 178, 250, 271
Scranton, Pennsylvania: 109, 172
Scribner's Monthly: 100, 102, 142
Seattle, Washington: 230, 250, 252
Severance, Solon: 106
Seward, William H.: 22, 65
Shakespeare, William: 28, 46, 106, 194, 199
Sheridan, General Philip H.: 202
Sherman, General W. T.: 202
Sickles, General Daniel E.: 202
Silver City, Nevada: 29, 55, 56
Smith, Mrs. E. Oakes: 98
Smith, Henry Nash: 200
Smollett, Tobias: 198
Smythe, Carlisle G.: 241, 242, 254-55, 259
South Africa, lecture engagements in: 263-65
Southampton, England: 160, 265
South Bend, Indiana: 212, 225
Sparta, Wisconsin: 115
Spencer, Herbert: 177, 206
Spokane, Washington: 249
Springfield, Massachusetts: 41, 127, 212, 217

Stanley, Henry M.: 174, 233
Stanton, Elizabeth Cady: 98, 143, 147
Stebbins, Rev. Dr. Horatio: 19, 146
Steubenville, Ohio: 170
Stewart, Senator William M.: 27, 74, 75, 82
Stoddard, Charles Warren: 35, 174, 184-85, 186, 188, 225
Stone, Lucy: 22
Storrs, Emory: 201
Stowe, Harriet Beecher: 75
Stuyvesant, New York: 110, 117
Swift, Jonathan: 198
Sydney, Australia: 105, 252, 253-254, 259

Tacoma, Washington: 249-50, 251
Tahoe, Lake: 125, 185
Talmage, Rev. De Witt: 20, 100, 101, 253
Taylor, Bayard: 98
Third Annual Message: 29, 32
Third House of Nevada: 24-27, 29-32, 35, 55
Tiffany, Rev. O. H.: 20
Tilton, Elizabeth: 195
Tilton, Theodore: 98, 194, 195
Titusville, Pennsylvania: 116, 117
Toledo, Ohio: 115, 163, 211, 218, 219
Toombs, Robert: 200
Toronto, Ontario: 212, 218, 224
"To the Person Sitting in Darkness": 275
Train, George Francis: 98, 144, 175, 195
Tramp Abroad, A: 18, 198, 221, 242
Trenton, New Jersey: 117, 136
"Triflers on the Platform": 142